PEGGY ASHCROFT

Michael Billington has followed Peggy Ashcroft's acting career for many years with dedicated attention and in 1987 made a widely-acclaimed television profile of her for Channel 4. He is theatre critic of the *Guardian* and *Country Life*, writes regularly on the London arts scene for *The New York Times* and is a frequent contributor to radio and television arts programmes including *Kaleidoscope*, *Critics' Forum* and *Third Ear*. His previous books include studies of the comedian Ken Dodd and the dramatists, Tom Stoppard and Alan Ayckbourn.

'A full-scale portrait, beautifully designed and controlled, by a major drama critic of our day.'
J. C. Trewin

see ½ way down
P.72.

By the same author

The Modern Actor
How Tickled I Am
Performing Arts
The Guinness Book of Theatre Facts and Feats
Alan Ayckbourn
Stoppard : The Playwright

MICHAEL BILLINGTON

PEGGY ASHCROFT

Mandarin

A Mandarin Paperback

PEGGY ASHCROFT

First published in 1988
John Murray (Publishers) Ltd
This edition published 1989
by Mandarin Paperbacks
Michelin House, 81 Fulham Road, London SW3 6RB

Mandarin is an imprint of the Octopus Publishing Group

Copyright © Michael Billington 1988

A CIP catalogue record for this book is available from the
British Library

ISBN 0 7493 0113 9

Reproduced, printed and bound in Great Britain by
BPCC Hazell Books Ltd
Member of BPCC Ltd
Aylesbury, Bucks, England

Contents

Illustrations

Acknowledgements

THIS BOOK COULD NOT have been written without the help of a large number of people.

Obviously, I owe the deepest debt to Dame Peggy herself: for agreeing to entrust so much of her life to my hands, for the loan of so many vital cuttings and, above all, for dispensing tea, sympathy, help and information at so many critical points in the writing. Without her active support, the book would simply not have been possible.

I also owe a profound debt to Derek Bailey, the best of producer-directors, and his cherished colleagues at Landseer Films with whom in 1986 I made a television film, *Dame Peggy*, which was a major starting-point for this book. Michael Kustow, Commissioning Editor for the Arts at Channel 4, was also a pillar of support during the making of the film.

Dr George Rylands CH gave me many valuable insights and also the loan of precious correspondence from the archives of King's College, Cambridge. His kindness was matched by that of Angela Findlater who lent me notes, cuttings and photographs assembled by her late husband, Richard, for his own projected book on Dame Peggy.

For their promptness, diligence and exemplary research, I also owe a lot to Adrian Neatrour, Sally Hibbin, Nicola Russell and the staff of the Shakespeare Centre in Stratford-upon-Avon. Barry Bliss also did an admirable job in combing the photographic files.

Not the least pleasure of writing a book such as this is the chance to talk to and correspond with many of Peggy's friends, colleagues and admirers. My especial thanks to: Harry Andrews, Frith Banbury, John Barton, Julian Bream, Anna Carteret, Mark Dignam, Fabia Drake, Robert Eddison, Sir John Gielgud, John Goodwin, Marius Goring, Sir Alec Guinness, Sir Peter Hall, Margaret Harris, Sir Rupert Hart-Davis, Jocelyn Herbert, Lord Hutchinson, Rachel Kempson, Christopher Morahan, Robert Morley, John Neville, Trevor Nunn, Tim Pigott-Smith, Harold Pinter, Sir Anthony Quayle, Donald Sinden, John Schlesinger, John and Wendy Trewin, Harriet Walter.

My deepest thanks also to my publishers, Jock Murray and John Murray, who applied whip and spur at precisely the right moments and who gave me much practical help; to my Arts Editor at the *Guardian*, Roger Alton, who generously tolerated my absences; and to my wife, Jeanine, who tolerated my presence even when I was engrossed entirely in writing the book.

Illustration acknowledgements

Front cover illustration, Zoë Dominic
Plates 1, 2, 3, 4, 15, Ashcroft Collection; 5, Raymond Mander and Joe Mitchenson Theatre Collection; 6, Angela Findlater Collection; 7, 8, Harvard Theatre Collection (Angus McBean); 9, BBC TV; 10, Gordon Goode; 11, Royal Court Theatre; 12, Zoë Dominic; 13, Granada TV; 14, National Film Archive, London; 16, Edward Maur.

CHAPTER ONE

The Mystery Begins

'ACTING' SAID PEGGY ASHCROFT to me one wintry afternoon in 1986, 'is a mysterious business.'

We were sitting in a borrowed house in Camden Town alone except for a lighting-cameraman, sound recordist, make-up girl, production secretary and producer-director (Derek Bailey). We were, in fact, in the midst of a four-day, ten-hour conversation later edited into a profile called *Dame Peggy* and shown on Channel 4.

The more we talked, the more I realised several things. One is that Peggy Ashcroft's career, spanning sixty years, is like a history of modern British theatre. It embraces the Old Vic under Lilian Baylis in the early 1930s, the famous Gielgud seasons at the New, the Queen's and the Haymarket in the 1930s and 1940s, the West End commercial theatre of the 1950s, the Royal Court under George Devine, the Shakespeare Memorial Theatre under Anthony Quayle and Glen Byam Shaw, the Royal Shakespeare Company under first Peter Hall and then Trevor Nunn, the National Theatre in its move to the South Bank. Wherever any new movement or venture has got under way, Peggy has always been there.

I also realised how unfair it was that the story of Peggy Ashcroft's career had gone largely untold in hard covers. Eric

Keown in 1955 wrote a slim, appreciative monograph that took us as far as *Hedda Gabler*. It ended with a lament for the dearth of living dramatists capable of writing roles that would challenge her and with the hope that there would still be 'good new plays for Peggy Ashcroft to transform with her own personal glory'. Since then she has not only given some of her finest classic performances, such as Margaret of Anjou. She has also allied herself to some of the most experimental living writers such as Beckett, Pinter, Duras and Albee. On top of that she has carved out a new career in television and films, winning awards and continents full of new admirers for her Barbie Batchelor in *The Jewel in the Crown* and her Mrs Moore in *A Passage to India*. It is ironic to think that, despite a couple of Broadway appearances in 1937 and 1948, Peggy Ashcroft was largely unknown to American audiences until her Indian summer in front of the cameras.

What follows is not an intimate personal biography. It is an impression of a career built up through my own observations as theatregoer and critic, through Peggy's own testimony and through the recollections of other critics and her colleagues and friends. Such a method has its dangers. The hero of Mario Vargas Llosa's novel, *The Real Life of Alejandro Mayta*, records: 'One thing you learn, when you try to reconstruct an event from eyewitness accounts, is that each version is just someone's story and that all stories mix truth and lies.' But Vargas Llosa's hero is involved in a quest for the true character of a Peruvian revolutionary. My search is for the key qualities of a radical English actress who, I believe, has had a big influence on the theatre of her lifetime and whose career has implications far beyond self-fulfilment.

If the book focuses largely on Peggy's public career, it is for two reasons. One is that it is her acting which has made her famous. The other is that Peggy is a very private person. In a publicity-crazy age when every minor TV starlet's dirty linen is aired in public, she prefers to be judged by the quality of her work rather than of her life. 'Imagine you're talking to the public over your tea-table,' an editor once suggested to her. 'But I wouldn't have the public to tea,' was her crisp and forthright reply.

Despite this almost Edwardian reticence, she has, during a number of encounters, talked to me candidly about her career.

She has also tactfully discussed her three marriages: to the publisher Rupert Hart-Davis, to the director Theodore Komisarjevsky, and to the lawyer Jeremy Hutchinson. (John Gielgud told me that in the late 1930s rumours of a somewhat improbable marriage between himself and Peggy were bruited on the evening-paper billboards. 'Peggy,' he added, 'had the good taste never to refer to the episode.') Although she didn't relish the prospect of talking about her marriages, she had the shrewdness to recognise that there are points where the private life and the public career overlap and that the one can often only be understood in relation to the other. By her 25-year marriage to Jeremy Hutchinson, she has two children: Nicholas, who now runs the English section of the National Theatre School (founded by her old friend, Michel Saint-Denis) in Montreal as well as a summer company in British Columbia, and Eliza, who lives with her family in France. There is a family pact that Peggy won't talk about them nor they about her. But again, in conversation, she has made it clear that career decisions were often affected by the need to bring up a young family.

This book is primarily a theatrical study. Even so I cannot begin it without some impressions of the woman who is its subject. I first got to know her through excursions to her quiet Hampstead home – Sickert paintings on the wall, poets ancient and modern on the shelves, usually the latest copy of *Index on Censorship* on the table – on behalf of various radio programmes and journals like the *Radio Times*.

I was instantly struck by several things. Most obviously, her youthfulness, as if her spring-like spirit were making mockery of autumnal fact. Also her combination of modesty about her own talent with firmness of opinion about certain plays and characters. When I went to see her to write a preview piece about Stephen Poliakoff's TV film, *Caught on a Train*, she plied me with questions. What did I think the film was about? Was her performance a little bit ham? Was her accent convincing? But on another occasion I confronted her with my view that *Romeo and Juliet* is a badly flawed play because the spirited Juliet that Shakespeare created would have had the gumption to go off with Romeo when he was banished rather than be left behind. I was shot down, if not in flames, then at least with experienced fire.

During our many encounters, I have also become aware of her dislike of fulsome flattery. In December 1985 Peggy gave a *Guardian* lecture at the National Film Theatre. She had just recovered from a severe bronchial illness and had every reason to cancel but, characteristically, agreed to honour her commitment. As her interlocutor, I rounded off the session (always the most difficult part) by invoking a phrase used as the title of a radio tribute broadcast on her 70th birthday: 'The Beauty of Her Character'. The result, to my astonishment, was a fist brandished at me in mock, or perhaps not so mock, anger and a fiercely whispered rebuke of 'Michael, how could you?' Most actresses, and actors, would have relished the ego-massage implied in such a title: to Peggy, it smacked of hyperbole and extravagance.

Peter Hall, describing her working methods, told me: 'She does not like talking. She likes doing.' That applies to her whole approach to her career. But, eventually, in late February 1986, she agreed to sit down with me in front of a television camera and talk about her work. Each day we would have a light lunch and then, for two hours or so during the afternoon, I would draw out her memories. I noticed her total comprehension of – and sometimes possessiveness towards – characters she had played. I remember one particular golden afternoon when she talked about Hedda Gabler, Cleopatra and Margaret of Anjou as if she had played them yesterday rather than decades ago. They were people she knew intimately – in the way a novelist might know his or her creations – rather than simply roles she had played.

She also talked engrossingly about the 'family' of actors, directors and designers with whom her career has often been entwined: John Gielgud, Edith Evans, George Devine, Michael Redgrave, Anthony Quayle, Alec Guinness, Komisarjevsky, Michel Saint-Denis, Glen Byam Shaw, Motley. It has since been hinted to me by those not in the family, such as the director Frith Banbury, that there was often a slight resentment at its exclusivity. What strikes me is the diversity of talent this unofficial group actually includes. And, talking to Peggy, I began to understand the continuity that is part of the strength of British theatre: particularly the way in which from 1930 to 1960 a group of like-minded friends and associates created a classical tradition before the big institutions arrived. Even a single-minded visionary like

Peter Hall was, in his foundation of the RSC, in many ways giving a practical form to dreams that had been entertained before him.

Continuity and togetherness are vital for Peggy. 'I was rather a solitary child,' she once told me, 'and, apart from enjoying school, I was never one of a big family.' In her work I believe she has found the permanent alliances sometimes lacking in her life; and in recent years she has rejoiced to find herself working with old friends such as Fabia Drake and Rachel Kempson (Lady Redgrave) in *The Jewel in the Crown* and Alec Guinness whose calm, Buddha-like presence was a consolation during the prolonged, difficult location-shooting of *A Passage to India*. 'The past,' writes L.P. Hartley in *The Go-Between*, 'is a foreign country – they do things differently there.' For Peggy this is untrue. The past is the foundation of the present; and proof of the evolutionary quality of the British theatre.

Working closely with her, I noticed several other qualities. Her refusal to generalise about acting (or *in* acting for that matter) and her unwillingness to lay down laws. The closest she got to that was a reiteration of Ellen Terry's dictum that acting is based on the three I's of Imagination, Industry and Intelligence. I noticed her habit of turning the question back on the interviewer to avoid making any *ex cathedra* statements about acting. And I also noticed the quiet determination that underlies her modesty. When I trespassed on no-go areas such as her working relationship with David Lean on *A Passage to India*, her mouth would tighten slightly at the corners. At the behest of my producer, I also remember launching one morning in a Stratford-upon-Avon garden into the whole subject of critics, only to be greeted with an abrupt closure of the conversational shutters. With Peggy, you always know where you stand.

As one actor pointed out to me, she has a born dislike of vulgarity: also of reckless journalistic intrusiveness. But I would not wish to imply that she was uncooperative. Having once committed herself to a project, she enters into it with total enthusiasm and gives of herself unsparingly. Stratford-upon-Avon, where we did two days' location filming, seemed to release something special in her. When we entered the RSC's new, magnificent, pale teak rehearsal-room above the Swan Theatre,

with its superb views of the Avon and the spring-green War-
wickshire countryside, she almost skipped with delight. When I
asked her if she envied the young actors working there today,
the light in her eyes gave me the answer I needed. A walk by the
Avon up to Shakespeare's church had her lamenting the death of
the swans who had suffered lead-poisoning from fishermen's
weights: apparently even Oscar, the terror of the Avon, was no
more. And, although she is not given to dewy-eyed nostalgia,
Stratford uncorked memories of canoeing up the river to work
(something the management eventually put a stop to) and of
supper-parties on the river after the play. Margaret ('Percy')
Harris, one of the trio of designers who made up the firm of
Motley, told me that at Stratford Peggy 'was always having
parties or taking people out for picnics on the river or having
cricket matches or something. She never let it become dull. She
always added to the enjoyment of the season.'

Enjoyment, with an insatiable curiosity about people and
things, is a crucial part of her character. Anna Carteret, who
worked with her in *John Gabriel Borkman* at the National and
who, as Christopher Morahan's wife, had an Indian holiday
towards the end of the filming of *The Jewel in the Crown*, recalls
two heady weeks of sightseeing in her company:

'Each day – with Geraldine James' husband, Joe Blatchley –
we'd set off in search of adventure. One day we'd say we're going
to visit the Hanging Gardens of Shalimar. Another day we'd say
we're going to do Willow Lake. We would be besieged by those
little boats coming to sell us things like rugs or jewellery or furs.
As they accosted us, Peggy and I vowed we would look ahead
and not buy anything. But there was one day when a man selling
furs came along and gave us the full story about having fourteen
children and Peggy said, "I'll just have a look at that little black
fur." She put it on her head and was obviously tempted. She
asked, "What animal is this?" and the man said "Cat, madam"
and she shrieked "What!" and threw it off her head back into the
boat. Another day I was so hot that I rowed out to the middle
of Willow Lake and just jumped in with all my clothes on. When
I got back to the hotel, Peggy said, "O, I wish I could have done
that!" and I could well believe it.'

Anna Carteret's point – vouched for by all of Peggy's friends –

is that she is fun to be with and an ideal company member. Peter Hall, who has known her well for 30 years, told me: 'She's like granite. If I were asked the old question of who would be your ideal companion if you were marooned in a boat in the Atlantic, Peggy would certainly be one of my top choices. She'd rise above it.' Off-stage or screen, some actors are slightly disappointing to meet because they fail to match one's conception of them. As Hazlitt wrote, 'today kings, tomorrow beggars, it is only when they are themselves that they are nothing.' Peggy has far too much character, commitment and moral integrity for that to be true of her.

But my theme in this book is Ashcroft the actress, and it may be helpful to begin with a sketch of the qualities that have carried her to and kept her at the top of her profession.

First, there is attack: the capacity to tackle a role head-on, establish clearly its physical lineaments and drive straight to its emotional centre. Olivier has attack, in abundance. So has Ian McKellen. And Peggy has the ability – by means of voice, gesture, carriage – to establish early on the terms on which a role is to be played. Her Cleopatra – to Michael Redgrave's Antony – in red ponytail wig and bright orange and purple robes was, from the first running entrance down a flight of steps, a passionate, wily woman of Greek extraction. Her Imogen, played at Stratford when she was close to 50, was the physical embodiment of a pure, breathless love. With the help of a distinctive French 'r' sound, her Margaret of Anjou instantly established the character's foreignness and sense of displacement in the broiling, fractious English court.

Peggy's range has widened enormously over the years and there are many different weapons in her acting armoury. But it is fascinating that John Gielgud, who first saw her on stage in 1928 in *The Silver Cord* and whose career has so often run in tandem with hers, seized on her attack when he talked of her in his Radio 4 autobiography, *An Actor and His Time*. He was asked which actress was the nearest to his great-aunt, Ellen Terry:

'Well, I suppose Peggy Ashcroft, because she has the same kind of shimmering radiance and irridescence and a kind of forthright, trusting quality: I know of no other actress with quite that gift. I used to say that she butted you like a little calf in the stomach. And in her Juliet I always remember the way she kind

7

of flung herself at the Nurse and flung herself at Romeo. There was something enormously defiant – it was a sort of feminine thing – and yet in no way truckling to the man that I loved about her. She has a fighting spirit without any pugnaciousness. She had it in *The Heiress* very much and in *Hedda Gabler*. She takes a part, as Olivier does, by the throat and she absolutely puts it over the way she wants to and that I admire so much because I never feel so certain of how to do something or how to bang in on a part in that way. But both these performers have that great gift of taking a performance and almost wringing its neck before you're aware of it.'

What is intriguing is how many other observers detect in Ashcroft the Ellen Terry qualities. Alec Guinness told me that the young Peggy had, whether consciously or not, the Terry gift of eagerness and impulsiveness. And, unprompted by me, Peter Hall also seized on the same parallel when I asked him to pin down Peggy's greatest quality:

'She's always been the juvenile. She still is. That extraordinary immediacy and passionate naïveté she's carried into old age in the most remarkable way. There is still a child inside her. I think that's the greatest thing about her acting. It makes me think that there is a particular Englishness which is to do with extreme passion and extreme sexuality contrasted with a wide-eyed English quality. It's a common factor in English actresses. It's what Ellen Terry was about. It's what Edith Evans was about, certainly in comedy. It's what Peggy is about and Judi Dench and Vanessa Redgrave. I remember taking Jean Renoir into the back of the Stratford auditorium where we watched Vanessa's Rosalind. He said, "Oh my God, these English women, when they are sexy, they are sexy."'

The second of Peggy's qualities I would single out is her dedication to truth in acting. What does one mean by 'truth'? The extreme positions on this subject were stated long ago and the debate about them has gone on ever since. Quintilian in the first century argued that the actor moves others only by being moved himself. In other words, to make others weep you must first weep yourself. Denis Diderot in *The Paradox of Acting*, completed in 1778, claimed that you can only be a great actor through the condition of self-mastery and the ability to express feelings that are not felt, feelings perhaps even that you could not feel. My own position on this matter is akin to that of the American critic, Stark Young, who believed that in all the theatrical arts there had to be a governing idea, and that this was as true of acting as anything else. Whatever disguises he adopts, Young argued, the actor is always himself. 'But,' he went on, 'he is himself only as a medium for his idea. He uses himself, his body, his voice and the elusive personal quality that goes with these, exactly as Titian uses paint or Haydn sound, to create a form for his idea.'

In Peggy's acting everything is dictated by the governing idea of the character she is playing. In the end, it is not so very far from the basic Stanislavsky principle of acting. I believe we often get Stanislavsky, the great Russian director and theorist of acting, wrong. We use him, Americans especially, to justify a restless, psychoanalytic, soul-searching approach to acting. That is partly due to an accident of publishing. Stanislavsky's *An Actor Prepares*, which deals mainly with the internal aspects of acting, was published in the West in 1936 while *Building a Character*, which deals chiefly with the external side, was not published till 1949. What is fascinating is that when you read his great autobiographical work, *My Life in Art*, you find that in describing the qualities of the ideal actor he uses very similar – indeed almost identical – words to those others use about Peggy.

Hall talks about her 'passionate naïveté'. Gielgud talks about her 'trusting quality'. Now hear what Stanislavsky has to say: 'Scenic truth is not like truth in life; it is peculiar to itself. I understood that on the stage truth is that in which the actor sincerely believes. I understood that even a palpable lie must become a truth in the theatre so that it may become art. For this it is necessary for the actor to develop to the highest degree his imagination, a childlike naïveté and trustfulness, an artistic sensitivity to truth and to the truthful in his soul and body.'

Stanislavsky's prerequisites are Peggy's qualities.

Her third key attribute is her voice: light, clear, musical, sensitive to verse, capable of infinite modulation. Kenneth Tynan often attacked her Kensington vowels. Others have pounced on her vocal mannerisms (all actors have mannerisms). To me, she combines clear articulation with a built-in sense of rhythm and stress: vital qualities at a time when actors seem to be getting more physically expressive but less rich in vocal texture. There are certainly a number of actors around today – Donald Sinden, Judi Dench, Ian Richardson, Alan Howard, Derek Jacobi – who have an innate sense of phrasing and who know how to use their voices with the pliability of musical instruments. But young actors often find themselves moving straight from drama school into Fringe theatre or television where vocal projection is little required and then discover they are stranded when thrust onto the big Stratford stage where they have to hurl iambic pentameters to the back wall. The problem, I believe, goes even deeper: we live in a culture where there is little regard for the spoken word, where reading aloud is a dying habit and where vocabulary is being pathetically diminished. As an American professor pointed out to me recently, even sentence-structure is now affected by television: asked to summarise the plot of a play or novel, students often resort to a series of arbitrarily-linked images rather than coming up with a cohesive, defined statement.

Peggy grew up with a childhood love of reading and speaking verse which has bred in her an instinctive musicality (though, paradoxically, she says she can't sing to save her life). But there is nothing cool or passionless about her verse-speaking. 'Like most great actors,' Peter Hall told me, 'her verse-speaking is idiosyncratic. John Gielgud marks the end of a line by braying. Peggy marks the end of a line by ponging (hitting the final syllable hard). Edith Evans used to mark the end of a line by swooping. But they all have a way. Most of that generation became great verse-speakers by doing so much Shakespeare that Shakespeare finally mastered them. One of the problems now is that people don't do enough Shakespeare so that Shakespeare never masters them. They continue to wrestle with it and are thrown to the ground by it.'

It is also significant that a critic and theatre historian of Peggy's generation, J. C. Trewin, remembers as long ago as 1929 with *Jew Süss* being enchanted not only by her naturalness but also 'by a voice so clear and light and true that I've never forgotten it. I remember coming out of the theatre and saying, "When am I going to hear her again?"' Not, you notice, when am I going to *see* her again. Peggy doesn't put sound before sense. But I have noticed that she brings to the preservation of verse-speaking standards the same gutsy enthusiasm she does to libertarian causes. Alec Guinness recalls, a little wryly, a Christmas he and his wife spent with her at Ludlow in the late 1930s devoted to reading verse aloud ('not', he says, 'one of my favourite activities'). In 1943 she took the initiative in forming the Apollo Society which did a lot to revive interest in the speaking of verse. And even today she doesn't need much prodding to talk about verse-speaking at Stratford and her own preference for actors who have the priceless gift of clarity.

Peggy will talk readily about subjects like that. What she hates talking about is herself, which is why for years she has kept even the most eager biographers at bay. The book that follows is, therefore, primarily a study of her extraordinary career. But it also attempts to place her in the context of her theatrical times – times which she has helped to shape and modify – and to explore the curious two-way process of acting: the way the characters played permeate the private person while at the same time the moral character of the individual is manifested in the public work. Acting, according to Peggy, may be mysterious. But I don't think that should deter one from trying to pluck out the heart of its mystery.

CHAPTER TWO

In the Beginning
Was the Word

TRAVEL TO CROYDON through London's south-west suburbs today and you end up in what looks like a miniaturised Denver: a town centre filled with anonymous, looming tower-blocks and made no easier of access by a one-way traffic system where your ultimate destination always seems to be on the other side of the road. To get where you want, like the man in Donne's poem seeking Truth, you 'about must and about must go'.

It was obviously a more beguiling place when Peggy (christened Edith Margaret Emily) Ashcroft was born there on 22 December 1907. She remembers it as 'a sort of quiet, rather large market-town where one was always within easy reach of the Downs. I remember it as what I call John Betjeman land reminding one of those leafy descriptions he has of churches and little woods with primroses and bluebells.' Betjeman – born just over a year before Peggy – in fact wrote lovingly about old Croydon with its Victorian villas, surrounding woodland and family continuity:

> In a house like that
> Your Uncle Dick was born:
> Satchel on back he walked to Whitgift
> Every weekday morn.

Betjeman was hymning a Croydon that still had links with the past, including Archbishop Whitgift's Hospital of the Holy Trinity, built in 1596 for the relief of the maimed, poor and needy. Above all, it was a Croydon still fringed by countryside:

> Boys together in Coulsdon woodlands,
> Bramble-berried and steep,
> He and his pals would look for spadgers
> Hidden deep.
>
> The laurels are speckled in Marchmont Avenue
> Just as they were before,
> But the steps are dusty that still lead up to
> Your Uncle Dick's front door.

This was the world Peggy was born into, and her background was the epitome of a modestly comfortable, mildly bookish, middle-class England, though one inevitably shadowed by the trauma of the First World War. Her father, William Worsley Ashcroft, was a land-agent whose job was to value large properties. Her mother, formerly Violet Maud Bernheim, was part Danish, part German-Jewish. Even more significantly, Peggy's mother was a keen amateur actress who had taken elocution lessons in Folkestone from the formidable pioneer of poetic speech, Elsie Fogerty, who in 1906 founded the Central School of Speech and Drama in the Albert Hall: only the strict Victorianism of her own mother had prevented Violet Bernheim from taking up the stage as a career. Peggy also had a brother, Edward, who was her elder by three and a half years and who had a passion for literature and reading which he assiduously passed on. In later life, Edward Ashcroft went on to have a distinguished public career writing for *The Times* (he did their obituary of General de Gaulle) and as head of the French Section in the BBC's External Services. Two of his five children, Margaret and Chloe, went on the stage; and his granddaughter, Katharine Schlesinger, has quickly made her mark as an actress in theatre and television.

Peggy's Croydon childhood was a brief idyll shattered by the War. Even on an income of £300 a year the family were able to support a nanny and cook-general; and life for the young Peggy was made up of such gentle pursuits as skipping, bowling the hoop, reading and going for long country walks to see the new Croydon Airport being built. But the reality of the War first came home to Peggy when an empty house in the Ashcrofts' road was given over to Belgian refugees from whom she heard first-hand stories of the invasion of their country. In 1915 her father joined up, her mother became restless in his absence and life for Peggy became a ceaseless shuttle between Croydon, rented rooms in London and a house in Bournemouth belonging to Violet's mother. Peggy caught only occasional glimpses of her father when he was on leave. But his death in action in 1918 was a devastating blow, and it is not hard to imagine that Peggy's later belief in the importance of extended theatrical families – in the shape of permanent companies – was, in some way, a compensation for the secure family life cruelly destroyed by war.

In one thing, Peggy was fortunate: she grew up with an instinctive passion for poetry and plays. At the age of seven, she went to the family shelves and picked out the most beautifully bound book, which happened to be a volume of Tennyson. It fell open at *The Lady of Shalott* and its insistent, incantatory rhythms ('On either side the river lie/Long fields of barley and of rye') meant that Peggy soon learned it by heart. She also discovered for herself *Lamb's Tales from Shakespeare* and was entranced both by the fairy-tale plots and the larger-than-life characters. At the age of ten, she was given a leatherbound copy of *Palgrave's Golden Treasury* by her enlightened paternal grandfather, and from that she graduated to the Greek Myths (she had a particular liking for *Jason and the Golden Fleece*), Anthony Hope's *The Prisoner of Zenda*, the stories of Saki and eventually Shakespeare himself and Shaw.

'My grandfather,' Peggy recalls, 'had a passion for Shakespeare and a passion for Wordsworth and I can remember the terrible arguments between him and my brother. He thought Edward was horribly modern because he preferred Browning to Wordsworth.' Under her brother's tutelage, Peggy later moved on to Herrick and Donne. But one cannot over-estimate the importance for her future career of growing up in a family where poetry was something to be memorised, read for pleasure and argued over; and, in our own semi-literate, video-filled, computer-game age, one looks back with envy to a time when families were divided by such serious issues as the merits of rival poets.

There were also occasional excursions to see the Shakespeare touring companies that criss-crossed England earlier this century. Even as a child Peggy had a sharp critical eye for violations of the truth: 'I remember vividly seeing my first production of *The Merchant of Venice* at the Winter Gardens Theatre, Bournemouth, when I was about eleven and being absolutely horrified that such a very large woman as the Portia could possibly say "My little body is a-weary of this great world." But I was entranced by Shylock. I didn't see another Shakespeare play until my teens and that was when the Charles Doran Company came to Croydon. I had the great pleasure of seeing Ralph Richardson in the Doran Company and that was very illuminating. I saw him play Henry V and Mark Antony and was absolutely entranced by him, in love with him in fact.' She could scarcely guess that before her teens were out, she would be sharing a stage with her idol; or that Richardson was singularly ill-at-ease in the roles he was assigned by the Doran Company and was nicknamed by his fellow-actors 'Bonzo' after a savage Staffordshire bull-terrier drawn by a famous cartoonist of the time.

Peggy not only went to the theatre. She also started to read about it avidly, and discovered two contradictory influences. On the one hand, her imagination was fired by reading about the romance of the Henry Irving–Ellen Terry partnership at the Lyceum in the 1880s and '90s. Irving employed the best players, painters and musicians of his day, made Shakespeare a box-office hit and created a theatre of colour and spectacle.

But at the same time as Peggy was sitting in the Croydon Public Library reading and romancing about Irving's Lyceum, she also discovered the work of Irving's most trenchant critic, Bernard Shaw. Peggy saw the touring Macdona Players in Shaw's plays, and devoured Shaw's theatre and music criticism. It must have come as something of a shock to her to read Shaw's excoriating attacks on what he saw as the decorative prettiness and interpretative falsity of Lyceum Shakespeare: 'Sir Henry Irving,' Shaw wrote in 1895, 'has never thought much of the Immortal William and has given him more than one notable lesson – for instance in *The Merchant of Venice* where he gave us not "the Jew that Shakespeare drew" but the one he ought to have drawn if he had been up to the Lyceum mark'.

Shakespeare was Peggy's childhood passion. Shaw became her portable university in that she would make a point of tracking down authors he referred to (though she says she never got as far as Nietzsche and Schopenhauer). As if this were not enough to lead her inexorably towards the theatre, she also encountered at Woodford School, Croydon, one of those inspirational teachers who figure in the lives of most actors and actresses. She was Gwen Lally, an ex-actress and subsequent pageant-director, who was then the school's elocution mistress. At the age of 11, under her own initiative, Peggy played Portia in her own presentation of the ring scene from *The Merchant of Venice*. From then on she and a fellow-pupil two years her senior, Diana Wynyard (who became a lifelong friend), carved up the leading roles in Miss Lally's annual Shakespeare productions. Peggy was Cassius to Diana's Brutus, Katherine to her Henry V, Shylock to her Portia. For her Shylock, Peggy faithfully copied reports of Irving's performance and even persuaded the firm of Nathan's to let her have a costume modelled on the great man's.

But the Shaw bug was not to be shaken off.

'I had an English teacher at school,' Peggy remembers, 'called Miss Grundy. I got on well with her except that she had a passionate dislike of Matthew Arnold and Shaw so I wrote a ten-page essay in defence of Shaw which rather surprised her. One forgets just how shocking Shaw was thought to be at that time. My mother disapproved of my reading him in the house. And when Diana, my brother and I decided to do our own version of *Candida* we adventured to London to see the play at the Everyman Hampstead. We then staged the play in aid of a hospital in Sevenoaks as we couldn't possibly have done it at school.' The audience was treated to Diana as Candida, brother Edward as the moralising parson, Morrell, and Peggy herself as the poetic intruder, Marchbanks. It was her first recorded charity show, though her failure to convince the audience that she was a man dissuaded her from further male impersonations.

In retrospect, Peggy's choice of profession seems inevitable. She had a mother with suppressed theatrical leanings. She had a built-in love of Shakespeare, poetry, the sound and texture of language. She also discovered through school plays that 'it was very exciting to be someone else'. Peggy even remembers the *coup de foudre*, the exact moment when the thunder struck: 'I was outside a grocer's shop in George Street, Croydon. I said to myself "I'm going to be an actress" and then I went into the shop. I don't know what made me think of it at that precise moment. Perhaps it was because I was rehearsing Cassius. I do know I was thirteen at the time.' Even then she possessed the born actor's instinct for hoarding up experience and turning it to use. She remembered an excellent bit of business in the Charles Doran version of *Julius Caesar* in which the actor playing Cassius wrenched a wreath off the bust of Caesar and hurled it venomously to the ground. It went straight into her own performance.

There was, however, nothing of the hothouse flower about Peggy. At school she enjoyed netball, tennis and cricket. She enjoyed writing English essays. What she didn't enjoy was swotting for exams. So at 16 she decided she must leave school to go on the stage. A horrified reaction ensued. The headmistress at Woodford wanted her to stay on and take School Matric; but not even the open bribe of a chance to play Hamlet (and what a performance that might have been) in the next school play could dent Peggy's resolve. Her mother – who had herself been prevented from going on the stage – begged her to stay on at school. It was useless. Peggy revealed an obduracy and toughness that she has often shown at crisis-points in her life. 'I was quite certain,' she says, 'I was going to win the argument. Something told me I really had to persist. Anyway there wasn't much of an alternative. I had to earn a living because my mother by that time had only a war-widow's pension to live on.'

Once Peggy's decision was made, her destination was clear: the Central School of Speech and Drama run by her mother's old teacher, Elsie Fogerty. Application was made, and not even Miss Fogerty's daunting enquiry of 'Little girl, why aren't you at school?' at the interview could shake Peggy's determination. Miss Fogerty, herself the daughter of an architect who strongly disapproved of the stage, was one of those tough, pioneering bachelor women who did so much to influence the British theatre in this country. It was Miss Horniman who had kick-started the

English repertory movement in Manchester in 1908 and Lilian Baylis who had single-handedly taken over the running of the Old Vic in 1912, turning it into an instrument of the Lord and cultural enlightenment. Miss Fogerty, stately, plump and dowager-like, was cast in the same mould. And Laurence Olivier, who was part of the same Central intake as Peggy in 1924, has left a very sharp impression of her: 'Her eyes were strong, very dark, almost almond-shaped but by no means always kindly. Her looks were those of a serious person; her nose was right for her face, sizeable with an even, downward curve. Her voice was predictably remarkable; its pitch was that of a richly skilled bass-baritone.'

It is startling to learn that Peggy, often quoted as one of Central's alumni, really didn't think much of Fogey's training and her stress on the Voice Beautiful. 'I learned very little about acting there,' Peggy says firmly. 'One had classes in voice, physical deportment, fencing, Greek dancing and so on. But while one's voice and body were trained, one's approach to theatre and drama was not. The agony of doing some Swinburne translation from the Greek with Elsie Fogerty was excruciating. As far as I can recall, we never did a single play. We only ever did scenes. Larry and I each got a silver medal for some silly piece about a Mr and Mrs Inkpen in a dialogue competition; and in the end of term show we each got a gold medal from Athene Seyler for playing Shylock and the clerk of the court in the trial scene from *The Merchant*. But this was hardly the real stuff of an actor's training.'

Peggy was irked by the whole set-up at Central but later, she says, it was transformed by the brilliant drama directorship of George Hall. In her time, the school was made up of 90 girls and 5 boys: that meant the boys got the pick of any parts going. A further irritation was that the boys were able to leave after a year while the girls did a minimum two-year course.

She was, however, far from hostile to the boys on the course. She found a natural ally in her fellow student Laurence Olivier: she feels they both had well-developed voices even before they got to Central (indeed Peggy had been informed by Elsie Fogerty that hers was too deep) and both chafed secretly against the old Fogey tradition. As Peggy points out, this may explain their joint attachment to realistic acting in later life.

Whether they were right to chafe against their training is another matter. Once a year, for instance, the students had to stand on the stage of the Albert Hall, speak to the Royal Box and be heard. Out of that must have come one of the most priceless gifts for an actor or actress: a voice that can hit the back of a theatre effortlessly. But, apart from their shared sympathies, there was even then an athletic energy and sexual aura about Olivier that attracted Peggy. 'It was clear,' she says, 'that he was going to be something remarkable. He had this terrific vitality. He was rather uncouth in that his sleeves were too short and his hair stood on end but he was intensely lively and great fun.'

The other male student Peggy got on well with was George Coulouris, who went on to have a distinguished career with Orson Welles's Mercury Theatre. Some girls at Central were wary of him because he was rumoured to be an impassioned Greek who kept a knife down his sock, though in fact he came from Manchester. Peggy found he was one of the few people she could have an intellectual conversation with. 'The fact is,' says George Coulouris, 'she was the only person who didn't scare the pants off me. I felt I was surrounded by Colonels' daughters with posh accents who looked down on me as a plebeian clodhopper from the north – whereas I knew I was a terribly intelligent fellow who thought he recognised a similar attribute in Peggy. I don't remember what we talked about: Stanislavsky, Gordon Craig, something like that. What was evident was that Peggy was the star girl student in Fogerty's mind just as Olivier was the star boy.'

Peggy may not have been academically inclined ('At school I funked exams'). But she was exceptionally bright, well-read, idealistic.

In 1924 – during Peggy's first year at Central – Constantin Stanislavsky's *My Life in Art* was published in Britain. This quickly became Peggy's Bible. Here was a book that described the cultural vitality of Russia at the turn of the century, that charted the painful evolution of a great company in the Moscow Art Theatre, that pinpointed the creation of a new drama in the works of Anton Chekhov and that, above all, demanded of the actor dedication, concentration, imagination and a systematic approach to work. At a time when the English theatre was dominated by commercial flotsam and by the gentlemanly Gerald du Maurier approach to acting that could be described as restraint run riot, the book became for Peggy and others of her generation a blueprint for Utopia. It proved that great things in theatre are only achieved by the shared convictions of permanent companies: something that became the central tenet of Peggy's faith. It also argued that acting was too serious an art to be a matter either of casual inspiration or well-honed technique, vital as that was. Stanislavsky wrote passionately about the actor's need to develop 'an artistic sensitivity to truth'. It seemed a long way from classes in Greek dancing in a dusty wing of the Albert Hall.

But it was Stanislavsky's description of the agonised birth-pangs of the Moscow Art Theatre with its commitment to 'youth, fanaticism, the ability to work and the revolutionary spirit in the sense of artistic rejuvenation' that really fired Peggy's soul, and from her reading of *My Life in Art* in the mid-1920s one can date Peggy's lifelong commitment to the idea of the company and the joy of permanence. 'That,' she now says, 'became one's focus. When one went into the theatre one realised it wasn't going to be like Irving's Lyceum. One hoped instead it would be like the Moscow Art Theatre but it took a very long time to become part of a company of that stature and permanence. But I think it was that idea that excited me most from the beginning.'

Russia at the time seemed the source of all that was most dynamic in theatre. Shortly after reading Stanislavsky's book, Peggy went to see a landmark season of Russian plays directed by a little-known Russian emigré, Theodore Komisarjevsky, early in 1926 at a pocket-handkerchief sized theatre in Church Road, Barnes, in the London suburbs. Komisarjevsky, whose sister Vera had played Nina in the first ill-fated production of *The Seagull* in St Petersburg in 1896, was a member of a famous Russian theatrical family and had directed many plays and operas in pre-Revolutionary Russia. In 1919 he emigrated to England and at first seemed an intellectual gadfly, designing costumes for J. B. Fagan's repertory productions and doing work that created a minor buzz around the fringe London theatres.

But the four Russian plays he directed at Barnes, on minimal budgets of around £100 each and in a tiny space, alerted critics and a discerning public to his directorial and scenic genius. In

January 1926 came Chekhov's *Uncle Vanya* with Jean Forbes-Robertson as Sonya. It was followed in February by the British première of *Three Sisters* with John Gielgud as a handsome Baron Tusenbach oddly at variance with the text ('The English public must have a romantic hero,' Gielgud was bluntly informed by Komisarjevsky). In March there was Leonid Andreyev's melodramatic *Katerina* with Komis changing the scenery right up until curtain-rise and finally in April Gogol's *The Government Inspector* with Charles Laughton. Gielgud remembers that the company were all paid £10 a week, shared a single dressing-room, played twice daily and drew fashionable London south of the river.

Peggy, as a penurious student, was amongst those who made the trek to Barnes and, more than 60 years later, still remembers the impact the productions made. 'With the two Chekhov plays especially,' she says, 'one knew one was seeing something the like of which had not been seen on the English stage before: everyday life recreated with total fidelity. Komis also had a wonderful eye for lighting and I can still recall the leaping shadows of the fire reflected on the bedroom wall during the third act of *Three Sisters*.' James Agate, drama critic of the *Sunday Times* and later to become a permanent thorn in Peggy's side, pinned down the nature of Komis's breakthrough in his notice of *Katerina*. It wasn't merely, he suggested, the miracle of movement and grouping Komis accomplished on a ten-foot stage: 'Mr Komisarjevsky achieves more than this; it is the whole web of sight and sound which he presents so that the play becomes an orchestrated score. This is beauty in which dramatist and producer have an equal hand.'

For Peggy herself, the Barnes season was the start of a lifelong love of Chekhov, a fascination with Komisarjevsky – who later became her guru and husband (in that order) – and an awareness that the combination of great texts, fine acting, imaginative lighting and design could raise theatre to an exalted, almost spiritual level.

She had to wait a long time for her dream of a permanent company to be fulfilled. She did not, however, have to wait long for her professional début. One of the roles she played at Central as a student – in between the detested Swinburne Greek tragedies – was Margaret in scenes from J. M. Barrie's haunted fantasy of

1917, *Dear Brutus*. She was spotted by a London agent. And when Muriel Hewitt – Ralph Richardson's first wife – was whisked out of the cast of a Birmingham Repertory revival of Barrie's play in May 1926 to appear in *The Marvellous History of Saint Bernard* at London's Kingsway, Peggy was quickly despatched to Birmingham to take her place.

It is worth pointing out that Peggy, even at 18, was no theatrical innocent. She knew full well the reputation of Birmingham Rep, founded by Barry Jackson in 1913, as a graduate school of British acting. She had also seen and adored H. K. Ayliff's celebrated modern-dress production of *Hamlet* which had transferred from Birmingham to London in 1925. For Peggy it was a gimmick-free version that gave her a fresh perspective on the play. In the London press it yielded not only predictable headlines ('Shakespeare in Plus Fours', 'The Gloomy Dane with a Cigarette') but also produced a priceless review in the *Men's Wear Daily* which complained that 'Hamlet's evening kit was a sheer disgrace'.

At Birmingham Peggy found herself thrust into Barrie's whimsical, unnerving play about a group of ordinary people shown lamenting what, in other circumstances, they might have been (hence the Shakespearean title). A sprite, Lob, is on hand to grant Barrie's people their wishes. But the point is that, even if fate had given them what they desired, nothing would have changed. Character, says Barrie, is the only destiny.

Playing the artless Margaret ('She is as lovely as you think she is and she is aged the moment when you like your daughter best,' writes Barrie), Peggy found herself in distinguished company. The director was the veteran Abbey Theatre actor, W. G. Fay. The brass-voiced Edward Chapman played the character of a roguish philanderer, Purdie. But the real thrill came from playing opposite Ralph Richardson (only five years her senior) as fantasy-daughter to his childless, would-be artist, Will Dearth. Richardson, with his unique gift for investing ordinariness with a touch of mystery and magic, was said to have reached tragedy at the end of Act Two when he realises his daughter is a mere Midsummer Night woodland wraith; and it is not hard to imagine Peggy, who knew something about the chilling separation of fathers and daughters, investing Barrie's

22

sometimes poignant, sometimes sentimental lines with a natural truth. Peggy herself is now dismissive about her professional début: 'It was a terrible shock to the system because I felt absolutely hopeless and knew I was hopeless too.' All the same, one would give a lot to have seen her and Richardson playing Barrie's moving second-act climax when Dearth disappears into the woodland night humming gently and Margaret ('out of the impalpable that is carrying her away') cries in desperation, 'Daddy, come back; I don't want to be a might-have-been.' Peggy's performance may not have matched her own dreams. But, in one respect, Barrie's play was prophetically accurate. Character, with the occasional nudge from fortune, was to be her destiny too.

CHAPTER THREE

London Calling

AFTER HER BIRMINGHAM DÉBUT in *Dear Brutus,* Peggy returned to Central School to complete her studies in the summer of 1926. But any thrill she may have felt at being released at last from the discipline of voice-classes and Greek dancing was offset by the shattering emotional blow of her mother's death that same year.

At the age of 19 Peggy was not quite alone in the world. She was close to her brother, Edward, but he was living abroad studying in Switzerland. She also went to live with devoted guardians first in Hindhead, Surrey, and then in Addison Crescent, Kensington. But it is fascinating to discover that friends in her early years as an actress, such as Fabia Drake, often referred to her in letters and diaries as 'little Ashcroft' as if she had a faintly orphaned quality. Like many solitary young girls, Peggy found release in writing poetry, setting down her thoughts exactly as they came to her, often at dead of night. The poems she remembers from this period are often influenced by pantheistic Words-worthian ideas about the union of the soul with nature. A verse of one runs:

> O Earth you have given me this body –
> A beautiful prison. Soon you will make it outworn
> Then my spirit will flow liquid and soft,

Sinking into you. Then I shall be no more
Only a sound and a scent of you, Earth.

Romantic, wistful and death-haunted, this hints at the young
Peggy's delicate sensitivity. Another poem from this period
which, thanks to Peter Fleming, found its way into the pages of
the *Spectator*, is a rather more effusive celebration of the joys of
nature:

But you are green and giving and like grass,
Restful and taking rest.
So soft you are that when you walk in trees
You move among them only as a wind,
A stream of life, a rhythm of the air.

But Peggy's poetic spirit was accompanied by a burning desire
to get work in her chosen profession; and, with the help of a
family friend, Walter Peacock, who worked for the agent A. D.
Peters, she set about the management of her career with single-
minded practicality. 'My rule,' she says, 'straight out of drama
school was to accept whatever was offered. I did a play even if I
hated it. Choice was a luxury that came later.'

What kind of theatre was Peggy coming into? Certainly one
that bore little relation to the high-minded idealism described by
Stanislavsky in *My Life in Art*. The faults of the commercial
theatre of the inter-war years were well described by S. P. B. Mais
in an article in a 1926 edition of *Theatre World*. Mais listed his
complaints under three headings.

First, there were the audiences. 'Let there,' he insisted, 'be no
more dressing up in the stalls, no more idolatry in the gallery, no
more pandering to the over-sexed (or should it be under-sexed?)
spinsters of the pit with their demand to be shocked at all costs.'
Then there were the actors and actresses who often had a greater
appetite for play and publicity than for work: 'Actors are too
fond of golf and actresses of being photographed sitting on the
edge of mountains.' Finally there were the managers who were
obsessed by one idea only: 'That if a play is vulgar it is bound to
be a commercial success and that, if a play is a commercial success,
it cannot be artistic.'

There were, of course, cultural oases: Lilian Baylis's Old Vic and Nigel Playfair's Lyric Hammersmith. But, in the words of another theatre magazine, *The Curtain*, 'The hope of the drama seems to lie in the little theatres.' In our modern arrogance we tend to assume that the teeming London Fringe of today was the product of pioneer work by bearded Americans like Charles Marowitz and Jim Haynes in the late 1960s. In fact, the foundations of the Fringe were laid long before in places like the Everyman, Hampstead (a converted drill-hall), the Gate Theatre in Floral Street, the Garden Theatre in St John's Wood, the Pax Robertson Salon in Chelsea; or in the dozen or so Sunday-night play-producing societies that tried out new work or foreign plays that the Lord Chamberlain considered unfit for public consumption. The virulent commercialism of the West End has always bred its own alternative, and it was the little theatres of the 1920s that played Gogol and Calderon, Cocteau and Capek, Kaiser and Joyce.

Proving that character is destiny, Peggy made her London professional début in May 1927 through the simple expedient of going round the little theatres looking for work. The play was an adaptation by Joseph Conrad of his short story, *One Day More*, first given by the Stage Society in 1905: the venue was a tiny theatre, seating 100, in New Compton Street called Playroom Six. The play itself was a short, stark tragedy much praised on its first appearance by Max Beerbohm who said that it was a pity duffers ceaselessly wrote plays while those, like Conrad, who might improve our drama generally held themselves aloof from it. Peggy found herself playing Bessie, an innocent young girl chosen by a crazy old man next door as the destined bride of his sailor son when he returns home from the sea. The son comes back. The father fails to recognise him. Bessie is roughly kissed by the wandering matelot and watches him go, realising the pitiful absurdity of her hope that he might be her husband.

Peggy was seen by only a handful of playgoers, but her unaffected simplicity as Bessie made a sufficiently strong impression to start a chain of events that kept her in steady work for the next few months. Mrs Cecil Chesterton gave her a good notice in her brother-in-law's publication, *G. K.'s Weekly*, and wrote a letter about her to Nigel Playfair, the actor-manager then running the Lyric Hammersmith. Charles Bennett, who acted opposite Peggy in *One Day More*, instantly gave her a part in a new play he had written for the Everyman, Hampstead, a slightly more prestigious venue where in 1924 Noël Coward had starred in *The Vortex*. Bennett's play, *The Return*, was something of a whimsical oddity: it dealt with the spirit of a child, born dead, which took the place of a young poet killed in the trenches. It offered Peggy the chance to play another of the waif-like heroines, such as Barrie's Margaret, that were to come her way quite often in her early years. It also earned her a good notice in *The Stage*: 'Mary had a poignantly emotional portrayal from a promising young actress, Peggy Ashcroft.' Then in July 1927 – thanks to the helpful introduction to Nigel Playfair – it was on to the little Q Theatre on Kew Bridge for a comedy he was directing, *When Adam Delved* by George Paston. Peggy is now briskly dismissive about it: 'a perfectly awful part in a frightful play', she says. Still, by knocking on doors and taking her chances when offered Peggy had very quickly got a toehold in the world of little theatres where then, as now, work bred work.

People took to Peggy very quickly. Having directed her at the Q Theatre, Nigel Playfair gave her an introduction to his friend, the dramatist John Drinkwater, who was looking for someone to play the female juvenile lead in his comedy, *Bird in Hand*, at Birmingham Rep. This was a highly popular play in its day about a squire's son who falls in love with a Gloucestershire innkeeper's daughter. For Peggy there was the triple attraction of playing a romantic lead, of returning to Birmingham Rep (which then transferred many of its productions to the West End) and of being re-united with her old friend from Central, Laurence Olivier, who was cast opposite her.

Olivier was a permanent member of the Birmingham company and had already made his mark playing Chekhov's Uncle Vanya (at the age of 20), Shakespeare's Parolles and Goldsmith's Tony Lumpkin. He wasn't exactly thrilled at the prospect of playing the squire's son, Gerald Arnwood, in the Drinkwater: a part he later referred to as 'a moth-eaten juvenile' (Sample line: 'Good evening Mrs Greenleaf, Mr Greenleaf. I was wondering whether Joan would care for a drive; it's a lovely evening'). But for Peggy it was a happy summer in Birmingham.

She remembers a trip across to Stratford with Olivier and John Drinkwater to see *Antony and Cleopatra* in the Greenhill Street cinema (the original theatre was gutted by fire in March 1926) and for a magical dinner at Hall's Croft. In an article she wrote in a book celebrating Olivier's 80th birthday, Peggy also quelled inevitable speculation about her relationship with her stage partner: 'Romance? No – only in retrospect . . . many years later Larry told me that when we went to tea with a member of the Rep company in his digs in Birmingham and our host had retired to the lavatory, only the sudden pulling of the chain prevented him from proposing.' Peggy doesn't think Olivier was serious; though it's worth noting that when *Bird in Hand* was revived in London a year later, he proposed to Peggy's successor in the role of Joan Greenleaf, Jill Esmond, within three weeks of meeting her, and eventually married her.

Even if Peggy and Olivier were content to remain just good friends, Peggy's performance in *Bird in Hand* earned her an approving notice from R. Crompton Rhodes in the *Birmingham Post*: 'Miss Peggy Ashcroft's Joan was a charming, sensible, straightforward impersonation: the part, naturally drawn, was naturally acted.' Her quality of unactressy naturalness was one critics were to seize on for years. Those looking for portents might also be amused by Rhodes's passing rebuke to Olivier: 'only one moment was he out of character and that was his sentimental kissing the door of his sweetheart's room'.

Interestingly, Peggy never had the long slog in regional rep then considered crucial for an actress's development. Instead she returned to London to play the small part of the maid, Betty, in Nigel Playfair's 1927 revival of his famous production of *The Way of the World*. Nowadays we tend to play Congreve's circuitous classic for its sexual realism, or see it as a harsh study in legalistic transaction. Playfair's approach was altogether more romantic. Pictures of Doris Zinkeisen's sets suggest a curlicued, bandbox prettiness. Playfair's charade-like approach also involved having the theatre orchestra dressed in white wigs and period costume while footmen dandy-minced around the stage lighting or extinguishing candles. But the glory of Playfair's production – which had started life at the Lyric Hammersmith in 1924 – was Edith Evans's Millamant. Peggy was her second understudy and each night watched her performance from the wings with rapt fascination. She never spoke to her at Wyndham's ('I was way below the salt'). Equally she never forgot Edith Evans's verbal precision and consummate comic style. J. C. Trewin, then a young critic up from the West Country, saw the performance straight after going to a rugby match and purloined a phrase of Colley Cibber's to describe this Millamant: 'a swan upon waving water'.

While still playing Congreve's chocolate-house waiting-maid, Betty, with the single line 'Turned of the last canonical hour, sir' (one that still puzzles her), Peggy fitted in a quadruple bill one Sunday night at the Arts in January 1928. Peggy was in two of the four plays: Shaw's *The Fascinating Foundling*, which got her a favourable mention in *The Times*, and W. B. Yeats's *The Land of Heart's Desire*, written in 1894 on Irish nationalist themes. Rupert Brooke's *Lithuania* and Strindberg's *Simoon* made up a bizarre quartet of one-acters, but one that typified the adventurousness of the little theatres of the Twenties.

For a 20-year-old actress who had only been six months in the business, Peggy had achieved a good deal: she had been in constant employment, played the little theatres, a major Rep and the West End, got briefly noticed and won some important friends. But her big break came in the spring of 1928 when she got her first substantial role in a tour of Sidney Howard's American play, *The Silver Cord*. No sooner had she signed up for this than she was approached about doing the West End run of John Drinkwater's *Bird in Hand*. Slightly to her chagrin, the management would not release her; but one suspects she was better off in Howard's brilliant domestic drama than in Drinkwater's lightweight class-comedy.

The Silver Cord – which opened in New York in 1926 and at the St Martin's in London in September 1927 – was defiantly umbilical, since the play is about a destructively manipulative mother and her half-castrated sons. The monster-heroine, Mrs Phelps, seeks to destroy the engagement of her son Robert to Hester and the marriage of her other son David to his wife Christina. When Christina accuses her of being little more than a civilised cannibal, she replies, 'I would cut off my hands and burn out my eyes to be rid of you.' Finally she drives Hester to suicide but David manages to sever the tie that binds.

In London the dragon-mum was played by Lilian Braith-waite: a tall, dark, formidably witty woman who had once greeted James Agate's equivocal compliment that she was the second most beautiful woman in London with the retort, 'I shall cherish that, coming from our second best dramatic critic.' In the West End Marjorie Mars played the fiancée Hester and Claire Eames (Mrs Sidney Howard) Christina. For the post-West End tour, Miss Braithwaite retained her starring role but Peggy took over as Hester and Fabia Drake as Christina.

Fabia Drake – Peggy's senior by a couple of years and a woman of remarkable zest and curiosity – remembers the difference between the West End version and the tour: 'No one has ever been as good as Marjorie Mars at the raging hysteria of Hester and at displaying a blazing fit. On the other hand, she was nothing like as good as Peggy at the human Hester. This person was much truer, much more real and clearly a far more important actress.'

During the three-month tour – in which Peggy was seen by her adored grandfather in Croydon and by an important rising star, John Gielgud – Fabia and Peggy became good friends. They remain so today though their recollections of crucial incidents totally diverge. Fabia Drake recalls: 'On that tour I made a very improper suggestion which has been proved totally wrong. Peggy was already very classically minded and was anxious to play the big roles. I said to her, "You'll have to change your name. You can't go on calling yourself Peggy Ashcroft. You must call yourself Margaret Ashcroft." She wasn't impressed since Edith Evans and Gladys Cooper had got on very well despite having unfashionable names. Of course, she took no notice of me. What she did say to me at the time – and it revealed a very deep ambition, she is intensely ambitious – is that she wanted some day to have a theatre named after her. That, of course, has happened. She won't remember this, but I was most impressed.'

Not only can Peggy not recall such a remark; she says, in the most vigorous and categorical terms, that she could not possibly have entertained such a wild and improbable idea as having a theatre named after her. Such things simply didn't happen in Britain. But although she is adamant on this point, it would be surprising if, as a well-read and theatrically knowledgeable young actress, she did not have her eyes set on the classical peaks. With Ellen Terry – who died in 1928 – then a cherished memory and with Edith Evans and Sybil Thorndike respectively 19 and 25 years older than Peggy, there was a glaring vacancy in the English theatre for someone capable of tackling Shakespeare's young 'golden girls'. Gwen Ffrangcon-Davies had made her mark as Juliet and Cordelia. Jessica Tandy was just starting on her career, following in Peggy's footsteps at Playroom Six and Birmingham Rep. But in those days of West End cup-and-saucer comedy the British theatre was short of young actresses capable of measuring up to the major classics. Unconsciously, since childhood, Peggy had been training herself for this role.

But, even if there was room at the top, Peggy had to wait some time before showing her classical mettle. From September 1928 to September 1929, she enjoyed a run of parts in a variety of plays: no sweet chits in West End ephemera but a mixed bag of parts dotted around the London Fringe adding up to a valuable portfolio.

In September it was back to the Q for *Earthbound* by Leslie Goddard and Cecil Weir: in Eric Keown's words, 'another supernatural freak in which the spirit of a pirate clashed with an occult Indian who possessed the monstrously unfair advantage of being equipped with spectacles for detecting astral rays.' A month later came the role of Kristina in Strindberg's *Easter* at the Arts: a rare piece of Strindbergian optimism though one critic remarked it might have been written by Calvin in a kindergarten. Peggy played the hero's dutiful fiancée, Kristina: Gwen Ffrangcon-Davies had the rather better role of his sister, the daffodil-clutching Eleonora who, according to the author,'realises the idea of Christ in man'. Peggy's shuttle round London took her in November 1928 to Playfair's Lyric Hammersmith for the Granville-Barkers' adaptation of *A Hundred Years Old* by the Quintero Brothers: placid, sentimental stuff with a good role for Horace Hodges as the centenarian hero, but not much in it for Peggy. The big disappointment was that Granville-Barker himself took a hand in the direction but didn't do very much. To Peggy, he was an idol both for what she had heard of his legendary Shakespeare productions at the Savoy in 1913–14 and for his newly established *Prefaces to Shakespeare*. But by now, spurred on by his American

31

wife, he was backing out of practical theatre work. 'I have an image of him,' says Peggy, 'sitting in the Lyric circle with his gloves on. I kept waiting for a director to appear but he never did.'

Young actresses need work; and Peggy's practical philosophy of taking anything and everything that came her way and of learning her craft through doing soon began to pay off. The first sign of a major critic coming off the fence and declaring the arrival of a distinctive new talent came in April 1929 when Peggy went back up the hill to the Hampstead Everyman to take on the lead role in a modern tragedy, *Requital*, by Molly Kerr: 'She is beautifully played by Miss Peggy Ashcroft, a young actress whose work bears all over it the stamp of an uncommon charm and ability,' wrote W. A. Darlington in the *Daily Telegraph*.

Of even greater significance for Peggy's career was the fact that an actor in the Everyman company, Austin Trevor, had been engaged later in the year to play in *Jew Süss* with Matheson Lang at the Duke of York's. Trevor generously took Peggy to see the famous actor-manager and she was asked to read The Song of Solomon to the star in his dressing-room. Hearing her, nearly six decades later, reading 'Stay me with flagons, comfort me with apples' for our television profile with extraordinary suppleness and warmth, one is not surprised that her audition-piece went straight to Lang's heart. She was eventually to get the role of Naemi and come to the notice of playgoers and critics who had not been assiduously trekking round the London suburbs from Kew to Hammersmith.

If Peggy's career was to undergo a dramatic transformation in 1929, so too was her private life. While waiting for *Jew Süss* to get under way in the autumn, she did a summer tour of *She Stoops to Conquer*, playing Constance Neville. Also in the company was a tall, good-looking young actor, Rupert Hart-Davis, with an Eton and Oxford background, brief acting experience during a 1927 Old Vic season with Jean Forbes-Robertson and a number of literary friends. Peggy, although she had turned down one proposal of marriage from a distant cousin, was inexperienced in matters of the heart. But in Rupert Hart-Davis she found someone who shared her own eager passion for poetry and drama. Both partners now look back on their youthful marriage from the vantage-point of true friendship.

'The tour of *She Stoops*,' Peggy recalls, 'lasted three weeks during which Rupert and I fell in love and became engaged. It was the first romance of my life, the first relationship, and we formed an instant bond but it was more intellectual than physical. It was a very idyllic romance which was stillborn. We got married on 23 December 1929 the day after my 22nd birthday. But although the marriage did not last long, the fruits of it were that we formed a deep and long-lasting friendship. Rupert came from a very different background to mine and introduced me to a new circle of literary friends. On his side, Rupert came to realise that the stage was not his true métier: through Jean Forbes-Robertson he got to meet her husband Jamie (Hamish) Hamilton and went on to a wonderful career in publishing.'

The impression one gets is of a *mariage blanc* based on a profound spiritual kinship; and the impression is reinforced in the highly entertaining exchange of letters in later years between Rupert Hart-Davis and his former Eton teacher, George Lyttelton. The letters are discursive, literary and full of a sense of warm comradeship. On the whole, they steer clear of the deeper private emotions but there is a highly revealing letter written by Rupert Hart-Davis in July 1960 just after he has seen Peggy playing in *The Taming of the Shrew* at Stratford. It was the play in which he himself had first appeared as a non-speaking servant at the Old Vic. He writes:

'This fact, combined with Peggy's astonishing youthfulness and beauty in the part, took me back forcefully, and with exquisite melancholy, to the time when we and the century were in our twenties. This in its turn made me long to write down some impression of those days. My love for Peggy, which will be with me always, was (I now see), chiefly an intellectual and spiritual passion, tied up with poetry and music, drama, youth and spring. Basically it wasn't a physical passion at all – which is why the marriage foundered – but all the rest is still there although we seldom meet, and a brief visit like this can be an inspiration. Forgive me for pouring it all out to you: it is still very much in my mind, and you are my conscience.'

You could hardly have a more touching tribute to a first love; and the affection on both sides still burns deep even if their literary tastes have now slightly diverged (Peggy points out that she doesn't think that Rupert would care much for Brecht or Beckett or Pinter). But it is interesting to note how news of their engagement was received by others: in particular, Fabia Drake, who in the summer of 1929 was touring the North American continent in an incredible, nine-play Shakespeare repertoire. Fabia heard the news of Peggy's engagement from her parents. She wrote back to them: 'I agree with you that the latter [the engagement] is a mistake so early. She is such an infant and so very keen and ambitious that she will find it hard to run everything at once. Still, she is an orphan and her only brother married last year so I suspect she feels rather alone in the world and wants to have a background. Anyway, I do hope it will be a success.'

Peggy now says that her only ambition at the time was to do good work in the best company. She also denies that she got engaged to acquire a 'background': the reason was pure romantic love. But what is significant is the way Fabia Drake refers to Peggy as an 'orphan'; obviously there was about her at this time a touching innocence and vulnerability (alongside a clear-headed professional determination) that was to prove a trump card in her first major role on the West End stage.

The role of Naemi in *Jew Süss* was an ideal one in which to make a big impact: it gave Peggy the chance, in one memorable scene, to show maidenly virtue under siege. Ashley Dukes's adaptation of Lion Feuchtwanger's huge rich plumcake of a novel was not much more than lavish melodrama and far removed from the 'complete picture of a complex social organism' which Arnold Bennett had discovered in the 1927 English translation of the book. But, in Peggy's case, it was melodrama which worked. Naemi is the daughter of the wily, wealthy Josef Süss Oppenheimer who is the power behind the ducal throne of Wurtemburg (the year is 1737). In the big scene the Duke comes to seduce Naemi in the keep of Süss's castle in the forest of Hirsau and so frightens the pure, Scripture-reading girl that she takes a header into the courtyard and plunges to her death.

Shaw, had he been writing in the *Saturday Review*, might have made mincemeat of the combination of melodramatic plot and balletic spectacle (with Harold Turner and Pearl Argyle dancing Mars and Venus). Audiences on the pre-London tour in August and September clearly loved it: Rupert Hart-Davis remembers packed houses in Birmingham and Glasgow. One person who caught the play in Manchester was an enthusiastic young theatregoer just down from Oxford who was struck to the very soul by Peggy's performance as Naemi. He was Harold Hobson, who two decades later was to succeed James Agate as drama critic of the *Sunday Times*. But even 50 years after seeing *Jew Süss* he recalled it in detail and described Peggy's performance as one of the seven times in his life he had felt 'in the presence of greatness'. His eloquent description of her performance is worth quoting in full not only as a record of his youthful sensitivity but because it also explains and pins down a vital element in her mysterious power:

'I drove across the Pennines from Sheffield to Manchester to see this play; or rather to see Matheson Lang. Lang's magnificent presence, his stupendous bass voice, had enthralled me several times before; and I dare say that my provincial outlook was awed by the fact that he was cousin of the Archbishop of York, the mighty, later-to-become king-removing Cosmo Gordon of Canterbury.

'In the first three acts of *Jew Süss* I thought Lang to be superb. No other actor has ever been able to present like Lang the secular travail, the never-ending misery, the unrelenting ordeal of the Jewish people. This is curious for, as in those days I was only too much aware, Lang was closely connected with one of the great Christian churches. On that evening the throb of an age-long agony was as powerful as ever in his voice and I was profoundly stirred. And then the miracle happened. The curtain rose on the fourth act – at least this is how I remember it – to show a platform on a high tower; and in the centre of this platform, exalted, isolated from the world, the clear, cold light shining on her, sat a young girl Naemi. This was Peggy Ashcroft. Why did it seem to me that the lightning had struck, that the revelation had come, that all that had gone before was only a prologue, an introduction to what really mattered, to the thing that would always last and illuminate?

'Naemi was neither a long nor a spectacular part. To Lang was given the tumult and the action, the magnificence and splendour and tragedy and melodrama. Naemi had only to sit still and read the Hebrew scripture. But there is great art in sitting still, in utter repose, in absolute quietness of mind and spirit. Few people can do it. Few people can give the audience in full measure the peace and stillness of their own being. Peggy Ashcroft can and could and on that night did.'

All criticism is a form of autobiography and tells us as much about the writer as the subject. But, even allowing for the impressionable nature of an aspiring critic with a lifelong penchant for the religious, this is wonderfully revealing. It tells us that Peggy, besides the many gifts she was to develop later, was endowed from the start with a specific moral gravity: that she could magnetise an audience as much by the quality of her character as by the armoury of her technique. At a time when young English actresses tended towards a mannered artificiality Peggy commanded attention through a serenity that seemed to come from within.

When *Jew Süss* opened at the Duke of York's on 19 September 1929, expectation was immense. The novel was famous throughout Europe. Matheson Lang was a star. The play even had some vague claim to seriousness in a West End of fun and froth where *Rose Marie* was packing out Drury Lane, Bobby Howes and Binnie Hale were skittering through *Mr Cinders* at the Hippodrome and Ben Travers's *A Cup of Kindness* frolicked at the Aldwych. On the whole, however, the critics were unimpressed by the piece ('plums pulled out of Dr Feuchtwanger's colossal pudding' was how Agate described it) but full of admiration for the acting, not least from Peggy. What the boy-Hobson had discovered in Manchester, London realised for itself: that here was an uncommon young actress. The anonymous critic of *The Times*, while ironically puncturing the melodramatic preposterousness of the plot, led off his discussion of the actors with especial praise for Peggy: 'But we should need to be blind to miss the distinction of Miss Peggy Ashcroft's performance which, though of no great substance, did give integrity to one character and communicate an emotion not directly theatrical.'

This last phrase is significant: it suggests that, even in a piece of sumptuous melodrama, she managed to escape the dead hand of factitious emotion. Other critics were equally struck by her dying fall. As Peggy remembers it now: 'I backed away from the wicked Duke, went up to the window sill and then fell backwards onto a conveniently placed mattress. It probably looked more dangerous than it actually was. What I also remember is that I was caught and helped to my feet by one of the young supporting actors who was none other than Alistair Cooke.'

Peggy might be said to have plunged rather than risen to stardom. But it was not merely her athleticism that hooked people. It was her ringleted Jewish beauty, her suggestion of spiritual purity and, in the case of J. C. Trewin, her voice: 'What fascinated me – and I don't think it is hindsight – is that speech in those days was so affected among the *ingénues*. It seemed to me that no girl on stage ever spoke naturally and I still remember listening to Peggy in her big scene and saying "Good heavens, this is a new voice to me and how uncannily natural this is".'

Jew Süss ran for 211 performances at the Duke of York's, though Peggy left before the end of the run with tonsilitis. But her performance as Naemi won her her next big opportunity on the London stage. During the run of the play, Paul Robeson arrived in London to discuss a forthcoming West End production of *Othello*. One night Robeson's producer, Maurice Browne, took the star and his wife to see *Jew Süss*. Afterwards they all agreed they had found the Desdemona they were looking for, though Peggy did not get the part immediately: 'I had to be auditioned. That was rather an alarming audition because I was expected to do the Willow Song and the thing I can't do to save my life is sing in tune. However, I did get the part and that was thrilling because Paul Robeson was a folk-hero, a legendary figure to us all in those days. So it was a chance to play with him and to do my first Shakespeare in London. You can imagine that was very exciting but it was also desperately disillusioning because it was a perfectly terrible production.'

On paper, the production's prospects looked good. Maurice Browne had a creditable track-record as an actor-manager. Though English-born, he had worked a lot in America and fought strenuously for an alternative to commercialism, founding the Chicago Little Theatre in 1912. His management of the Savoy had also started well in 1929 with the success of R. C. Sherriff's *Journey's End*. Paul Robeson was also a powerful artist who had the right bass thunder in his voice for Othello and who had twice already taken London by storm: in O'Neill's *The Emperor Jones* in 1925 and in the 1928 production of *Showboat*, in which his rendering of 'Ole Man River' stopped the show. Robeson and Peggy apart, the cast included Sybil Thorndike as Emilia and the up-and-coming Ralph Richardson as Roderigo.

What went wrong? Basically, the attempt to do a major Shakespearean tragedy with an inadequate director. Robeson, who had at first turned down the role of Othello because he felt he lacked Shakespearean experience, was beguiled into playing it on the promise of a wonderful Iago and a great director. What he actually got was Browne himself as Iago and his first wife, Ellen Van Volkenburg, as director. According to Rupert Hart-Davis this was the problem:

'The tragedy of the whole thing was that Robeson had a wonderful ear and could instantly reproduce any intonation he was given. But Miss Van Volkenburg was incapable of giving him anything. She was in fact a pretentious dud. Yet when Othello cried out,"I would have him *nine years* a-killing", you could hear the audience draw in its breath in terror.'

Not merely was Robeson under-directed. He was also handi-capped by an Elizabethan costume of padded trunks, square shoes and a ruff that made him look broad and bulky, and by a text that was not so much badly cut as severely maimed. Out went such jewels as Othello's 'It frights the isle from her propriety' and huge chunks of Iago – including, incredibly, his envious, tell-tale description of Cassio, 'He hath a daily beauty in his life'. The painterly sets by James Pryde (a friend of Sickert and Nicholson who had worked on posters for Henry Irving) were also dull, cumbersome and murkily lit. Much of the action took place on a remote flight of steps cutting the action off from the audience, and the lighting was so dim that on one occasion Ralph Richardson planted an electric torch in his sleeve simply to get his stage bearings. As if this were not enough, while Peggy was bravely persevering with the Willow Song, a great 14-foot-high bed was being trundled into place like a battleship. On the first night at the Savoy in September 1930 all the critics complained about the aural bombardment going on behind the back-cloth while Desdemona was singing. Eventually peace was restored when the brass-lung'd Sybil Thorndike told the head scene-shifter in her best stentorian tone, 'Don't start moving the bed till I begin my speech. I can shout you down.'

The production exemplified the difficulty of doing one-off West End Shakespeare with an unversed director. For Peggy, however, the production offered both a vital Shakespearean launching-pad and, in the immediate future, something of a contractual cage. Maurice Browne had signed her up on a three-year contract. Its terms were that she got paid £16 per week as Desdemona but, if she was employed by anyone else over the next three years, Browne himself would take the extra money: a rather one-sided arrangement that was to curtail her immediate Shakespearean future.

For the moment, however, Peggy was thrilled to be playing Desdemona. The key question, in the absence of much directorial help, was how to interpret her. Down the centuries opinions have changed greatly about the part. The old view was to see her as an alabaster angel or wilting lily and one eighteenth-century actress pronounced that 'gentleness gives the prevailing tone to the character'. More recently, an anti-Desdemona faction has grown up. Peter Conrad, writing in the programme for the Royal Opera House's magnificent 1987 *Otello*, described Shakespeare's Desdemona thus: 'She remains only too querulously human: flirtatious on the quay at Cyprus, obstinate and bossy, convinced that she is the little woman who makes possible the great man's success.' That, however, is a rather misogynistic over-reaction to the view of her as a vacuous moppet.

Peggy's idea of the part was based on two key notions: in her own words, Desdemona is 'basically a girl with great spirit'; at the same time, she is passionately in love with her husband. Everything in the text supports Peggy's reading. It is all there in Desdemona's opening speech to the Senators:

> That I did love the Moor to live with him
> My downright violence and scorn of fortunes
> May trumpet to the world. My heart's subdued
> Even to the very quality of my lord.

In other words, she has the strength and courage to defy both her father's wishes and social custom in marrying a member of an alien race: her motivation is pure love. For Peggy, Desdemona's later passionate defence of sexual fidelity to Emilia is further proof both of the character's strong will and her marital devotion. At the start of her Shakespearean career, as so often later, Peggy was able to suggest a sexually-charged femininity that was in no way passive or languorous.

The major critics were quick to grasp the point. Ivor Brown sounded the keynote in the *Observer*: 'On the credit side, and an exquisite foil to Robeson's Othello, is Miss Peggy Ashcroft's Desdemona, a wife as simply innocent as her lord. No emptiness of the pretty flaxen puppet here but a true woman opening the petals of her wonder and her love to the African sunlight of her hero's triumph. All the scenes between these two are of a rare partnership and, when tender, beautifully so.' Even James Agate in the *Sunday Times* – at this stage one of Peggy's admirers though later her sharpest critic – wrote of 'Peggy Ashcroft's exquisite Desdemona'. But one of the most handsome tributes to her performance came in later years from a perceptive observer in the Savoy stalls, John Gielgud. Writing in *Early Stages* in 1938, he described the murky ineptitude of the production with its gloomy sets and off-stage clatter. 'But,' he wrote, 'when Peggy came on in the Senate scene it was as if all the lights in the theatre had suddenly gone up. Later, in the handkerchief scene, I shall never forget her touching gaiety as she darted about the stage, utterly innocent and light-hearted, trying to coax and charm Othello from his angry questioning.' And today he remarks that 'Everything she did on stage seemed right and natural.'

About Robeson's Othello opinion was – and still is – divided. Peggy herself says he took a lot of care in his speaking of Shakespearean verse and that it was remarkable to lie on her death-bed every night and listen to his final speech. George Rylands, a legendary Cambridge director-don and now one of Peggy's closest friends, still has reservations about Robeson's speaking: 'The trouble with Robeson was that the rhythm of music is not the same rhythm as that of Shakespeare's blank verse. The full emotional tide was not going in on the blank verse wave. What I do remember is that there was an audible intake of breath when Peggy rushed into the arms of his Othello; which is exactly as it should be.' In the racial climate of 1930 there was, in fact, a *frisson* at the spectacle of a black man and a white woman embracing on a public stage. Frith Banbury, who saw the production as a young actor, confirms that 'we were so thrilled and excited to see a black actor playing the part that we didn't care too much about any imperfections in the execution.'

But not everyone was quite so thrilled. Agate in his review argued that there was no more reason to get a Negro to play Othello than a fat man to play Falstaff, and one detects a touch of subconscious racism in his emphasis on Robeson's physical awkwardness and the fact that 'his hands appeared to hang below his knees and his whole bearing, gait and diction were full of humility and apology, the inferiority-complex in a word'.

If there was a hint of racism in Agate's review, there was an audible blast of it in the response of some members of the public to the presence of a black actor as Othello. For Peggy, then a slightly sheltered, apolitical, middle-class girl who knew little of the world beyond Britain, it came as a violent shock to encounter the ugliness of open prejudice:

'I had never thought consciously about racism. So I was absolutely amazed that Sybil and I used to get rather unpleasant letters saying "East is East and West is West and no more theatres where you play for me after this". The fact that Paul Robeson, who was acclaimed as a great singer and a great artist in this country, was not welcome in the Savoy Hotel was also enormously shocking and surprising to me. I heard from Paul himself something about the racist situation in the United States and I think my first feelings about racism were aroused in that play.'

And not only her feelings about racism. Peggy was both spiritually charmed and physically enthralled by Robeson. And she recently expressed her sentiments – to the authors of a new Robeson biography – in carefully chosen words: 'The many manifestations of racism made it more than a theatrical experience. It put the significance of race straight in front of me and I made my choice of where I stood. It was also a lesson to me in the power of drama to encourage a portrayed emotion to become a fantasy of one's own. How could one not fall in love in such a situation with such a man! Othello and Desdemona – fighting together in adverse circumstances. My first lesson in having to distinguish between what is for real and what must be simulated. The play only ran for six weeks and then the Robesons left

England so that our friendship was short-lived, and though they came to see me in various plays when they visited London our communications were few.'

The experience of playing Desdemona was, in every sense, momentous. It was Peggy's sixteenth role in three busy years on the professional stage. But it was the part that launched her as a Shakespearean heroine, that won the approval of the critics and the interest of Walter Sickert who asked for photos of her and Robeson and who was to paint her many times in future years. But, no less importantly, it alerted Peggy to injustice and oppression in a way that had a profound effect on the rest of her life. Desdemona saw Othello's visage in his mind; and Peggy listened to Robeson's stories of American racial prejudice with the same transfixed, adoring attention that Shakespeare's heroine brought to Othello's rather more romantic traveller's tales.

CHAPTER FOUR

Pupil and Master

IN THE SAME WEEK that *Othello* opened at the Savoy, a rather startling little book appeared in print: *A National Theatre* by Harley Granville-Barker. It envisaged a permanent structure, costing around half a million pounds, situated on the South Bank between County Hall and the new Charing Cross Bridge. It would ideally have three auditoria: a large one seating 1800 for the production of plays like *Antony and Cleopatra*, a smaller one seating 1000 for more intimate pieces and comedies such as *The Importance of Being Earnest* and a 200-seater for experimental pieces. What is impressive is how close Granville-Barker's blueprint was to the National's eventual structure: what is equally striking is that it was to be almost 50 years before the dream became a reality.

It was the kind of theatre that Peggy, as an idealistic young actress, dreamed of but in 1930 it seemed a far-off Utopia. The sole home of classical drama in London at that time was the Old Vic and it was there that one might have expected Peggy to go after her acclaimed Desdemona. Here there is some divergence in the records. Harcourt Williams, who was director of the Vic from 1929 to 1933, gives the impression in his book *Four Years at the Old Vic*, that when Peggy did eventually join the company in 1932 it was after a good deal of pleading on his part and a

43

certain amount of evasion on hers. Peggy's recollection of events is entirely different:

'In the summer of 1930 I was approached by both John [Gielgud] and Ralph [Richardson] to join them at the Vic for the new season that autumn. Maurice Browne, however, refused to let me go because I would have earned no more money than I was getting as Desdemona and he would have lost out. Obviously I would have been there in its heyday instead of coming at the end of the Williams regime. I only got out of the Maurice Browne contract in 1931 when I was in a play by Edgar Wallace: he discovered the terms of the contract and threatened to expose it in his column in the *Sunday News* unless it was torn up.'

So instead of capitalising on her success in Shakespeare, Peggy spent a rather frustrating eighteen months in a series of commercial plays (three of them disastrously short-lived) that did little to advance her career. As she says, it was typical of the haphazard way in which the theatre was organised at that time.

Inwardly impatient at the restrictions placed on her by the Browne contract, Peggy followed her Desdemona with a juvenile role in a new Somerset Maugham comedy, *The Breadwinner*, that opened at the Vaudeville in September 1930. This was another instalment in Maugham's attack on the emptiness of marriage and the inhuman bondage of domesticity. A kind of *Doll's House* in reverse, it was about a London stockbroker who walks out on his parasitic children and pretentious wife in order to start a new life. Ronald Squire, an expert light comedian with a voice like a squeezed soda-syphon, and Marie Lohr played the husband and wife, Jack Hawkins was the son and Peggy the daughter who packs her father's tailcoat when he decides to leave in case he finds work as a waiter. Critics, with maidenly *pudeur*, professed to be shocked by the line in Scene Two when Judy Battle says: 'Don't you know that since the war amateurs have entirely driven the professionals out of business? No girl can make a decent living now by prostitution.' The drama critic of *The Times* declared that 'Peggy Ashcroft is made to say things of fantastic callousness' and Hannen Swaffer attacked the piece in his Sunday column declaring that Peggy had blushed as she spoke the offending words. The real problem, however, was that Maugham's misogyny made the character a deeply unsympathetic one. Frith Banbury, an indefatigable playgoer, recalls that Peggy looked a trifle strange with her hair in earphones and that she was not overly persuasive. Small wonder since the play, which ran for 158 performances, was chiefly a hymn to naked male selfishness.

Coming out of *The Breadwinner* in 1931, Peggy found herself confronting a frustrating, standstill period both in her work and in her life: one of the very few in her career. Her marriage to Rupert Hart-Davis had foundered. She was still frustrated by the Browne contract, and she found herself in a series of short-run flops adapted from foreign works.

Her first engagement of that year, however, came when she was invited to complement the cast of an Oxford University Dramatic Society production of James Elroy Flecker's *Hassan* at the city's New Theatre: women undergraduates had first been allowed to take part in productions in 1927 but, because of their supposed shortcomings, it was still the practice to invite down young professional actresses. Unfortunately, the production itself was a débâcle. Flecker's piece of Oriental exotica – written in a style of empurpled rhetoric – was way beyond the scope of Oxford undergraduates. Basil Dean, who had directed the original 1923 London production, merely supervised the Oxford version, leaving the 12-hour-a-day rehearsals to his Stakhanovite stage-manager, Gibson Cowan, who earned the nickname of 'Back-on-it' through his habit of making the cast go endlessly over the lines. Not even an undergraduate cast that included Giles Playfair (the son of Nigel), William Devlin and the England Rugby captain and future MRA leader, Peter Howard, could save the day. 'Bad speaking is prevalent . . . the result is disastrous,' wrote W. A. Darlington in the *Daily Telegraph*: the two imported professionals, Peggy and Thea Holme, as Pervaneh and Yasmin, were left stranded.

But the trip to Oxford had one significant benefit for Peggy: it introduced her to a stocky, unusually mature undergraduate who played the Caliph in *Hassan* with some distinction and who walked the streets of Oxford sporting an immense brown overcoat, a muffler and cane. This was George Devine, with whom Peggy struck up an instant rapport. Peggy was intrigued by his un-English quality (Greek on his father's side, Scots-

Canadian on his mother's), his obvious maturity and his passion for the theatre: the two of them talked endlessly about the Komi-sarjevsky Chekhov productions they had both seen at Barnes. And when, immediately after *Hassan*, Devine and Giles Playfair engaged in a battle royal for the OUDS Presidency, Peggy canvassed eagerly for the idealistic Devine rather than for the son of her former patron. Devine won the Presidency by 48 votes to 45. Even more importantly, Peggy found a new friend who shared her vision of a company theatre based on something more exalted than box-office receipts.

For the moment, however, it was back to the roulette of West End theatre and for Peggy the rare, dispiriting experience of being in a hat-trick of commercial flops. First she found herself playing a religious novitiate, opposite Ronald Squire, in an ill-fated Edgar Wallace version of *Charles the Third* by Curt Götz at Wyndham's. The one good thing was that the Wallace connection allowed her to escape from the tentacles of Maurice Browne, when Wallace discovered the terms of his restrictive contract.

Next her critical champion, Bill Darlington, asked her to be in his adaptation of *A Knight Passed By* by a Dutch author, Jan Fabricius. The play itself passed by in five nights at the Ambassadors. But, although it was a box-office disaster, it attracted professional theatre people: so much so that when the box-office manager was incautiously asked how the play was going he replied 'Magnificently – we're turning away paper (i.e. complimentary tickets) at every performance.'

Completing the dud trio was *Sea Fever* at the New Theatre in June. This was an adaptation by Auriol Lee and John van Druten of Marcel Pagnol's Marseilles trilogy. But life on the Quai de la Joliette did not translate well to St Martin's Lane; and, although Peggy herself was praised for the sincerity of her performance as the fish-girl, Fanny, whose lover finally abandons her for the sea, it was generally felt that an atmosphere of Kensington gentility prevailed and that the actors reeked more of toothpaste than of garlic on the breath. Frith Banbury, as a spectator, remembers that Peggy and her leading man, Maurice Evans, were 'suburban middle-class'. Peggy herself recalls that the actors all wanted to use a regional accent but were brusquely informed that they had to do the play in standard English.

An irksome, wasted year for Peggy – one in which she might have been playing Shakespeare at the Vic – was rounded off by a six-week autumn run at the Haymarket in yet another foreign play: *Take Two from One* adapted by the Granville-Barkers from the Spanish Sierras, though clearly staying in the foothills. The play, full of old Spanish customs, involved Gertrude Lawrence and the young Peggy struggling for the affections of Nicholas Hannen who loved them both and who ended the piece, Piran-dello-style, by jumping off the stage into a neighbouring box. Granville-Barker was rapped over the knuckles by the critics and told to stop interpreting 'minor matters from Madrid'. For Agate the low point in this Hispanic farce was the scene where Gertrude Lawrence had to burst into a drawing-room in the costume of an African savage which, he said, was 'like a production number in a Cicely Courtneidge musical'.

For Peggy, there was one minor consolation: the piece was directed by Komisarjevsky. The art-theatre god from the Chekhov seasons at Barnes and the apostle of an inner realist style of acting was not much in evidence in this production. Nor, despite Komis's formidable amatory reputation (not for nothing was he known in theatrical circles as 'Come-and-seduce-me') was there at first any hint of romance. 'The play,' says Peggy, 'was far from a success and I got little satisfaction out of doing it. All I remember about Komis's direction is that the day after the first night I ran into him at the Stage Door and he said "You were very good." This came as a shock because he had torn me apart in rehearsal. He told me the reason was that he had washed his hands of the stars and decided to concentrate on me. It wasn't until the following year that our relationship really started.'

In a marking-time year that did little to encourage a love of the commercial theatre, Peggy had at least worked with two men who had some vision of an alternative theatre: Komis and George Devine. On the larger horizon, the complacent insularity that is the perennial curse of British theatre had received one of its periodic shocks. La Compagnie des Quinze from the Vieux Col-ombier in Paris had been imported to London by Bronson Albery for a season in André Obey's *Noé* and *Le Viol de Lucrèce*. The Quinze were acrobats, mimes and musicians whose balletic style enlarged the whole definition of acting and had a powerful impact on a new generation of theatre practitioners: it became a matter of love, honour and Obey. The company also brought to England Michel Saint-Denis: the nephew of the troupe's founder (Jacques Copeau), a good actor and a figure of monastic dedication. In years to come he was to found the London Theatre Studio, and become part of the ill-fated Old Vic Centre and a director of the RSC. He was also to direct, and become an intimate friend of, Peggy, whose idealism accorded with his own. The year 1931 may have been a slow one for Peggy, but there was a hint of change in the air and a sense amongst certain visionary individuals that it was time to pump new life into the comatose British theatre.

What Peggy herself needed most, after a fitful and dispiriting eighteen months, was a major classic role. The opportunity came with an invitation to play Juliet in an OUDS production of *Romeo and Juliet* in February 1932.

It was, in every sense, a momentous production: one that forged vital links between a group of people whose professional lives were to be interconnected over the next three decades. If there was a sense of family in the upper echelons of British theatre, it had its origins in this production.

For a start the OUDS Committee, under the Presidency of the imaginative George Devine, took the bold step of inviting John Gielgud, already a pillar of the Old Vic and a West End star playing nightly in *The Good Companions* at His Majesty's, to direct his first production: his mercurial, quicksilver mind and impeccable visual taste marked him out as a shrewd choice. As his costume designers he chose three rather shy, retiring girls from Kent who had come to his attention with their character-sketches of the Old Vic 1929–30 Company: Elizabeth Montgomery and the sisters Margaret ('Percy') and Sophia Harris, known as the firm of Motley, thus began a long association with Gielgud. Apart from Peggy, who soon established herself as his first choice leading lady, Gielgud also brought in Edith Evans to play the Nurse. And amongst the OUDS's own talent there was the handsome Christopher Hassall as Romeo, George Devine exercising his Presidential prerogative and casting himself as Mercutio, Hugh Hunt (who went on to run the Old Vic during a stormy period) as Friar Lawrence and the Chorus, the noble-voiced William

Devlin as Tybalt and Terence Rattigan as one of the maskers. What is staggering, in hindsight, is how much of the future of the British stage this encompasses and how the friendships Peggy formed with Gielgud, Devine and the Motleys were to be of enduring significance.

For Peggy it was a happy time both personally and professionally. There was the fun of Oxford itself in the Spring term and the chance of mingling with the students: one OUDS member who vividly remembers meeting her at 'one of those classic Oxford parties where we all stayed up till six in the morning' was her future third husband, Jeremy Hutchinson. But there was also the chance to discover a role that Peggy was to make very much her own in the 1930s. 'I see Romeo and Juliet,' she says, 'as in themselves the most glorious, life-giving people. What you have to take into account is their ages. She is a girl of 14, Romeo is a boy of 16. I discovered in playing her that the essential thing is youth rather than being tragic. I think she's a victim of circumstance. The tragedy is simply something that happens to her.'

Peggy had the advantage of playing opposite a young, student Romeo. In contrast to her experience with the Savoy *Othello*, she also found herself in a production based on fluency of action and simplicity of design. The setting, a triple-arched affair backed with drapes and a central raised doorway, was economical but effective. Gielgud, imbibing the lessons of Harcourt Williams and his mentor Harley Granville-Barker, kept the action moving forwards at a great pace. He also, as you would expect, encouraged his young actors to relish the sound and music of the language. William Devlin said of him that 'he really *taught* us rather than produced us: the right method for intelligent undergraduates with flexible voices.' Lord David Cecil, forty years later, said it was 'easily the best performance of the play I have seen.' The major Fleet Street critics came rushing up to Oxford and decided that it was the best thing the OUDS had done in years. Darlington in the *Daily Telegraph* wrote that: 'It happens again and again in this production that one seems to hear Mr Gielgud's voice on the stage — which means not that the undergraduates are slavish imitators but simply that they are indeed learning to speak verse and are sensitive enough to recognise a master when they hear him.'

As for Peggy's Juliet, the quality that critics seized on was the very one she was hoping to convey: not so much total technical perfection as youthful ardour and intensity of feeling. 'Above all,' wrote Darlington, 'this Juliet is in love – not rehearsing phrases but passionately in love.' *The Times* critic concurred, saying that she was not only the youngest and freshest Juliet of his experience but the one who was most vehemently in love: 'The high music of that love's despair sometimes tests her too far but its melancholy is a rapture and its delights are delight itself.' Significantly he added that 'in comedy Miss Ashcroft can go where she pleases', suggesting that Peggy found in the character a gaiety that actresses often miss and prophetically putting his finger on one of her greatest gifts: the ability to find in 'tragic' characters like Cleopatra and Hedda a sharp-tongued irony.

The only person who didn't much enjoy this production was poor Terence Rattigan. Playing one of the maskers who enter after Juliet's presumed death, he found that on the first night his solitary line 'Faith, we may put up our pipes and be gone' got a big laugh from the audience. He tried it with a different emphasis each night of the run, but the same thing happened, until by the final performance he was muttering it inaudibly. It never seems to have occurred to anyone that the line, in context, actually is quite funny.

Clearly the memory of his embarrassment scarred Rattigan for life. In his play, *Harlequinade* which is set backstage during a tour of *Romeo and Juliet*, he included the character of the bit-player who has the same trouble with the line. And twenty years later when Peggy came to do Rattigan's *The Deep Blue Sea* she found that he was still haunted by the recollection of his OUDS fiasco: 'Terry told me,' she says, 'that when he came in after Juliet has taken the potion and he had this one line to say, he thought I had an expression of such utter disapproval on my face that it daunted him. I explained that it wasn't disapproval but that I was desperately trying not to cry when Edith had to say "Honest good fellows, ah put up, put up, for well you know this is a pitiful case." That was the literal truth and so it became an instant bond between myself and Terry.'

After their Oxford triumph, the company were invited by Bronson Albery to give two extra Sunday performances of *Romeo and Juliet* at London's New Theatre in aid of Lilian Baylis's Old Vic–Sadler's Wells Fund. The idea was that a cheque would be handed to Miss Baylis on stage at the end of the show by the incoming OUDS President, Hugh Hunt, who was playing Friar Lawrence. The problem was that the Friar's habit (in the days before he began to be played as a bicycling worker-priest) had no pockets, so it was arranged that George Devine as Mercutio should look after the cheque and hand it over to Hunt at the curtain-call. Devine forgot all about it and so an embarrassed Hunt had to press an empty palm to Miss Baylis's pretending it contained the cheque. Not having any of this nonsense, Lilian Baylis cried in a sarcastic voice that carried well into the stalls, 'Come on, dear, where's the cheque?'

One interested spectator at that performance was Komisarjevsky, who was then in the process of setting up a Sunday night Stage Society production for May of *Le Coçu Magnifique* by Fernand Crommelynck. Peggy's work he already knew; though it is fair to say that until that night he had little idea of the depth of feeling she could convey on stage. But he was also taken with the performance of Devine as Mercutio. Shortly afterwards he sent for him with a view to casting him in his Sunday night show and was somewhat surprised when a stocky, apparently unprepossessing young man walked in. 'Oh no I don't want you, you're not the man I'm looking for,' said Komisarjevsky. 'I'm looking for the man who played Mercutio.' To which Devine replied 'But that was me' and was immediately cast in the show.

It was during rehearsals for *Le Coçu* that Peggy – her marriage to Rupert Hart-Davis now over, though without any loss of mutual affection – came under the spell of the Russian magus; and after the production was over, they lived together in a flat in Berkeley Gardens in Campden Hill that became something of a mecca for idealistic young actors. Peggy leaves one in little doubt that her relationship with Komis and their subsequent marriage were fraught with difficulty, but she makes it equally clear that she learned from him a much more methodical, disciplined and analytical approach to acting.

Komis's production of *Le Coçu Magnifique*, closely modelled on a Constructivist version directed in Moscow ten years earlier by Meyerhold, had a characteristic inventiveness. The play itself is about a village scribe and poet who is so infatuated with his beautiful, innocent bride, Stella, that he convinces himself no man could resist her. Madly jealous, he forces her to share her bed with every man in the village in the hope of unmasking her true lover. Amongst the queue of lovers lining up outside the house was Anthony Quayle, who told me: 'There was a great line of extras who had to walk on as the cuckolded hero offers his wife to the villagers. It was a typical Komis production: people entering on bicycles, a jazz band on stage squatting on what looked like a clothes-horse. There was also a great walkway up to the house and all these people dressed in different clothes – fishermen in oilskins, cabdrivers, peasants in corduroys, you name it, all going up to the house where she conferred her favours.'

Quayle – who, like Devine, was to become a regular visitor to the flat in Berkeley Gardens – talks about Komisarjevsky with a rapt adoration that convinces one of his theatrical genius and explains why he exercised the spell he did on the still-maturing Peggy:

'I was reading the other day a paper an American scholar sent me about the production of *The Merry Wives of Windsor* that Komis did at Stratford in 1935. Falstaff had a Tyrolean hat and there were Viennese-operetta-like yodellers. It was a pastiche of absurdity: the kind of thing they're doing now at Stratford with great success. Komis was there ahead, ahead, ahead. He was a really remarkable man, a draughtsman and designer as well as director. His was the entire and total concept. Even Peter Brook can't do everything. He plays around with a tape-recorder and makes squeaks and squawks and noises but in the end he has to have someone to do the music. He can't do it all. Komis could. He was Russian, had a very Slav face with a bald dome and slanting eyes. He looked a bit like Lenin without a beard. He had a funny, sharp fox-face with a little pointed nose and a sly, humorous look. I was in a musical he directed at the Q Theatre in 1931 and in an adaptation of Louis Golding's *Magnolia Street* he did at the Adelphi in 1934. He was very quiet, never shouted, just waddled about with his feet turned out. Always wore a brown tweed jacket and grey flannel trousers. There was no finger-cracking or shouting. He was responsible for de-romanticising English acting. Everything was to do with reality and the truth of human relationships. This is what he was endlessly on about. He was really a product of Stanislavsky. He was only half a generation on from him. He had a very far-ahead concept of what should happen in a theatre. They should have put him in charge of Stratford long ago. It would have been a towering theatre. Instead they gave him one production a year during Bridges-Adams's time in the 1930s. It was pathetic they didn't trust him because he was the best director they had – almost ever. So there you had Peg from her first flowering being influenced by this very intellectual man.'

Komisarjevsky's intellectuality also concealed an impish, mercurial humour. Margaret Harris recalls that in *Magnolia Street* Anthony Quayle was required to take a brick and hurl it through a plate-glass window. Komis was not satisfied with the way he did it and asked for another window to be brought so that he could show him how. Komis still felt the action wasn't quite right and smashed another six windows purely because he was enjoying himself so much. Miss Harris adds that: 'In a dance sequence in the show he made a very large actress called Molly Hamley-Clifford dance with a midget because he enjoyed the contrast between this tiny little man and this huge woman: the climax of the sequence was that she fainted and fell on top of him and nobody could find him.'

For Peggy the relationship with Komisarjevsky – who was 50 as against her 24 years of age when they started living together – was serious and productive, though later filled with pain. 'With Komis,' she told me, 'I always felt that I was the pupil and he was the master and he was very inspiring. I learned from him how to approach a part, how to analyse a role, how important it was to understand the director's whole conception of a play. I realised from him that the whole is more important than the individual part. I would say that Komis crystallised certain things for me. He knew exactly what he wanted a production to be: he knew the tempo, the interpretation, the precise musical rhythm of a play.'

In fact, Peggy was to work with Komisarjevsky only on three further occasions. But with his Stanislavskyan background, his wide knowledge of plays, his vision of a more enlightened theatre, he was obviously a tremendous intellectual stimulus as well as a source of advice and encouragement. When Peggy talks about him now it is with tremendous gratitude for everything he taught her as well as with a slight sadness at the volatile brevity of their marriage. But possibly the most significant admission is when she says, 'He made me realise that to be an actor is to be a perfectionist.' That is a vital clue to the mystery of Peggy's art: her profound and dedicated application.

In the summer of 1932 Peggy's perfectionism was applied to a somewhat shaky vehicle: an Eden Philpotts Dartmoor tragedy, *The Secret Woman*, at the Duchess. The most significant fact about the play was that it had been banned in 1912 by the prurient Lord Chamberlain who objected to a speech in which a husband explained to his wife, pretty circuitously, the facts of life. Protests followed from Shaw, Henry James, Granville-Barker, Gilbert Murray and many more and the play was eventually given its first public showing at Birmingham Rep in 1922. But when the piece finally arrived at the Duchess ten years later, its display of rustic passion pleased not the million and it soon closed.

For Peggy it was no great matter since she was by then committed to the biggest challenge so far in her young career: joining the Old Vic as leading lady in September to play ten leading roles in the space of nine months. It was both a ludicrously demanding assignment and an invaluable experience for an actress of 24 with her eyes firmly set on a classical career. It was Mecca with a hidden treadmill.

Harcourt Williams in his book claims that he decided after seeing Peggy's Oxford Juliet and talking to Edith Evans that he wanted her for the Vic, but that she eluded him. He rang her up in the spring: she was unsure. A week or so later he saw her at the theatre. 'She was in the stalls,' he writes 'and I was in the pit. In the interval she waved to me and hurriedly left the stalls. I left the pit and made an effort to join her. We never met. She told me afterwards that on seeing me it had suddenly come to her that after all she *must* come to the Old Vic. And then, not being able to find me, she had let the wretched Fates cut the thread.'

Peggy passionately denies that she played hard to get. She says she was angry and annoyed about missing her chance of joining the company in 1930. When the offer was renewed two years later she obviously talked it over with Komisarjevsky, who was her mentor, tutor and lover, but she had no real inner doubt. On paper, it was a young actress's dream. Accepting a salary of £20 a week and with her Stanislavskyan Svengali to advise and encourage her, she set out by bus that autumn from Campden Hill to try and win the battle of Waterloo Road.

CHAPTER FIVE

Ten at the Vic

ONE MORNING IN MARCH 1929 a promising Shakespearean actor called Harcourt Williams had sat down to breakfast to discover a letter from Lilian Baylis inviting him to take over the post of Producer (Artistic Director in modern parlance) at the Old Vic.

He nervously took the job on and went about it with admirable intentions. His aims were to break down the slow, deliberate method of delivering Shakespeare's verse, to demolish the habit of speaking Shakespeare with a windmill of waving gestures to indicate 'period', to further the revolution begun by William Poel and Harley Granville-Barker of presenting the play without breaks to accommodate tons of decorative scenery. With his habit of munching Bemax in the stalls during rehearsals, he was an eccentric and lovable man, and his first three seasons showed his success in attracting the brightest young acting talents of the time. Those were the years of Gielgud's Hamlet, Lear, Macbeth, Romeo, Richard II and Hotspur, of Richardson's Iago, Bottom, Toby Belch, Petruchio, Enobarbus and Caliban.

By the time Peggy joined the Vic company in 1932, however, Williams was in his fourth consecutive season of turning out productions at a huge rate on pinched Lilian Baylis budgets. 'I must find some money,' Baylis said to Williams one day. 'I keep praying for money but the Almighty only sends me penny collections.' Every expense was spared, and Williams was a tired man.

Peggy's marathon season at the Vic can be looked at in two ways. At the age of 24 she was getting a chance for a first, or even second, go at some of the great Shakespearean roles: Portia, Rosalind, Imogen, Juliet. On the other hand, she was playing these roles in a pell-mell repertory with a three-weekly turn-around and in rough, but by no means always ready, productions. She looks back on that Vic season now with decidedly mixed feelings:

'I suppose,' she says, 'it was like most repertory theatres except that there was the pressure of a national press night every three weeks. When I went for my first interview and was given my line of parts it sounded very, very exciting but little did I know that I was really biting off more than I could chew. I felt I could never catch up. It was like always running for a train. The conditions of work were extremely strenuous and travelling across London was very tiring. I lived in Notting Hill Gate at the time and I had to get to the theatre at ten in the morning and, when I was playing, I'd arrive home at ten-thirty at night. There was no underground and almost no-one had a car in those days so it always meant a long bus journey.'

Fortunately Peggy had Komisarjevsky at home to sustain her. She discussed her roles with him as they came up. She would even discuss grouping and stage positions with him at night and try to smuggle some of his ideas tactfully into the next morning's rehearsal. Above all, he made her see that she was serving a vital apprenticeship. The season may have been, in Peggy's words, 'a desperate aim at an impossible target' but, as an actress, she had the perfectionist ideal instilled in her by Komisarjevsky.

The season would have been easier if Peggy had had a Gielgud or a Richardson opposite her. In fact, her leading man was Malcolm Keen: a perfectly sound actor but the pressures of a helter-skelter season so got to him that on the first night of *The Winter's Tale* he went on as Leontes with the book in his hand. Around Peggy there was a not inconsiderable young company including Alistair Sim, Marius Goring, Roger Livesey, Anthony Quayle and George Devine. But her old friend, Devine, often found himself cruelly miscast, and Anthony Quayle even now paints a graphic picture of the hectic, low-budget improvisation that characterised the British theatre in those days before subsidy:

'Productions at the Vic that season were appalling. I talked once to the resident designer, Paul Smyth, who was a cobbler-together of whatever he could find. He told me he had a budget of £28 per production. There was also a famous Wardrobe Master, Orlando Whitehead, who would rummage around for whatever he could get but it was all old stuff from the Benson productions. Anything, anything went. A monk's habit, there it is, get on, there's your monk's habit. If it's too long or too short, well get your mother to take a tuck in it. If you fancied wearing green earrings, you went off to Woolworth's and bought them. It was truly awful.'

For all that, the season got off to a bright start in September with Shaw's *Caesar and Cleopatra*. The idea of opening a Shakespeare-dominated season with Shaw had been handed down from on high by the Old Vic Governors and Miss Baylis was none too pleased. Neither the play's title nor Shaw's name was allowed to disfigure the posters outside the building, and on opening night Miss Baylis told an enthusiastic audience that their reception made her a little jealous for Shakespeare. Shaw's attitude to the whole venture also reveals what an old deceiver he could be. On a brisk walk over the Malvern Hills earlier that summer Shaw had told Harcourt Williams that the theatre was done for and that we had better pack our trunks and go home. But, after seeing the production, Shaw sent a congratulatory note to Williams revealing just how much he cared about theatrical effect: 'The death of Ftata was well staged; but next time put a mess of rose-pink under her neck and when Cleopatra, lifting her head, gets her hands into it, let her lift the roof with a scream. Then slam down the curtain ...'

Peggy, whose first and last professsional appearance in a play by her teenage idol this was to be, scored a great success as Shaw's kitten-queen. In pictures of the production she looks beautiful with her Princess Nefertite head-dress showing off her extraordinarily long swan-like neck. The Old Vic audience took to her instantly: one paper noted that she received the kind of welcome which the outer world reserves for visiting Hollywood stars. But what really counted was her ability to characterise the role and to realise that Shaw – in reality the sexiest of writers – created a heroine who combined a spankable erotic playfulness with shrewd mental agility. Charles Morgan in *The Times*, more than any critic, got the point: 'This is no doll when you get to know her but a petulant child quick to her immediate advantage, shallow in long judgement, cruel as a kitten, dangerous in her follies. Not, let us say at once, a pleasant child for she would have been at home in the highest Jamaican wind but an engaging trickster with the spark of life fairly aglow in her'. Peggy's auspicious début was only marred by an accident at a matinée when she dashed her toe against an iron counterweight and broke a bone which led to her missing a few performances' and some rehearsals for the next show in the rep, *Cymbeline*.

This turned out to be a disaster. Harcourt Williams admits that he bungled it pretty badly. The set was too far upstage, Peggy's enforced absence threw the rhythm of rehearsals and poor George Devine was disastrously miscast as the juvenile lead, Posthumus Leonatus. Quayle to this day has a recollection of him sitting in front of his dressing-room mirror with tears streaming down the yellow make-up (making him look like a 'jaundiced Arab') that he thought appropriate to a romantic juvenile. Peggy and Marius Goring had persuaded Williams that Devine should be given a break from character-parts, but his stocky, bullish build was against him and when Imogen followed his exit in the first scene with the line 'I chose an eagle' the Vic audience dissolved in laughter.

Imogen was the role Peggy most wanted to play when she went to the Vic. She got good notices for her performance, not least from Ivor Brown in the *Observer*, who said that she 'caught loveliness on the wing and made the Fidele scenes delicious'. Yet she also found the character terrifically hard work because the other characters are rather shakily drawn and Imogen therefore has to push the play along almost single-handed. She points out that Ellen Terry had a precisely similar reaction. Miss Terry adored Imogen, saying that 'her impulses are always wholehearted ones too – she never does things by halves' while, at the same time, writing to Shaw that she felt she could never fly in the role and that she knew what the part ought to be but could never bring it off. Peggy adds that Judi Dench later confessed to her 'I found it very tough playing Imogen.' Three generations of actresses seem to have had problems with the character. Yet it remains Shakespeare's most touching portrait of female constancy.

Peggy's gallop through the Shakespearean heroines continued in November with Rosalind in *As You Like It*. Williams's production, evoking the forest through a geometric hillock made out of rostra from the previous season's *Lear* and blue-net curtains in a half-circle, suffered from the Baylis scrape-and-save philosophy. Critics seized on the bare, windswept nature of this Arden stripped of vegetation: a place where the Banished Duke and his cronies had only threepennorth of fruit for supper. Williams also records that, in the wrestling scene, he put spectators between the audience and the combatants to camouflage the lack of wrestling-skill of Orlando and Charles. Our theatre has come a long way since then: nowadays we never have less than a complete Hoxton Baths bout with one of the wrestlers invariably ending up in the front stalls. Peggy herself got rather mixed notices. Ivor Brown said she gabbled in the chop-logic scenes as if they bored her (more likely, it was early-season fatigue) and Agate, accusing her of draining the part of poetry and depth of feeling, dismissively described her as 'a nice little girl in a wood'.

The person who responded most warmly to her Rosalind was, in fact, the painter Walter Sickert. Sickert, born in Munich in 1860 and a leading figure in the Camden Town group, had spent three years as an actor before studying art and had himself been painted in the character of Romeo by Sir Johnston Forbes-Robertson. In his later years he was increasingly drawn to theatrical subjects and especially to Peggy: during this Vic season he painted her in *As You Like It*, *She Stoops to Conquer* and *The School for Scandal*.

'I always knew when he was in the house,' says Peggy. 'If he liked a line he would break into solitary applause, usually at the matinées. He would also bring a photographer with him who, when nudged by Sickert, would audibly snap us in a particular pose: in the case of Rosalind it was when I was putting a chain round the neck of William Fox as Orlando. I remember he did a painting of me in *The School for Scandal* which he entitled 'The

Divine Peggy' though I thought I looked rather like a monster hovering over the footlights. But he was very kind and also very perceptive. I would often go to lunch with him and his wife and he would give me some of his sketches. He often wrote little notes at the bottom saying things like 'Quayle excellent as Morocco – one day he'll play Othello.'

While playing Rosalind at the Vic, in the daytime Peggy was also rehearsing a role said to be twice as long as Hamlet's and one of the most arduous in the history of the theatre. Each actor at the Old Vic was allowed time off for the course of one play. But instead of using the time for recuperation, Peggy spent the three weeks preparing for a taxing three-week run at the Kingsway of *Fräulein Elsa*: a story by Schnitzler which Komisarjevksy had adapted and was now directing. In effect, it was a stupendous monologue broken up by music and devices such as the turning pages of a huge book, the scenes being its illustrations. What made it startling at the time was that the heroine dropped her cloak and appeared in the nude. It seems typical of Peggy's pioneering spirit that she thus became the first serious actress in Britain to bare rather more than her soul for the sake of her art. Peggy herself tells the story:

'It's the monologue of a girl who is staying in a Swiss resort. Her father writes that he is about to be made bankrupt but he asks his daughter to approach a man he knows who is staying in the hotel for financial help. The supposed philanthropist is just a dirty old man who says he will give her father the money if she will meet him and take all her clothes off. She can't face the prospect so she takes some laudanum. Then instead of meeting the man in the woods, she goes down to the hotel lounge where he is waiting, takes off her cloak and falls to the ground and never recovers consciousness. Komis staged it so that my back was to the audience at the crucial moment. I was suitably covered in front for the near-onlookers and I fell to the ground as the cloak came off. It was entirely discreet.'

Alec Guinness was amongst the interested spectators and remembers there was a sudden intake of breath in the audience as Peggy dropped the cloak and was momentarily glimpsed in the buff before the black-out. 'It caused,' he says, 'quite a bit of shock and stir and a touch of Mrs Whitehouse outrage at the time.' But, presented under the auspices of the Independent Theatre Club, it was safe from prurient spectators or investigation by the moral watchdogs; more remarkable was Peggy's stamina and her readiness to explore the tortuous mental anguish of Schnitzler's heroine. It certainly knocked on the head the Agate image of her as simply a demure *ingénue*, a nice little girl in a wood.

Once again, however, Peggy was caught up in a non-stop whirl of acting. After *Fräulein Elsa*, it was straight back to the Vic to play Portia in *The Merchant of Venice*: the one production of the season that seems to have inspired happy memories both amongst those who were in it and those who saw it.

There were two prime reasons for this. It was directed by John Gielgud. It was designed by the Motleys. Shrewdly realising that he could never single-handedly break the Baylis rule of Victorian pauperism, Harcourt Williams invited Gielgud to undertake his first professional production; and, although he could only be present for five rehearsals, Gielgud (then playing in the West End in *Musical Chairs* and filming *The Good Companions*) left his signature all over the production. A rehearsal drawing by Roger Furse shows Gielgud, willowy in brogues, pointing an imperious finger at a Portia in thigh-length boots and billowing cloak; she herself is delaying a green-gowned Shylock in the act of knifing an Antonio surrounded by Venetian popinjays. It looks enticing, and worlds away from standard Old Vic tat.

Miss Baylis was horrified by the outrageous extravagance of the Motleys, who spent all of £90 on decor. But the production, though it looked good, was put together out of cheap materials. The setting was a simple affair of fluted columns, curtains and rope balcony, all carried out in unpainted hessian. The costumes were equally inexpensive. Shylock's robe was made out of dish-cloth at $3\frac{1}{4}$d a yard. Other costumes were made out of mosquito netting, painted linen and black tailor's canvas. Gielgud added music from Peter Warlock's Capriol Suite to give the whole production a free-flowing, fantasticated quality. The effect, on those used to the Vic's patchwork drabness, was stunning.

Anthony Quayle says: 'It was the first play I was in there that was designed: behind everything there was a brain.' Alec Guinness greatly admired Peggy's Portia and thought the production 'looked wonderful though every sort of kitchen rag was dyed and used.' J. C. Trewin was equally taken by Peggy's Portia: 'There was a Shakespearean voice and manner at the time and you didn't believe the people were human. At the Vic they were. I'd just been reading Granville-Barker's *Merchant* essay and he speaks of Portia as "an enchanted princess" and to me Peggy Ashcroft was just that. I remember old Joseph Thorpe in *The Times* said he had never heard the "quality of mercy" speech spoken as she did, quite naturally with her hands behind her back and not attempting to orate. That struck me as extremely odd because all the Portias I had seen until then would go down stage-centre and address the audience and give it all they had. I remember thinking at the Vic the speech arrived so suddenly that I couldn't believe we'd got there.'

Peggy herself, who believes passionately that *The Merchant of Venice* is a fairy story which has to be played for real, is rather more muted in her reactions: 'I think John at the time was very influenced by Komis and his innovations at Stratford. I wasn't too sure about the production because I felt it was fancy-dress and I didn't know what period we were in, though I did like my costume as the Doctor's Clerk. As for the quality of mercy speech, I remember having once been very annoyed when a girl at Central School asked if she could cut it. I tried to do it not as an aria but as a way of advancing the argument.'

Reading the notices today one is struck by the cyclical nature of debates about Shakespearean production. Agate, putting on his old fogey hat, objected strenuously to the fantastication by Gielgud of the Belmont scenes, comparing them to a Cochran revue or a Lifar ballet as 'a procession of Eton-jacketed pages speed the parting Arragon with *coups de derrière*.' It sounds slightly camp, but fun. Agate was on stronger ground in claiming that the youthfulness of the Old Vic company, with the exception of Malcolm Keen, made it look like a nursery – but 'a nursery for what?' This was a fair point, since the Old Vic at the time was the only place in London where there was anything remotely resembling a classic repertory. Ivor Brown, however, made the even better point that the record of Shakespeare on the English stage was mainly one of violent assault; compared with happy endings for *King Lear* or the eighteenth-century treatment of *The*

Tempest as an operetta in need of additional lyrics, Gielgud's transformation of Belmont into a Never-Never Land was forgiveable. A similar argument is repeated today every time a Young Turk at Stratford give us a *Two Gentlemen of Verona* with a swimming-pool and shades or a *Romeo and Juliet* with jazz and jacuzzis. The truth is that there is no single, right way of doing Shakespeare and that, if the plays are acted with intensity, they will survive the singular vision of their directors. What Gielgud clearly did with *The Merchant* was to liberate the play from stale convention and provide a framework for an intelligent, refined and refreshingly natural Portia from Peggy.

This was the high point of the Vic season: something that showed what might be achieved with a strong directorial and design concept and the expenditure of a bit of cash. But after the mercy of Gielgud's quality, it was back to the rum-ti-tum of the Williams rep and, for Peggy, a hard slog through five roles in the first four months of 1933.

A decent *She Stoops to Conquer* with Peggy as Kate Hardcastle was followed by a feeble version of *The Winter's Tale*. Malcolm Keen's Leontes was struggling with his lines, flu had spread through the cast and Paul Smyth's set for the Bohemian revels suggested, according to one witness, a smug poster advertising cheap residencies in the Home Counties. Peggy's Perdita was rewarded with bland epithets like 'exquisitely graceful'.

Given the strain of rushing from one part to the next, it is no surprise that three weeks later Peggy found herself nearly voiceless for the first night of John Drinkwater's *Mary Stuart*. Not that the play gave her many rich opportunities for characterisation. Drinkwater's heroine was nothing like the fiery woman of history who could and did ride sixty miles a day and whose last letter to Elizabeth is a masterpiece of stinging irony. In his version she was simply a sweet and noble woman singularly unhappy in her choice of men: 'Miss Peggy Ashcroft,' said *The Times*, 'could not lift Mary above the level of the conventional heroine of romance.' The major critics, probably to Peggy's relief, absented themselves and went to see Ludmilla Pitoeff in *Mademoiselle Julie* at the Arts.

Peggy did, however, score a triumph with her second Juliet in the space of just over a year. Harcourt Williams's production was a shabby, dull affair compared to Gielgud's at Oxford. Marius

Goring's Romeo was, on his own admission, rather callow and immature. But Juliet is a role that Peggy seems to have been born to play. She also claims that every time she played it, the character somehow got younger. Ivor Brown in the *Observer* was in no doubt as to her quality: 'Miss Peggy Ashcroft's Juliet is the best performance I have seen her give at the Vic. She has the magic. She has also the experience and can establish that transition from piping innocence to the full-throated cry of the tragedienne which has always made Juliet's part so sharp a test of dramatic scope and range. Miss Ashcroft's Juliet never seems to be the wrong age. Despite limitations of vocal pitch, her delivery of the grand speeches is extremely moving.'

By now the end of the season was in sight. Peggy gave her Lady Teazle in *The School for Scandal* and steeled herself to the thankless task of playing Miranda in *The Tempest* with Harcourt Williams both directing and playing Prospero. There is not much any Miranda can do except be a good listener as her father replays his whole life story and exude wan, virginal innocence in the presence of Ferdinand. But in one of Williams's better productions – free from wires and flashes and puffs of smoke, and never allowing Prospero to dwindle into a desperate conjurer at some aquatic children's party – Peggy was praised for speaking the verse as if it were new-minted.

What the Vic clearly lacked in this season (with the exception of the Gielgud *Merchant*) was any sense of creative excitement. By a fascinating conjunction, the same night that Williams's solid version of *The Tempest* was opening at the Vic (18 April 1933), Komisarjevsky's production of *Macbeth* was opening at Stratford-on-Avon. At Stratford, with basically only a week to get the shows on, rehearsal time was even tighter than in the Waterloo Road. But it is amazing what imagination can do. Reading the often hostile notices of the *Macbeth* now, one still gets a quiver of excitement. Sheets of twisted aluminium hung at the back of the stage. Light broke against these vertical cylinders making the characters look like shadowy beings flitting through a labyrinth of horror. The Witches were old women plundering corpses and skeletons on a gun-ringed battlefield while steel-helmeted soldiers passed by. Amplifiers drummed out the incantations which Macbeth's conscience speaks. 'Producer's Shakespeare,' snorted *The*

Times; and the same would probably be said today. But while Komis was doing something stirring at Stratford, his partner, Peggy, was involved in another decent, humdrum piece of Old Vickery.

It would be unfair to blame Harcourt Williams. While staying loyal to the Lady, he made it clear at the end of his book on his four seasons at the Vic that Baylis's pauperised repertory system was showing signs of metal fatigue. He suggests that constant cries of poverty can be overdone and the cultivation of 'a more confident outside' would attract the very money that was lacking. He also significantly hints that the old Baylis notion of luring the masses from the glamour of gas-lit pubs with high-minded entertainment was getting a bit dated. There was a new audience out there made up of 'middle-class school teachers, the intellectual new poor, the typist clerks of both sexes, young women who work all day in the city, students of every kind.' They wanted well-thought-out productions rather than buns and lemonade.

Baylis, to be fair, did begin to see that dowdiness was not a policy. The next season Tyrone Guthrie was brought in as director and imported stars like Charles Laughton and Flora Robson to give the Vic a bit more glamour. Even in the West End there was a hopeful portent. Gielgud's runaway success in *Richard of Bordeaux*, which opened at the New in February 1933, led to an extended contract from Bronson Albery and the chance to do classic plays in the commercial heartland which Peggy would soon be a part of.

For Peggy the Old Vic season had been 'a killing venture'. Inspired by Komisarjevsky at home with the ideal of perfectionism, she found that there was no time in rehearsal for read-throughs or discussion: it was all placing, placing, placing and getting the plays on with very few run-throughs. As a genuine artist with a vision of what might be, the season filled her with frustration, but at least it gave her the chance to place her marker on some of Shakespeare's major characters in the hope that she would come back to them later on. It also filled her with a conviction that there must be a better way of organising the theatre than this.

From Harcourt Williams himself her work elicited a generous tribute in *Four Years at the Old Vic*. Revealingly, the qualities he praised were precisely the ones that other directors would seize on for the next half-century: her insight, clear-headedness, honesty of method, freedom from false sentiment, avoidance of tricks. 'She has an eye,' he wrote, 'for line and colour and as an artist instinctively rejects the commonplace.' That is as true in the 1980s as it was in the 1930s.

One of the most eloquent tributes to her work at the Old Vic, however, is to be found in Laurence Kitchin's *Mid-Century Drama*. Mr Kitchin watched her work from the gods but with an all-seeing eye:

'Ashcroft's performances had the effect of very sweet wood-wind interludes in a robust symphony. Viewed by goggling students from the gallery, she had some of the glamour of the West End society most of them would never mix in, together with a distilled essence of sex that humanised the lyrical heroines, who seem too hearty or too knowing when the average actress attempts them. This enabled her to carry off the bedroom scene in *Cymbeline* without a snigger from anyone. Incapable equally of a memorable gesture or an ungraceful one, Ashcroft defined an acceptable standard for this range of parts which has never been attained since. Her voice fluted away with a quality of eagerness peculiar to her and subtly feminine. Her Juliet was the definitive performance of our time.'

What Kitchin says is highly revealing. Peggy did not impose herself on the parts through 'memorable gestures', statuesque poses or the sonic boom of the poetry voice. Her key qualities were femininity, impulsive eagerness, purity of character and passionate integrity. Even at this embryonic stage of her career, it is clear that Peggy was remarkable for what she was as well as for what she did; and that the soul of an artist managed to shine through the circumstances of the classical treadmill at Lilian Baylis's slightly fatigued Old Vic.

CHAPTER SIX

Anger and After

ON HER OWN ADMISSION, Peggy was not at this stage of her life much concerned with politics. Working with Robeson had made her aware of racial intolerance in both Britain and the States. A holiday in Germany in 1932 had taught her what was happening to the Jews: she had met Lion Feuchtwanger, the author of *Jew Süss*, who was in serious trouble with the authorities and who a year later escaped to France and ended up in rather embittered Hollywood exile. Wrapped up though she was in the Old Vic, she could also hardly fail to be aware that in January 1933 President Hindenburg had appointed Adolf Hitler German Chancellor and that in the March elections the Nazis became the largest party in the Reichstag with 288 seats.

But she was not a great newspaper reader and was too busy hurtling from job to job to take a consuming interest in world affairs. At the end of the Vic season, she was off to Twickenham Studios to begin a rather intermittent film career in Maurice Elvey's version of *The Wandering Jew*, playing the prostitute who unwittingly betrays the hero to the Inquisition: an experience that left her with no great desire to pursue a career in movies.

Peggy may have been apolitical, but she did have a spontaneous indignation at any manifestation of injustice, and this came to the fore on the momentous first night of *Before Sunset* at the Shaftesbury in September 1933. The play was adapted by Miles Malleson from a German work by Gerhart Hauptmann. Werner Krauss, a famous German actor whose roles included Richard III, Macbeth and Shylock, had been brought over to play the role of an old widower who falls in love with a young girl, is prevented from marrying her by his children and dies of a stroke while holding her hand. Krauss, who didn't speak a word of English, had learned the role phonetically. But that was the least of his problems. There were suspicions, amongst militant anti-Fascist groups in Britain, that he was a Nazi sympathiser and that he had been instrumental in getting the great director, Max Reinhardt, dismissed from his theatre in Berlin (this last was later found out to be untrue). With hindsight, it certainly seems an act of managerial recklessness to have imported him to play in the West End in 1933.

Recollections of that extraordinary first night of *Before Sunset* differ slightly depending on which side of the footlights one was, but it was clear that a section of the audience had come to demonstrate against Krauss's presence. Someone caught up in the ruckus was Peggy's old friend and colleague, Fabia Drake, who remembers the event as if it were yesterday:

'A group of people who suspected Werner Krauss of being a Nazi were giving away pamphlets outside the theatre and had filled the gallery. One of the pamphlets fluttered down to where I was sitting in the stalls. But the claque that was there to boo Krauss off the stage had no idea what he looked like. When an old gentleman called O. B. Clarence came on, they started to boo him, thinking he was Krauss. They booed him vociferously and ad nauseam. The curtain had to come down. Another elderly gentleman came on later in the scene and the same thing happened again. The storm of booing returned and chaos was come again. The curtain came down and this time it opened in the centre and Peggy appeared in a frenzy of rage. She had watched all this from the wings, respected the quality of Krauss as a player and was appalled at what was happening. I reminded her over the phone the next day what her speech was and I still remember how it ended. She said something like 'There are those of us here tonight who respect and admire the actor who is about to appear called Werner Krauss (groans and boos). Those of us who are here to respect and admire him, will they stay. Will the others KINDLY GO AWAY'. She shouted GO AWAY in her most passionate voice. She is passionate and that is why she has so many causes. The performance went on. We did survive, we did stay in the theatre and we did listen to the play. At that stage, I knew of Peg's ambition and of the power she brought to whatever she was interested in. But, as far as I knew until that moment, it was purely the theatre.'

Stirring stuff. But Peggy remembers it slightly differently. She says the curtain came down only once. There was a panic-stricken huddle backstage, the theatre manager was about to go on and call for order when an actress in the company, Edith Sharp, told him that he mustn't go on because he was one of the villains of the piece. 'Send Peggy on,' she said, presuming the play's innocent heroine would have more luck in calming the audience. For Peggy what followed was more of an instinctive protest than a sign of any great impassioned political awakening. 'I remember at the time,' she says, 'thinking how ridiculous it was that I went out in front of the curtain to make a speech wearing white cotton gloves.'

Peggy's action certainly proved there was spirit and fire under her quiet charm. (The *Morning Post*'s critic, Robin Littlewood, came back into his office that night crying 'Oh, we had an evening, we had an evening – it was held up by Little Miss Ashcroft.') The sequel to the affair is even more fascinating. It showed that the demonstrators, however violent their methods, were not far wrong in their diagnosis. Krauss, rather like Hendrik Höfgen in Klaus Mann's novel *Mephisto*, clearly was someone who collaborated with the Nazis in order to sustain his career. For Peggy too the consequences of the episode did not end with that first night in 1933.

'Krauss's Nazi connections,' she says now, 'were complex. It was only after I made the protest that I and the rest of the company realised he had connections with the Nazis though I never knew if he was a party member. But I do remember being sent a German paper that had the headline – ENGLAND'S NAZI ACTRESS DEFENDS WERNER KRAUSS. A year or so later Komis and I went to Berlin and saw Krauss playing King Lear. We went backstage to see him afterwards and he said "Would you like to meet HIM (meaning Hitler) tomorrow?" It was an invitation we managed to refuse. Some years later when I was at the Haymarket I was asked to sign a statement saying that Krauss wasn't a Nazi. He had been imprisoned by the Russians after the fall of Berlin but I simply couldn't bring myself to sign it because it was untrue. Then I had a rather odd experience in 1952 when I was telling the whole story to an actor while we were on tour in *The Deep Blue Sea* and, out of the blue, a German visitor came to the hotel bearing a note from Berlin saying "With Best Wishes from Werner Krauss." Three years later I was on tour in Vienna with John Gielgud in *King Lear* but although Krauss was playing there at the time I made no effort to contact him nor he me. But the real irony of the story is that only after making my protest did I discover that Krauss had Nazi sympathies.'

Perhaps the whole episode revealed Peggy's *naïveté*. It would be more charitable to say that it demonstrated her reflex hatred of intolerance and belief in the artist's right to be heard. But, apart from all that, the play got her a good notice from Agate who said that her schoolmistress-heroine was 'made of spirit, fire and dew'. Frith Banbury also remembers that the play was genuinely moving because of the plausibility of the May–December relationship: Krauss really was old and Peggy really was young.

In private Peggy was also, of course, living with a man twice her age. But much to everyone's surprise, not least her own, she and Komisarjevsky got married in the late autumn of 1933. Her friends were sceptical, since Komis was as notorious for his infidelity as he was admired for his genius. But Peggy, looking back without a trace of rancour, says simply: 'I was very unwilling to enter into a second marriage so soon after the break-up of my first. But I was finally persuaded by Komis and I'm afraid my reluctance proved correct: not much more than a year after our marriage he left me for a young American dancer. Many years later when he was living in America he wrote to me and said it could never have worked out because he was "a bloody foreigner". But that wasn't really it: I would say that he never felt happy whatever country he was in. I think it's fairer to say that he had no great regard for the matrimonial state even though he kept on entering into it: I never did work out whether there had been three or four wives before me. But, whatever pain he caused, he was a great inspiration to me both as an actress and a person, and he did a lot to shake up the English theatre and foster a much more realistic style of acting.'

One further tangible sign of Komisarjevsky's legacy was the artwork for the Phoenix Theatre in Charing Cross Road and the chain of Granada Cinemas, both built by Sidney Bernstein in the 1930s. At the Phoenix Komis added visual taste to a cream-and-gold commercial house and built in copies of pictures by Titian, Giorgione, Tintoretto and Pinturicchio. On the safety curtain there was even a copy, inappropriately perhaps, of Jacopo del Sellaio's 'The Triumph of Love'.

Peggy felt, instinctively, that she had made the wrong decision in agreeing to marry Komisarjevsky. Shortly after, early in 1934, she made one of her very few poor career choices in accepting the leading role of Vasantesena in *The Golden Toy* at the Coliseum. Ironically she had been recommended for the role by Werner Krauss because of her loyalty to him at the Shaftesbury. It just goes to prove Wilde's point that no good deed goes unpunished. For the show at the Coliseum proved to be Teutonic tosh based by Carl Zuckmayer on an old Hindu play, directed by Dr Ludwig Berger and featuring a live elephant, Rosie, assorted music by Schumann and a cast of two hundred including such oddly-assorted names as Ion Swinley, Ernest Thesiger, Wilfred Lawson, Nellie Wallace, Lupino Lane and Wendy Toye. John Gielgud, busy looking for a lead actress to appear in a new play by Emlyn Williams, was heard to remark: 'Peggy, if you can believe it, is going into that musical farrago at the Coliseum. Who does she think she is, Phyllis Dare?'

The question posed by *The Golden Toy*, none too strenuously, was whether it was possible for a girl to keep her heart virgin for her lover when fate had condemned her to belong to other men. The trouble was that the feeble story was swamped by mounds of papier-mâché scenery which kept twirling around in front of the audience on three revolving stages. *The Times* recorded with laconic dismay: 'The truth must be that the more Dr Berger's scene changes, the more it remains the same. There is an outer circle of spectacle, so to speak, and an inner; and while on the outer we move backwards and from one quarter of a nameless

Eastern city to another, the inner, though sometimes the trysting place of lovers and sometimes the haunt of furies, remains disappointingly reminiscent of rock gardens at Torquay with a dull, sub-aqueous light on them ... Miss Peggy Ashcroft is uniformly charming and sympathetic throughout the adventure but she is a graceful miniaturist working on a canvas that calls for the biggest of brushes.'

Dr Berger went on record as saying that he hoped to capture 'the scent, the sound and the spirit of India' but he clearly didn't get any nearer to the East than the Caledonian Market. Obviously the puzzle is what a graceful miniaturist and rising classical star like Peggy was doing in this piece of mystical malarkey. Her own answer is that the project was presented to her as a great artistic venture: a combination of Schumann, Berger and an Indian love-story. 'What one didn't realise,' she says, 'was how vulgar it was going to be. There was a song, for instance, built around Rosie called An Elephant Never Forgets. I also remember that the elephant was on stage in a stable and I was in another one next door and that during one of my big emotional scenes it very loudly pee'd.'

This is reminiscent of Sarah Bernhardt's pronounced aversion to having performing animals as colleagues. Her first remark, on receiving an offer to appear on the music-hall stage in a scene from L'Aiglon, was 'Between monkeys, not.' In retrospect, Peggy might have had second thoughts about appearing in a show where she was asked to share a stage with a pachyderm that at one point kicked a tambourine with panache. Even the human performers were not very reliable, sometimes exercising the variety artist's prerogative not to appear at all. Frith Banbury recalls a matinée: 'Peggy and Ion Swinley had the poetic parts and spouted the verse stuff at each other. Nellie Wallace was also in it. Then darling old May Hallett suddenly came on in the market-scene dressed exactly like Nellie Wallace who then re-appeared in the next scene. I went round afterwards and asked May what that was all about. Had Miss Wallace got stuck in the loo? I was told "No, she had someone to tea in the dressing-room and sent me on for the market-scene."'

After the exhausting tumult of the year at the Vic, Peggy's career marked time in 1934. Privately, she knew that her marriage to Komisarjevsky was a mistake. Professionally, there was not much on the horizon for an actress yearning to do the classics. After the débâcle at the Coliseum, she got the chance to play Shakespeare's Imogen and Isabella on BBC Radio. Her only other theatre work that year was a short run at Nancy Price's Little Theatre in John Adam Street in Pirandello's *The Life that I Gave Him*. Pirandello, then as now, was regarded as something of an exotic curiosity by the British theatre, which has always had a built-in anti-intellectual bias. What people forgot – until organisations like Miss Price's People's National Theatre reminded them – was just how theatrical Pirandello was. Miss Price herself played the role written for Eleonora Duse of Donn' Anna: a mother who tries to prolong her dead son's life by finishing a letter he had half-completed urging a married woman, Lucia, to leave her family and come to him. Peggy played Lucia who turns up, proves to be pregnant, at first believes her lover to be alive and only gradually realises that his 'life' is an illusion in Donn'Anna's mind. Peggy was praised for the precision with which she handled the grief of the final tragic scene. But a good performance at a small Fringe venue off the Adelphi was no substitute for the head-on collision with the great roles that an actress of her promise might expect in France, Scandinavia or the Soviet Union.

The year 1935 did not begin much more promisingly. Peggy went north to Glasgow for a pre-London try-out of a play by Beverley Nichols, *Mesmer*, which Komis was directing for the legendary showman, C. B. Cochran. As often happens in the theatre, everything looked better on paper than it turned out in reality: the real trouble was that Nichols's dramatic talents were not equal to the hypnotic fascination of his theme and the play was stillborn in Scotland. Mark Dignam, who was one of the understudies, remembers the whole affair with wry humour:

'The Austrian actor, Oscar Homolka, was Dr Mesmer and Peggy played the blind girl whom he mesmerised. I remember Peggy being rather *distraite* because it wasn't a successful play. Komis – the Peter Brook of his age – directed it, designed the scenery and costumes, did the music and everything. One scene was set in Mesmer's garden in Vienna for which Komis had real water flowing from a fountain. But on the first night the fountain overflowed and little pools of water started to form on the stage. The whole thing was a ghastly failure.'

Peggy herself, possibly mesmerised by Komis, undertook the production in a spirit of naïve optimism and has now virtually banished it from her memory. She does, however, remember that Homolka – a famous actor who had been directed by Brecht in *Baal* in 1926 –failed to turn up for the dress rehearsal and that search-parties had to be despatched through Glasgow to find him. It was shockingly unprofessional but maybe, in retrospect, Homolka's instincts were sound.

By the middle of 1935, Peggy's life and career stood at the crossroads. Komis, as other people had predicted, proved unsuited to the comforting imprisonment of marriage and abandoned her. As an actress, her demonstrable intelligence, attack and energy also seemed curiously homeless: outside the Old Vic, there was no permanent company to nurture an actress with classical leanings. The choice often lay between something European and adventurous in London's little theatres (where Peggy had paid her dues) or the commercial frippery of the West End. Peggy had shown she could carry a demanding classical season, had given proof of her skill in comedy and tragedy, had repeatedly shown her unaffected naturalness, emotional directness and belief in the word. But in the disorganised British theatre of the 1930s, the girl who had left drama school dreaming of permanent companies and Moscow Art Theatre idealism found herself at 27 still at the mercy of the freelance jungle.

Her saviour appeared in the shape of John Gielgud. During the summer of 1935 he was working on a projected version of *A Tale of Two Cities*. He had mapped out the scenario, Terence Rattigan was writing the dialogue, the Motleys were designing the costumes, Peggy was approached, and enthusiastically agreed, to play Lucy Manette. Then Sir John Martin Harvey wrote to Gielgud out of the blue announcing that he intended to revive his version of the same story, *The Only Way*, and begged him not to continue. So Gielgud suggested to the New Theatre manager, Bronson Albery, for whom he was on his second three-play contract, reviving *Romeo and Juliet*. Peggy recalls a breathless, late-summer phone call from Gielgud saying: 'I hope you don't mind not playing Lucy Manette. Would you mind playing

Juliet instead?' Thus are people's destinies settled.

For Peggy, Juliet in 1935 was a major turning-point. It made her into a star. It also gave her the chance to work in the nearest thing the West End could provide to a company. But, for Gielgud, setting the production up at short notice was problematic. The idea was that he and another actor would alternate the two main men's roles. Robert Donat was contacted. But he was planning his own version of the play. Laurence Olivier was mentioned. He too had a production on the drawing-board. Ivor Novello was also rumoured to be planning a *Romeo* of his own. London that autumn might have ended up with the quaint spectacle of four gentlemen of Verona. In the end, both Donat and Olivier selflessly abandoned their projects: Olivier, even more graciously, threw in his lot with Gielgud and agreed to alternate with him the roles of Romeo and Mercutio.

Why did the production turn out to be successful? For several reasons. For a start, Gielgud and the Motleys strove hard to get the setting right: the look of a production was always the starting-point for Gielgud. He and his designers – taking a tip from the abandoned setting for *A Tale of Two Cities* – decided to place Juliet's balcony centre-stage with the interior of the bedroom visible above it on a platform. Below stairs was a door leading to the street. Thus it was possible, through lighting-changes, to move swiftly from the bedroom to the balcony to ground level when it was time for the preparations for Juliet's marriage. Again the transitions to Friar Lawrence's cell, which remained in place at the side of the stage concealed by a curtain, were swiftly accomplished. Today we are used to fast-moving, permanent-set Shakespeare. In 1935 it was sufficiently novel to invite comment: at least one critic noticed how the play became an organic whole, rather than a collection of famous speeches. Gielgud, so often seen as a high-priest of traditionalism, was literally setting the pace for modern directors.

If the setting was permanent, the company was familiar. As Peggy shrewdly remarks, since 1933 and the success of *Richard of Bordeaux* at the New, Gielgud had virtually been given the position of actor-manager by Bronson Albery; except that, unlike the actor-managers of the past, what Gielgud sought to establish was a company of his peers. He had followed Gordon Daviot's

costume-drama with his own production of *Hamlet* in 1934 and
the lead role in André Obey's *Noah* in 1935; and it was from
those productions that he assembled his cast for *Romeo and Juliet*.
Harry Andrews went from playing the Lion in *Noah* to Tybalt,
the Prince of Cats, in *Romeo*; George Howe moved on from
Polonius to Friar Lawrence; Alec Guinness graduated from the
Wolf in *Noah* to Sampson and the Apothecary; George Devine
was the Player King in *Hamlet*, had two small parts in *Noah* and
enlivened the role of Peter in *Romeo* by playing it in a bowler
hat and with a number of Chaplinesque comedy tricks. It may
not have been La Compagnie des Quinze but it was a start. As
Peggy says: 'Instead of creating a good secondary company
around himself as the star, John really wanted to form a genuine
company: that was what one had dreamed about and he realised.'

Peggy's 1935 Juliet was her third to date and her best: the
older she got, the younger the character became and the more
she brought out the element of child-like impetuosity. A small
anecdote illustrates this. Towards the end of the following year
Peggy met a couple of Americans on a boat going over to New
York. It came out in conversation that Peggy had lately played
Juliet in London and the Americans recalled having seen the play
in 1932 at Oxford. Of course, they said, the girl who played it
was much older than Peggy. She revealed that it was her and she
had been five years younger.

Critics who had enjoyed the benefit of seeing Peggy's progress
as Juliet over the years were quick to spot the differences: in
particular, the way she deepened the tragic dimension while
retaining the hurtling adolescence. 'Finest Juliet of Our Time' ran
the headline in the *Daily Telegraph* on the morning of 18 October
1935. Tracing her development since her début in the role at
Oxford, W. A. Darlington wrote: 'Then she was utterly charming
as the young girl newly in love but she let the tragic Juliet evade
her. Now she gives us the whole portrait. Without losing a trace
of the lovely eagerness and innocence of the earlier scenes, she
rises to the tragedy and shows herself to be what one had always
thought she might someday be, the finest as well as the sweetest
Juliet of our time.' Not only had she thought herself into the very
heart and spirit of Juliet; she had also learned the art of speaking
verse so that the words seemed the only conceivable expression

of the idea, a point picked out by Peter Fleming in his review: 'There is a triumphant beauty in Miss Peggy Ashcroft's Juliet, a passion not to be gainsaid: from the first we tremble for the child who challenges with such a love the inauspicious stars. Technically her performance is perfection: there is no one like her for conveying the sense of a difficult passage without, so to speak, being caught in the act. She does more than make Shakespeare's expression of Juliet's thoughts seem natural: she makes it seem inevitable.'

Peggy didn't simply play Juliet: she appropriated her. Even now she is loyally protective towards the character and the play. *Romeo and Juliet*, I confess, strikes me as a flawed piece of work that falls apart after the death of Mercutio. The reason is that Shakespeare follows too slavishly the narrative pattern of his source: Arthur Brooke's *The Tragical History of Romeus and Juliet*, published in November 1562. To Brooke the tragedy was the work of Fortune who 'nothing constant is, save in inconstancie'. Shakespeare inherited the idea that it was a tragedy of circumstance rather than of character. He then proceeded to create two young lovers of such vitality that they burst apart the bounds of the story. When Romeo is banished, why doesn't Juliet go with him? If she had the courage to swallow a drug that gave her the appearance of death, wouldn't she have been brave enough to leave Verona disguised as Romeo's page? Shakespeare's Juliet is too intelligent to be a victim of Fortune.

Peggy will have none of this. 'I don't think intelligence is Juliet's main characteristic. I think she's passionate and impetuous, the same with Romeo. These are two children, the victims of the hate of their families. And that is the tragedy: that the hate of the parents destroys the children and the children are put into this appalling hotch-potch of hatred, intrigue, fighting, murder. If you're in the play, you find everything happens so quickly. Mercutio is killed, Tybalt is killed, Romeo is banished; it's kaleidoscopic, really, so I don't think you have to be logical and say "Well, this is what they should have done." The fact is they did what they did on the spur of the moment and it is that tragedy of children being crushed by other forces that I don't find illogical or impossible to believe.'

Peggy also laughs to scorn the idea that there is something a

bit morbid and death-fixated about Juliet: a girl who, as she takes
the potion, imagines waking up in the ancestral vault where she
might 'madly play with my forefathers' joints'. Rather flatter-
ingly, Peggy responds: 'You're talking like Bernard Shaw. On
the one occasion I met him, it was in a theatre box before I was
about to play Juliet. He said "I hear you're doing Juliet. I don't
know what you want to do a play like that for. It's all butchers
and bones." The real difficulty of Juliet is that it needs considerable
technique to take the pace of the play. There are a lot of speeches
that have to be taken swiftly because of the drama yet they are
also packed with intricate poetic images. You have to find a way
to digest the images and make them spontaneous.'

That is a vital clue to Peggy's art: the ability to absorb densely-
packed imagistic speeches into her being and then speak them as
if they came new-minted from her brain. It is the gift – crucial
in Shakespeare – of being poetic and realistic at the same time.

She was universally thought to have succeeded. Olivier, her
first Romeo, was widely thought to have failed. Where she was
praised to the skies, he was carved up by the critics for his supposed
insensitivity to the poetry ('plays Romeo as though he were
riding a motor-bike' ... 'his blank verse is the blankest I have
ever heard'). Olivier, whose first major test in Shakespeare this
was, offered to give up the part immediately. Convinced in
rehearsal that his interpretation of Romeo as an impassioned
Italian adolescent was correct, he was mortified by the reaction
of the overnight critics; but Peggy, as he recalls, was unwavering
in her support and encouraged him to continue through the
nightmarish early performances.

To this day, Peggy is vehement in her belief that it was a
daring and cruelly under-praised performance. Dismissing the
critical reaction as 'absolute rubbish', she says: 'Larry didn't
declaim the speeches as speeches because he was intent on acting
the part rather than speaking it, and that was a marvellous turning-
point. I think it was fairly innovatory then. He didn't play a
romantic, poetically spoken young hero. He was a very real
young man or boy and I thought he spoke it beautifully.'

To be fair, not all the critics were hostile to Olivier. Agate,
while attacking his lack of music, rejoiced in his facial mobility,
his play of arm, his smaller gestures ('Note, for example, how

lovingly he fingered first the props of Juliet's balcony and at the last her bier'). St John Ervine, who wrote a weekly theatrical essay in the *Observer*, also came out with two columns in praise of Olivier.

With hindsight, one can appreciate the difficulty of trying, in three weeks' rehearsal, to combine an electric naturalism with a feeling for the pulse of the verse: Olivier, a few weeks after the opening, sent for his old friend, John Laurie, and bluntly asked 'What is this thing called blank verse?' Peggy hints that Olivier was being *faux naïf*; he knew perfectly well. But in those days there was no directorial godfather like John Barton or voice-coach like Cicely Berry – as there is today at the RSC – to give actors practical instruction in verse-speaking. The production also highlights a technical and temperamental difference between Olivier and Gielgud that has lasted throughout their careers. Olivier's verse-speaking has always been a matter of an impressionistic highlighting of crucial lines (with Romeo it was 'Is it e'en so? Then I defy you stars') while Gielgud has always had a matchless feeling for the vocal architecture and linear structure of a speech. Gielgud, according to Peggy, was arguably the better Mercutio, and one senses there was a greater physical chemistry when she played Juliet to Olivier's Romeo. Frith Banbury, who saw both combinations, put it succinctly: 'Larry to me was *the* Romeo. You got the sex with Larry. They've really got to be in love, these kids.'

Beyond question, the production was a landmark for Peggy, and the theatre at large. It gave her star-status, alongside Gielgud, Olivier and Edith Evans. It provided security at a time when her emotional life, after the failure of two marriages, was in limbo. It also, on the material level, earned her £40 a week for six months (a tidy sum in those days) and enabled her to go out and buy her first car. As Anthony Quayle observes, it was through Gielgud's championship that she was able to rise so fast. He adds that 'it was John who led this movement to make the classics both fashionable and pay.' Asked in advance by a sceptical critic how long the production would run, Bronson Albery declared 'It will run for six months.' He was right. It ran for 186 performances, surpassing the record set by Gielgud's *Hamlet* at the New in 1934 which had 155 performances. Gielgud's triumph was to have shown that Shakespeare was box-office, that the plays could be done with speed and fire inside a permanent set and that it was possible to form the nucleus of a company even on the giddy carousel of the West End.

During the run of *Romeo and Juliet*, Peggy found time to do a few days' filming as the young wife of John Laurie's Scottish crofter in Hitchcock's *The Thirty-Nine Steps*. The momentum of her career – and the idea of the company – was also sustained by the fact that, almost as soon as the run of *Romeo and Juliet* was finished, she went straight into Gielgud's last venture at the New Theatre under the Albery banner: a superlative and acclaimed production of *The Seagull*, directed by Komisarjevsky, in which Peggy played Nina.

On paper, it looks a cloudless triumph. Here was Peggy in the West End doing her first Chekhov, surrounded by a family of actors who were all firm friends. Edith Evans was playing Madame Arkadina, Gielgud himself (having played Konstantin at the Little Theatre in 1925) was now Trigorin, Stephen Haggard, who had been in the ill-fated *Mesmer*, was Konstantin, Martita Hunt was Masha with George Devine as the bailiff Shamrayev and Alec Guinness as a wordless workman operating the pulleys on the stage-by-the-lake and later promoted to the tiny role of Yakov.

It was a happy production, but for Peggy herself it was also an extremely difficult one. On the personal level, there was the problem of working with her ex-husband, who had just left her. Also there was the knowledge, as she says, that 'Komis's sister, Vera, had been the original Nina in St Petersburg in 1896 and I felt that was an ideal I could never match.' On the technical level, there was also the problem that confronts all actresses playing Nina and that very few have managed to solve: how to make convincing the transition from the idealistic, life-hungry young girl of the first three acts to the provincial touring actress, pale with hunger and fatigue, who enters out of the storm in the final act. I tend to agree with a point made to me by Frith Banbury: that we now revere Chekhov so much that we overlook the fact that his treatment of Nina in the fourth act is 'a bloody bad bit of playwriting'. Konstantin tells us that Nina had a child, that it died, that Trigorin abandoned her and that, as an actress, she has been slogging round the provinces playing big roles crudely and without distinction. Then Nina herself enters out of the night and has to convey two years of personal and professional failure in about ten minutes. As Frith Banbury says: 'You can't just put all that into the last act and expect an actress to play it. It's rather like a line Irene Vanbrugh used to quote – Enter Madame X having just drunk a cup of tea.'

Peggy now talks movingly about the intense struggle involved in achieving Nina's transition, something clearly much harder than catching Juliet's progress from impetuous lover to tragic victim. Looking back over half a century, Peggy says: 'For a while, I never had the confidence that I could do what I wanted in the last act. I used to have a tiny sip of brandy before I went on to take off the edge of terror. Something I would emphatically not advise other actresses to do. As Ralph Richardson used to say, one should always drink after a performance, never before. I remember the great French director, Jacques Copeau, came to see the performance and he must have been very perceptive because he said to me "You are very good in the last act but you don't yet trust yourself. You have to know what you are doing and then do it." What I came to realise is that Nina identifies with the seagull. In the second act Konstantin kills a seagull and Trigorin weaves it into a subject for a story about a girl who lives by a lake and then is casually destroyed just like the seagull. That is why Nina, who in the final act is in a state of exhaustion and hysteria, goes back to the lake where they did the play.... I looked different in that last act. My hair was tied up rather than in a pigtail. *You have to look different but you have to show that it is still the same character*. The difficulty is that you have to come in at such a pitch of exhaustion and despair. Then you have to recover sufficiently to play the scene with Konstantin. Then you have the shock of hearing Trigorin's voice. But all through the scene is the idea of the seagull. I kept that visual image in my mind throughout and I felt, in the end, I achieved what I was after.'

That is a good example of how Peggy goes to work: finding in the text itself the solution to a crucial acting problem. As a footnote Gielgud, in his book *Early Stages*, provides an unforgettable image of Peggy backstage in that final act, sitting alone in a corner with a shawl over her head working herself up to her big entrance while the wind and rain effects whistled all around. Although Peggy suggests that it took time for her to achieve what she was after, critics on that memorable first night on 20 May 1936 seem to have had fewer doubts. Indeed, Charles Morgan in *The Times* seems to have totally understood what she was trying to convey: 'Miss Ashcroft's Nina has an enchanting freshness in the early scenes, and her tragic return has the supreme quality of being indeed not the coming of a stranger but the return of a girl we have known, changed by suffering but not obliterated by it so that what she was is visible always through what she has become.' All Ninas should have those words engraved on their hearts. And other critics shared Morgan's view. Alan Dent said of the final scene that 'Miss Ashcroft has never done anything quite so poignant as this' and Ivor Brown extolled her growth 'from the dewy innocence of the first acts to the pale, storm-pelted desperation of the last.'

The dissenting voice, as so often, was James Agate, who never seemed able to accept that Peggy was an actress to be judged by the transparency of her soul rather than the magnitude of her effects: it is what she was as much as what she did that made her so moving. But, on this occasion, it rather depended on which Agate one read. In his column in the *Sunday Times* he wrote beautifully about the play and about the Komisarjevsky production and kept most of his reservations till the final paragraph: 'Miss Peggy Ashcroft's performance of the earlier part of the piece was heart-rending. But alas when she came to the last scene there was not enough power in her to carry it through. This was just a child hit on the head by a bludgeon and this Nina had not lived those two years which she recounted. Obviously she would have thrown herself into the lake instead of going off to play lead at Omsk or Tomsk which is what she does.' The implication is clear: Peggy was playing the effect without the cause and producing a high-pitched desperation without indicating the ravages of time. But Agate also wrote another column, under the pseudonym of Richard Prentice in *John O'London's* and here the tone was somewhat different: 'Perhaps in Nina Miss Ashcroft has the hardest task of all. She triumphs, giving the early scenes an exquisite child-like quality and even winning through most of her appallingly difficult last act. The end of the play with the lovers parting in the stormy night – Konstantin to shoot himself, Nina to vanish like a seagull into the sky's steep commotion – has never before seemed quite so heart-rending.' Second critical thoughts? The hand of Jock Dent (Agate's companion-secretary)? Or critical schizophrenia, repairing on Friday the damage one has done on Sunday? Who knows.

The point is that Peggy fought – and thought – her way through to triumph with the aid of application, intelligence and a tiny tot of brandy (she firmly resisted Komis's injunction to the cast to drink a half bottle of champagne before curtain-up). It is only fair to say that Komis's production provided a perfect setting for her performance, and everyone else's. His design was exquisite: a garden for the first two acts with paths, pillars, banks of flowers and a rustic bridge; for the last two acts a double room (part library, part dining-room) so rich in atmosphere that, according to Gielgud, one felt one knew the rest of the house. He also had that musical control of tone, pace and tempo that is absolutely vital in Chekhov. Norman Marshall, himself a director very active in the Little Theatres of the 1930s, gives a vivid description of going to interview Komis to get his opinions on the English theatre. At first Komis seemed bored and grumpy: 'Then something I said suddenly aroused his interest and he sat down at the grand piano and started to improvise a tune. "It is an English theatre," he said. "The curtain rises. I hear a tune – something like this. The act goes on – and so does the tune, always at the same damn, dull pace. Now it is the second act. Still the same tune, still the same tempo. I cannot stand it. I compose myself for sleep. That is very easy – the tune lulls me to sleep. On and on goes that damned tune. But in the theatre it should not be so. It should be like this." Then he played his improvised little tune again with innumerable variations of tone and tempo. It was exactly what Komisarjevsky did in his own productions, giving them intricate patterns of rhythm.'

Peggy confirms this: indeed, she says ruefully, it was probably their piano he was demonstrating on. But Komis, like all great directors, also allowed his actors sufficient freedom to dictate their own tempo. Alec Guinness tells a famous story of Edith Evans in rehearsal as Arkadina, apparently missing a cue when the characters are watching Konstantin's play with their backs to the audience. She ignored a whisper from Gielgud and a hint from the prompter. No-one moved. Silence fell. Komis sat still. Then after four minutes, Edith gave a slight shiver as if touched by a chill breeze and said, with a mixture of sadness and callousness. 'Let's go in.' I beg leave to doubt (as does Peggy) the length of the pause, since four minutes on stage would seem like an eternity. But it makes the point that a Komis production was free from the deadly metronomic regularity of tempo of most West End theatre.

Even if it was not an unmixed joy, *The Seagull* confirmed Peggy's status in the front rank of English actresses. She was particularly sorry when Gielgud left the cast after eight weeks to prepare for his opening in *Hamlet* in New York early in 1937. Since her personal life was somewhat unhappy at the time, she was also intrigued to get an offer late in 1936 to sail to New York to appear in a new play by Maxwell Anderson, *High Tor*. The dramatist's wife was originally going to play the female lead but the director Guthrie McLintic, had said he would resign if she did. So Peggy was offered the role, cabled John Gielgud for advice and got the instant response, 'Play a mixture of *The Tempest* and *The Flying Dutchman*. Strongly advise.' – which just goes to show that Gielgud was still very much Peggy's guiding star, but that even the brightest star is something it is not always wise to follow.

CHAPTER SEVEN

The Spring Queen

PEGGY HAD NOT ALLOWED herself any time to contemplate whether she wanted to go to New York to appear in a blank-verse fantasy by Maxwell Anderson. She committed herself to *High Tor*, got her visa, packed and set sail all in the space of a few days. Only when she arrived and read the script did dismay set in: Anderson's play had a lack of reality to which she found herself totally antipathetic. The production had a good lead actor in Burgess Meredith. Its director, Guthrie McLintic – memorably parodied as the tearful, self-delighting director always blathering about magic-time in Moss Hart's *Light Up the Sky* – was a name. And when the play opened at the Martin Beck Theatre on 9 January 1937 it got respectful reviews, went on to run for 171 performances and eventually to win the New York Drama Critics' Prize for the best new American play of the season. It did, however, take eleven ballots for the New York aisle-squatters to come to a decision. In retrospect, one is only surprised it was so few.

High Tor did not exactly live up to Gielgud's advance billing. Its hero, Van Van Dorn (played by Meredith) is disgusted with civilisation. Having fought with his sweetheart, he flees to a hill that he owns overlooking the Hudson. There, along with a native Indian, he spends an eventful night. The couple encounter bank-robbers, land-developers determined to buy Van Dorn's hill, and the ghosts of old sailors. Come the dawn, the ghosts vanish, the robbers are apprehended and a profitable deal is consummated with the developers. Although Van Dorn may appear to have sold out to the forces of progress, he has not totally capitulated, for the Indian assures him 'Nothing is made by men but makes, in the end, good ruins.'

George Jean Nathan, the most trenchant of American critics, put his finger on what was wrong with the play: Anderson's determination to see poetry in everything, whether it was there or not. Nathan even scrupulously exposed the flaws in the Indian's aphorism quoted above:

'This last is the play's key philosophy. It sounds impressive enough but what sense does it make? If Mr Anderson has in mind the concrete, material things made by men, any number of such things as the Pyramids, the Sphinx etc, remain to confound his statement. And it must be such concrete, material things he is thinking of, because, first, his play points directly to that belief and because, secondly, he would recognise himself as being completely absurd if he argued that great art, which has been created by men, and great scientific achievement have not lived down the long lane of the centuries. The ruins of even material things are but the outward symbols of enduring inner accomplishment.'

Peggy's *bête noire*, James Agate, who in May did a three-week stint in New York on behalf of the *Sunday Times*, was even more brusque than Nathan in his criticism: he described Anderson's play as 'high fudge interlarded with bleak, totally unfunny humour.' But it is fair to say that Peggy herself was not taken in by Anderson's blank-verse hokum. Nor, sad to say, did she much enjoy life in the frenzied showbiz village of Manhattan. Fortunately, she had English friends in town such as John Gielgud and Harry Andrews. She met Ruth Gordon, Lillian Gish and the rather sad expatriate figure of Mrs Patrick Campbell then living in a little hotel on West 49th Street and memorably compared by Alexander Woollcott to a 'a sinking ship firing on her rescuers'. Along with Burgess Meredith and Hume Cronyn, Peggy also filled in the time by going to drama classes with a teacher named Benno Schneider and experiencing for the first time improvisation, which she thoroughly enjoyed.

'But,' she says, 'I lived in an apartment block in Washington Square for six months on my own. I feel you either sink or swim in New York and I sank. I never got used to the brilliant artificiality of New York and the fact that no-one seemed to have homes – one always seemed to meet people in restaurants. Possibly the most memorable time I spent was with Edward Sheldon who was married to the actress Doris Keane, and who had in his day been a very popular playwright. He was blind, had been stricken with paralysis and lived in his apartment stretched out on a bier. Every day friends would come and read the paper to him, tell him all the latest theatrical gossip and read books to him. I joined in not out of pity but because I so much admired his stoicism and courage. He gave far more to his visitors than they could ever give to him.'

But Peggy was not, and was never likely to become, a Broadway baby. Theatrically New York was much livelier in 1937 than it is today: at least then there was Maurice Evans in *Richard II*, Helen Hayes in *Victoria Regina, Babes in Arms, You Can't Take it with You, Tobacco Road*. But the hype, the star-worship, the belief that every new opening is an event of cosmic significance that are endemic to Broadway were miles removed from Peggy's fundamental belief in a theatre of organic growth and familial closeness. Broadway has many virtues: above all, the backstage feeling, as an actor once told me, that every performance there is like a first night. But it is still – and perhaps always will be – a theatre that craves success, hates failure and has little room for the patient growth that leads to first-rate company work.

The best thing to happen to Peggy in New York was an invitation from her mentor and friend, John Gielgud, to join him back in London in another attempt to forge a company inside a commercial framework. In the autumn of 1937 Gielgud planned to go into management at the Queen's Theatre with a four-play season comprising *Richard II, The School for Scandal, Three Sisters* and *The Merchant of Venice*. For Peggy it meant a goodish run of parts: Queen Isabella, Lady Teazle, Irina and Portia.

Even more importantly, it meant working with good directors – Gielgud himself, Tyrone Guthrie, Michel Saint-Denis – and with an astonishing, more or less permanent company that would include Michael Redgrave, Leon Quartermaine, Harcourt

Williams, Harry Andrews, Anthony Quayle, Alec Guinness, George Devine, Glen Byam Shaw, George Howe, Dennis Price and Rachel Kempson. Each production was to run for a minimum of eight and a maximum of ten weeks. The result became, in the words of Harold Hobson, 'one of the rarest blazes of theatrical light of the century.' But the Gielgud season was much more than a fiery comet tearing across the West End sky. It is no exaggeration to say that it laid the foundations of the work to be done at Stratford-on-Avon in the 1950s under Anthony Quayle and Glen Byam Shaw and thereby sowed the seeds that were to grow into the Royal Shakespeare Company and the National Theatre. If anyone can claim to be the architect of post-war British theatre it is John Gielgud. Anthony Quayle perceptively sees the English theatre of the 1930s as made up of the formation of little crystals: Devine's invitation to Gielgud to direct for OUDS, the Gielgud seasons at the New and the Queen's, the work being done simultaneously by Guthrie and Olivier at the Old Vic. Quayle also shrewdly makes the point that Peggy's progress to prominence in the Thirties was determined partly by Komis's intellectual influence and by Gielgud's abiding faith. 'Peggy,' he says, 'was always John's young leading lady. He helped her to achieve status. She was the spring-queen of the time.'

Peggy, for her part, was in seventh heaven: here she was back in London playing in the nearest thing England could provide at the time to an ensemble. And no greater proof of her devotion to an ideal could be found than her willingness to open the season in the thankless role of the Queen in *Richard II*. The character is almost never on stage, and when she is, apart from listening to the symbolic chat of the two Gardeners, she has little chance to appear more than suffering or ill-used. Equally impressive is that Peggy, with a pencilled line over each of her eyebrows to give her a medieval look, managed to make a distinct impact in a part Shakespeare almost forgot to write. Charles Morgan noted that 'she accepts a small part and plays it with admirable grace.' W. A. Darlington wrote that 'If anybody can make more of Richard's poor little anonymous Queen than Peggy Ashcroft, may I be there to see it when it happens.' Rachel Kempson told me that it was a performance of outstanding poise and J. C. Trewin says he can still see her in his mind's eye: 'For all her eagerness, she always moved most gracefully. There was never any feeling of "I am now going from A to B to C." One of the reasons why she made her name in the Thirties is that it was an artificial world and people weren't used to seeing an actress break the mould as she did.'

Although Gielgud was producer, director and star, there was no sense that this *Richard II* was simply a one-man show. Gielgud ensured, in fact, that he was captain of a team that batted all the way down. Michael Redgrave (who only three years previously had been a schoolmaster at Cranleigh) played Bolingbroke as a burly, virile contrast to Gielgud's poet-king but also, in his silence when upon the throne, indicated the inner torment of conflicting conscience: here was an actor of potential greatness. Leon Quartermaine's John of Gaunt had a voice of silk and a splendid poise of the head. Glen Byam Shaw's Mowbray was marked by its ambitious venom and Anthony Quayle lent the Captain of the Welshmen a touch of Celtic song. But Gielgud's direction was also masterly. Even before a word had been spoken, the air seemed heavy with turbulence, mistrust and incipient revolt. And there were some highly imaginative touches, such as the light blazing on Bolingbroke in the deposition scene illuminating Richard's 'sun of Bolingbroke'. Admittedly some thought that the Motleys' scenery and costumes were too lavishly pictorial: semi-realistic mock-castles and enough plants in the Duke of York's garden to populate a Westminster florist's. But, with Gielgud himself returning to a role he had first played at the Old Vic in 1929, it was a brilliant start to a season whose importance was recognised at the time. As Charles Morgan noted in *The Times*: 'Its failure would give disastrous opportunity to those who cry that the living theatre is a sick man that cannot save himself. Fortunately it is too good to fail.'

Failure would be too harsh a word to apply to the next production of the season: Sheridan's *The School for Scandal*, directed by the towering, hawk-like *enfant terrible* of the British theatre, Tyrone Guthrie. But this production, which opened on 25 November, was certainly a let-down for all sorts of reasons. Guthrie was wildly over-stretched, dividing his time between the Queen's, the Old Vic, where he was still the Artistic Director, and film-acting for Charles Laughton's Mayflower Company (he appeared as a credible missionary in *Vessel of Wrath* and an improbable busker in *St Martin's Lane*).

Peggy is the most forgiving of women and rarely says a harsh word about any of her theatrical colleagues, although she has pronounced likes and dislikes. But it is quite clear that she and Guthrie didn't see eye to eye (very difficult, anyway, when he was a looming six foot four inches in his stockinged feet). For Peggy building a character is a matter of patient research and exploration, always digging, digging, digging towards that core of truth. Guthrie, as a director, was less an explorer than a magician. His genius lay in marshalling large crowds of people like some inspired Royal Tournament pageant-master; his weakness lay in plays requiring a passionate emotional intimacy. Put twenty people on stage and he was the greatest director in the world; when two or three were gathered together, he was generally much less good.

Guthrie's inspired recklessness was not Peggy's style and she talks about him now with lips gently pursed: 'My doubts about Guthrie were exacerbated by the fact that, while we were rehearsing *The School for Scandal*, he was busy with the Old Vic and acting in a film. I remember, for instance, rehearsing the quarrel scene with Leon Quartermaine as Sir Peter Teazle and Guthrie simply said 'Oh, that'll be all right – we needn't do that again.' And we never did come back to it. I always felt that he was a mixture of brilliant genius and occasionally inspired amateur. When he was working at Stratford many years later I could never forgive the way during Gwen's [Ffrangcon-Davies] big scene in *Henry VIII* he had clerks audibly scratching away with a quill pen.'

It is clear that Guthrie never found a consistent style for Sheridan's surprisingly difficult play. According to Alec Guinness, there was considerable tension between the older actors who wanted lots of fluttering lace hankerchieves and fan-work and Guthrie who took a more uncompromising, down-to-earth attitude to the period; even the sets were an unhappy mixture of dusty, realistic drabness for the Teazles and impressionistic painted curtains elsewhere.

In mitigation, one can also say that Guthrie was caught up in events beyond his control. Two nights before *The School for*

Scandal opened at the Queen's, Michel Saint-Denis's production of *Macbeth* with Laurence Olivier was scheduled to open at the Old Vic. A disastrous dress rehearsal at the Vic led to a postponement of *Macbeth* for three nights: the first time such a thing had happened in the Vic's long history. Worst of all was the death of Lilian Baylis through a stroke. For Guthrie, Gielgud, Redgrave, Guinness and not least for Peggy, who had a deep affection for The Lady, it was shattering news, just as they were gearing themselves up to present or play period comedy. For both circumstantial and temperamental reasons, it was not a happy production and Anthony Quayle pithily summed up to me the reasons why: 'John Gielgud and Tony Guthrie were both great influences on the theatre of that time but they didn't get on: not at all, not at all. John is the most generous of men but I think he felt Tony let him down over *The School for Scandal* because he was constantly running from the Queen's to catch up with affairs at the Vic. Guthrie in his book admitted that he slightly short-changed the Gielgud company because the Vic, at that moment, was going down the plug-hole.'

Peggy herself does not count Lady Teazle amongst her best performances – a verdict readily confirmed by Agate, who said she was too innocent and kindly where she should be 'panting under a smother of acquired elegance'. A small symptom of her difficulty lay in her make-up. She admits that she has always been very bad at make-up and was taught nothing about it at drama school. She recalls Gielgud crying in exasperation at a dress rehearsal of the Sheridan: 'Peggy, I can't see your eyes – you look as if you hadn't got any make-up on at all. Glen, take her away and do her make-up.' At a time when actresses (and actors too) painted an inch thick, Peggy's naturalness clearly had a lot to do with her refusal to appear on stage looking like a wall of greasepaint.

For Peggy the real joy of the season was playing Irina in Michel Saint-Denis's production of *Three Sisters*: the high water-mark of British theatre in the period between the wars. Here, at last, was everything Peggy dreamed of. A great play; a great company, as responsive to each other's nuances as the members of the Moscow Art Theatre or La Compagnie des Quinze; a director who gave her the total confidence in her abilities she often lacked; ideal rehearsal conditions with one week spent reading the play and six more spent on total immersion in the characterisation. Seven weeks' rehearsal for a single play was something unheard of in the British theatre at that time: it was an application of Continental methods to the normally intractable British system and it paid superlative dividends.

Admittedly there were a few problems over casting to begin with. Gwen Ffrangcon-Davies had to be coaxed into playing the schoolmistress Olga. Gielgud had originally chosen for himself the role of Andrey and was never entirely settled as the romantic battery-commander, Vershinin. Michael Redgrave, instead of playing Andrey as hoped, was cast as Tusenbach and initially lacked confidence in his reading: the scales fell from his eyes only when he came to the Baron's speech about the migratory cranes in autumn and Saint-Denis told him 'You say this speech as if you mean something. You must mean *nothing*.' Peggy claims that even if Redgrave lacked confidence at the start, he finally achieved one of the finest performances of his career.

If there was a secret to the production's success it lay in the all-round strength of the cast – which included Carol Goodner as Masha, George Devine as Andrey, Angela Baddeley as Natasha, Frederick Lloyd as Chebutykin – and in Saint-Denis's fanatical attention to every detail.

Peggy recalls: 'I remember the hours Michel spent trying to achieve the timing of the music and the exact volume of sound at the end of the final act. He used a De Sousa march that seemed to fill every crevice of the theatre before fading into the distance. Also I have never seen a production of *Three Sisters* where you sensed so vividly the change of the seasons. The first act had the gaiety of Easter and springtime. Then it was winter for Act Two. Then it was a blazing hot summer night for the fire in Act Three. For the final act it was deep autumn. We would spend hours rehearsing things like just how hot it was going to be. I can still see Gwen clapping her hands to show the mosquitoes were biting: simple things like that gave you the atmosphere. It was this rapt attention to detail that made it a great production.'

The production's mastery lives on in the surviving still photographs. A famous one from the third act shows Redgrave as the Baron asleep with gaping mouth while clutching a cushion;

Peggy next to him with her head lolling in fatigue; next to her Leon Quartermaine as Soliony head slumped forward. Sitting on a sofa together, they represent the very ecstasy of exhaustion. Behind them stand Frederick Lloyd, spade-bearded and quizzical, as the army doctor and Gielgud's Vershinin, ramrod-backed and handsomely moustached. Everything looks precisely right.

Those who saw and wrote about the production testified to its perfection. Rupert Hart-Davis wrote: 'One cannot help feeling the company approach the much-described harmony of Stanislavsky's actors.' Lionel Hale said: 'They seem to have embraced their characters finally and naturally; they grow in them as flowers bedded in good earth.' But Harold Hobson in later years pinned down a good point when he suggested that the timing of this production – at a period when, for all Lord Halifax's appeasement of an ever more aggressive Hitler, war was becoming increasingly certain – added to its pathos and beauty. 'Michael Redgrave as Tusenbach and Peggy Ashcroft as the youngest sister,' Hobson recalled, 'made a very poignant thing out of their shy, embarrassed parting on a note of forced cheerfulness in the last act, just before the duel; and the fading music of the marching regiment, dying away into silence at the end of the play, was a sadly sufficient comment on the vanishing hopes of the entire Russian bourgeoisie before the sky darkened into revolution. This was the last evening of tranquil beauty that the British theatre was to know for many years, if indeed it was ever to know such a thing again.'

Peggy's final role in the Queen's season was as Portia in a production of *The Merchant of Venice* played under a white canvas dome designed by the Motleys and featuring Gielgud as a modest, restrained Shylock somewhat lacking in demonic fury. He also directed with the help of Glen Byam Shaw, and Peggy found it a better production, sharper and more lucid, than the fantasticated one he had done at the Vic in 1932. Her opinion is worth hearing, since by then she could have toured the country giving WEA Extension Lectures on the play. She had done it at school, at drama school and at the Vic; while critics tend to droop at the prospect of another jaunt to Venice and Belmont and at another round of *Take Your Pick* with those caskets, Peggy's spirits always seemed to lift at the notion of giving life to a fairy-tale and at donning breeches to become Balthasar. An extremely feminine woman, Peggy has always delighted in the male masquerading of Shakespeare's heroines, maybe because that is when the characters impose themselves on the action.

Critical reaction to her performance was divided on now familiar lines: that is, Agate versus the rest. In the pre-war period, before she began to show the breadth of her sympathy and the range of her technique, people either responded to her emotional directness and youthful allure or they didn't. She was a fast-developing actress: she had not yet become a great one. Of her critical admirers, none was more consistent than Charles Morgan in *The Times*, who wrote of this performance: 'Belmont is not overwhelmed by Venice and Portia is permitted to rule in her own country. Miss Ashcroft rules it with magic, giving Portia her miraculous youth, her sweetness, her wise gravity, her underlying spirit of laughter; carrying the court scene with a natural ease and humour, converting the whole part into a lyric and giving to the play a freshness such as we do not remember having seen upon it before.'

That is as clear a tribute to the young Peggy's qualities as you could hope to find. In an age of twittery artifice or Shakespearean *grande-damerie* and sonic boom, she invested the comic heroines with her own qualities: lightness, ease, the alternation of gravity and gaiety. For Agate, it was not enough. He saw Portia as arch and sophisticated, tiresome and something of a *pretensieuse*: an ideal part, as he said, for a leading lady who is young enough to look it. 'Now,' he went on, 'Miss Ashcroft's talent lies in conveying innocence and her chief difficulty is to look old enough to play anything. Whence it follows that I did not believe a word of her Portia throughout the entire evening. If, however, Portia is rightly represented as a child on the way to becoming a great lady, then Miss Ashcroft's performance was perfect.' But what is there in the text to indicate that Portia is a mature lady? Why shouldn't she be played as a young woman gradually discovering the delights and responsibilities of love? Ellen Terry, whose name Agate invoked, once said that she had tried five or six ways of playing the role. But Peggy was rebuked by Agate for not measuring up to his fixed ideal.

The odd bad notice did not, however, matter that much to her. What did was the fact that she had now been part of two historic ventures: the Gielgud seasons at the New and the Queen's. As she says, very simply, 'John's seasons changed the point of view.' They showed that the classics could be a box-office draw, that an identifiable team of actors could be held together in a freelance world and that great plays repaid minute examination. Gielgud had erected a signpost to the future. It pointed ultimately towards the RSC and the National.

Margaret Harris of Motley makes a similar point: 'John has never been given credit for what he did. Because I think he single-handedly put the English theatre back on the map. He led Peggy into doing the sort of work she's best at. He found Olivier as a classical actor and encouraged people like Alec Guinness, Harry Andrews and Anthony Quayle. He really did the most amazing work. Larry gets all the credit and John doesn't, which I think is a sign of John's innate modesty.'

By the end of the Queen's season in June 1938, Gielgud himself was tired and suffering from the triple strain of being manager, director and star of a commercially-based classical company. But several members of the Queen's company, led by Peggy, decided to re-form under the directorship of Michel Saint-Denis. By this time Saint-Denis had put down roots in England and was trying to foster an attitude to acting that derived from the methodical training of the Continent rather than the Olympian casualness of the British. In 1936 he and George Devine had opened the London Theatre Studio first in Beak Street and then in Providence Hall, Islington: the work included mime, improvisation and mask exercises then unknown in London drama schools.

Capitalising on his triumph with *Three Sisters* and with the financial backing of Bronson Albery, Saint-Denis planned to take over the Phoenix Theatre and announced a programme that would provisionally include *The Cherry Orchard, Uncle Vanya, The Wild Duck, Twelfth Night* and *Le Bourgeois Gentilhomme*. Among the players deeply committed to the venture were Peggy, Michael Redgrave, Glen Byam Shaw, George Devine and Marius Goring. Rather cloudier expressions of support came from Laurence Olivier and Ralph Richardson.

In the end, this idealistic venture lasted only from October 1938 to January 1939 and only two plays were presented: Bulgakov's *The White Guard*, translated by Rodney Ackland, and *Twelfth Night*. According to Peggy, a cardinal reason for the season's failure was its timing: it coincided with the Munich crisis and, as often happens in periods of national turbulence, people's minds were bent on things other than theatre-going. It was not a success financially, and although Bronson Albery was, in many ways, a saintly patron of the higher drama two commercial flops in a row were more than he could sustain. Saint-Denis's aborted project also proves the extent to which in the 1930s (and arguably even today) high ideals depended on the backing of box-office fire-power. Had Gielgud, Olivier, Richardson and Edith Evans thrown in their lot with Saint-Denis, who knows what might have happened?

Before writing the Phoenix season off as a failure, it is worth recording that *The White Guard* got very good notices, even if a lot of people professed not to know what was going on. The importance of the play lies in the fact that it was, in 1926, the first attempt to depict on the Soviet stage the enemies of the Bolshevik regime as human beings rather than monsters. Set against the background of the Civil War in the Ukraine from 1918 to 1919, it shows the White Russian intelligentsia coming to terms with the fact that they are on the losing side and that the Red victory is inevitable. The Civil War scenes are – to a British audience anyway – undeniably clumsy and confusing. The strength of the play lies in the family scenes set in the Turbins' apartment in Kiev, which are full of drink, love, despair, loneliness and that peculiar emotional volatility that is the hallmark of Russian drama. In the Soviet Union of 1926 the play was dubbed as 'indubitably decadent' and accused of 'discharging' rather than 'charging' the spectators' political fervour. The Moscow Art Theatre production, vilified for its content, was withdrawn after a run of three years. The Phoenix production, acclaimed for its sympathetic portrait of the White Russians, was withdrawn after a run of three weeks. Commerce clearly exacts a swifter, more brutal revenge than politics.

The tragedy was that the play was a perfect vehicle for Saint-Denis's talent. His handling of the first act, where people drop in and out of the Turbins' apartment, get drunk, philosophise, attempt suicide, sing and poeticise, explore heaven and hell simultaneously, had something of the symphonic realism of his *Three Sisters*. Redgrave got great notices as a stiff-backed military commander with a spectacular second-act death-fall (that left a permanent scar over his right eye as a memorial). Peggy as the central figure, Yeliena, was admired for her radiance and strength of spirit. Only in the usual quarter was she given a douche of cold water: Agate, while praising her intentions, crushingly remarked that she gave 'an exquisite performance of something which got no nearer to Russia than the handbag department at Harridges.' First she was too young for Agate. Now she was too English. She could not win.

Neither could the Phoenix project, despite the brave words of Redgrave when interviewed during the run of *The White Guard*: 'It must be judged not by the success or failure of this or that play but by whether, after a time, after trial and error, part successes and part failures, something does not emerge which will be good and consistent, new and lasting. I believe that Michel Saint-Denis must achieve this, not only because he wants it so much himself but because many actors and a large section of the public want it too.'

In fact, not quite enough of either wanted it. After the sad commercial failure of the Bulgakov, Saint-Denis directed *Twelfth Night* which opened at the Phoenix on 1 December. The cast he originally had in mind was a mouth-watering one: Olivier as Malvolio, Richardson as Sir Toby, Edith Evans as Maria. In the end, many of the first choices proved unavailable and the result was a good company rather than a great one in a fussy, overloaded production that was said to prettify Illyria in the manner of a fancy-dress ball. Peggy, capturing yet another of Shakespeare's comic heroines, was much praised for the charm and wit of her Viola and Michael Redgrave got excellent notices for his Aguecheek by following the Louis Jouvet line of playing him as an ass who knows he is an ass and takes the utmost delight in it. One always tends to link Peggy with Gielgud, but she also found a perfect partner in Redgrave, a fellow-Stanislavskyan, a highly intelligent man and an actor whose demonic inner turbulence found a perfect foil in her built-in *gravitas*. But, alas, *Twelfth Night* played to half-empty houses and doomed the Saint-Denis project. Reversing the myth, the Phoenix turned to ashes. But, as a minor historical footnote, it is worth noting that Shakespeare's comedy became only the second play ever to be televised live in its entirety from a theatre; Peggy remembers dashing off-stage and into the television caravan outside the theatre to glimpse the miracle of a play, of which she was a vital part, in progress.

Peggy was disheartened by the failure of the Phoenix season but in no way defeated. A less indomitable spirit might have decided that there was little hope for long-range seasonal planning and company values in the roulette-world of the West End. But Peggy had seen the future and she knew it worked. If anything, she became more determined than ever that she would be part of a theatrical system that had a vision beyond the success or failure of an individual play. It was difficult in England (as it proved impossible in America) to achieve the kind of politicised ensemble so beautifully described by Harold Clurman in his account of the Group Theatre, *The Fervent Years,* where he says 'A technique of the theatre had to be founded on life values.' But as the Thirties lurched towards their traumatic close, Peggy knew that her own best work had been achieved in settled groups that offered a familial closeness and a sense of shared purpose: groups that provided an emotional security that had often been lacking in her lonely adolescence and her not always happy personal life over the past decade. In Richard Findlater's phrase, she now became 'an actress in search of a company'. As a woman she also became someone seeking – and very shortly to find – the stability that had hitherto eluded her.

Meanwhile in 1939, with the shadow of war growing ever more visible, she threw herself unremittingly into work. She played Rostand's Roxane and Shaw's Raina on BBC Radio. She also went out on the road in a springtime tour of a play, *Weep for the Spring,* by the sensitive, immensely gifted Shelleyesque young actor, Stephen Haggard, with whom she had appeared in *Mesmer, The Seagull* and *The White Guard.* It was not, however, the ideal time to be presenting a play set in Germany against a Nazi background, even though it was a story of the frustration and despair of romantic young love: despite being directed by Saint-Denis and having a good cast, including Haggard himself, Athene Seyler and Nicholas Hannen, it predictably failed to reach London.

If in 1939 people didn't want to see plays set in Nazi Germany, what did they want to see? Harold Hobson makes the point forcefully in his book, *Theatre in Britain*, that at a time of apprehension and fear, progressive intellectuals were conspicuous either by their departure to America (as in the case of Auden or Isherwood) or by their Olympian irony (as with Cyril Connolly). In Hobson's view, it was the commercial theatre alone that fulfilled the proper function of cheering people up and he cites as an example John Gielgud's production of *The Importance of Being Earnest* which opened at the Globe on 16 August 1939. Bracketing it with J. B. Priestley's *Music at Night* and Emlyn Williams's *The Light of Heart*, he wrote: 'Theoretically these plays had no social relevance. They were plays of entertainment. But in practice their social relevance was considerable. Audiences left the theatre feeling braver and happier than when they went in. When they thought of the work of those progressives whose work *was* socially relevant, their emotions were quite different.'

I am not sure how just these strictures are. I can't believe that a new verse-play from Auden or Isherwood or a rousing column of criticism from Connolly would have made an iota of difference to the nation's morale. What is clearly true is that audiences in time of national crisis seek pleasurable escape; and in Wilde's cut-diamond farcical masterpiece, they found a sublime example. Gielgud's production had been played for eight matinées the previous February in aid of theatrical charities; now it came into the West End for a short run with Gwen Ffrangcon-Davies as Gwendolen and Peggy as Cecily Cardew joining the cast.

It was Peggy's début in Wilde and it was an inspired piece of casting: her lucidity, poise and downright belief in what she was saying was far funnier than that kind of arch, stilted delivery – as if they had a fishbone stuck in their throat – that some actresses think is appropriate for Wilde. So much acting is about cutting away the dead wood and finding the simplest, clearest, truest way of delivering a line: that is what Peggy is superb at. John Gielgud says that Peggy 'acted Cecily with a demure slyness that added to the part an *Alice in Wonderland* comment of farcical solemnity.' Agate, catching the play at Golders Green on its way into town, praised Peggy for playing Cecily with a sincerity that would be a little too much even for Ophelia which in his view was perfectly right. Seeing the play a week or so later at the Globe her most steadfast admirer, Charles Morgan, suffered a rush of simile to the head: 'She comes into the pageant like a rightly placed jewel, let us say a chrysoberyl, which changes colour with the light, now innocently olive-green, now an audacious pink.'

But it was that kind of production. Critics reached not just for their superlatives but for their full armoury of metaphor. Edith Evans's legendary Lady Bracknell was compared to an ambulatory Gorgon with a dead bird in her hat (could it be an albatross?), a sloop under full sail, an avalanche hurtling down a mountain-side. To Ivor Brown, she was 'like some great fowl from splendid and uncharted skies'. To Agate, 'she faces enormity very much as the whale must have faced Jonah, a little unprepared but by no means daunted.' She defined the contours of the role in a way that went unchallenged until Judi Dench's flirtatious and sexy performance at the National in 1983. But although, with the help of gramophone recording and film, Edith Evans's dowagerial bravura passed into legend, she by no means overbalanced an impeccably cast production. Gielgud's John Worthing had a superfine solemnity. Gwen Ffrangcon-Davies's Gwendolen had a faint aura of incipient dragonishness. Margaret Rutherford, offering a multitude of chins, was simply Miss Prism in the highest degree.

The production proved to Peggy – if it needed proving – that there is no inherent conflict between style and truth: that period style is not a kind of lacquer to be sprayed indiscriminately on to a play but something that grows out of understanding its rhythm, its tempo, its meaning. The production also increased her admiration for Edith Evans, that inordinately complex woman who seemed to combine a generosity of spirit in large things with a meanness in small ones. Edith used to refer to Peggy jokingly as her daughter, and Peggy was her inheritrix in the sense that she realised that sincerity and music in acting are not incompatible. 'The amazing thing about Edith,' says Peggy, 'is that if you were in a play with her or heard her speak, you could never read it again without hearing Edith's voice because she had very extraordinary cadences, but they were never anything but her way of finding the true way to speak that line. She also knew that acting's got to be precise; it must be actual and particular, not generalised.'

While still playing in *The Importance*, Peggy and Edith Evans both went into rehearsal for a projected new production of *The Cherry Orchard* put together by Hugh ('Binkie') Beaumont for the H.M. Tennent management. It was to be directed by Michel Saint-Denis and was a blatant, and wholly admirable, attempt to capitalise on the success of his *Three Sisters*. The cast was of the kind made in heaven but for once realised on earth. Edith Evans was Madame Ranyevsky, Ralph Richardson Lopakhin, Ronald Squire Gaev, Alec Guinness Trofimov, Cyril Cusack Firs and Peggy Anya; according to Guinness, Peggy's Anya was 'potentially wonderful'. It remains, however, one of the great might-have-beens of British theatre, for after a bare two weeks of rehearsal Binkie Beaumont assembled the cast on stage on the morning of Saturday, 2 September, and told them the production would have to be cancelled because of the imminence of war and the closure of the theatres. Guinness recalls going for a walk immediately after the announcement with Edith Evans who wailed sadly: 'What am I to *do*? I am an actress. I can't act with bombs falling. What shall I *do*?'

Peggy had no time for hand-wringing or lamentation. The war was as cruel a disruption to her career as to everyone else's, but she immediately set about making herself useful. In a BBC Radio feature with the splendidly Robb Wiltonish title of *The Day War Broke Out*, she remembered exactly where she was on the fateful Sunday of 3 September 1939:

'I had been staying with friends in the country in Huntingdon who had an evacuee centre for children. The point was that everyone, as soon as war was declared, was expecting a holocaust that never came and so children were quickly got out of the cities. I was driven down that afternoon and I remember arriving at this country house and being taken to the tennis court which had loose red sand. It was packed with toddlers who had been sitting there for a long time and who all had wet bottoms and runny noses, which I had to blow for them. It was before the birth of my own children and I found myself changing nappies for the first time in my life and putting children on their potties after every meal. A lot of the children had never seen the countryside before, I remember one little boy sitting on his potty and saying to me, in tones of great surprise, "Butterflies don't have potties, do they?"'

This was good preparation for the domestic life that was to occupy Peggy for much of the war. But in the last months of 1939, while the London theatres were closed, she went on tour with *The Importance*. Then, with the news that the West End would try to resume business as usual in the spring of 1940, Peggy went into rehearsal with Edith Evans and Alec Guinness for *Cousin Muriel* by Clemence Dane – 'a lousy play' according to Guinness. In this Peggy played, not for the first time, a young girl crossed in love. When the play opened at the Globe in March 1940 during the period of the phoney war, Peggy got good notices but was more insulted than overjoyed to find Agate saying it was the best thing she had ever done. It wasn't a good play. But John Gielgud remembers it nearly half a century later for one of those tiny moments of truth that have always characterised Peggy's work: 'She came on,' he says, 'in some kind of fancy dress with a clumsy skirt far too long for her and suddenly tripped over it with a furious cry of irritation so perfect that I thought for a moment it was an accident and not intended by the author.' It is significant that she could momentarily fool a consummate actor like Gielgud.

But of far more importance than the play and the role was the fact that in that wartime spring Peggy had fallen in love. It would not be quite true to say that it was love at first sight. Peggy had first met Jeremy Hutchinson, through their respective families, when he was 16. They had met again briefly at Oxford parties when he was an undergraduate and she was playing Juliet in 1932. But they fell in love during that strange, still, period of phoney war. Peggy was on tour in *Cousin Muriel* at the Theatre Royal, Brighton; Jeremy was doing officer-training for the RNVR at King Alfred's, Hove. What followed was, by his own account, a lightning courtship:

'I looked in the paper and saw that Peggy, whom I hadn't bumped into for eight years was playing in Brighton and I made my call at the Stage Door to see her. There was nothing premeditated about it: it was pure chance. We made a date to see each other and went for a long walk over the Sussex Downs. Partly I suppose because of the presence of war we had something of a whirlwind romance. After our meeting in Brighton, I went off to join Louis Mountbatten's destroyer fleet. But I got back to

London in the middle of the summer on leave, our romance continued and we got married on 14 September 1940. It was a memorable time because by then the bombing had resumed and we were
right in the middle of one of the worst air-raids of the war. We
got married in a Registry Office in Marylebone, had a reception in
my parents' house in Prince Albert Road and then drove off for
our honeymoon in Dorset through totally deserted London streets.'

It all has a touch of the romantic RAF movie *The Way to the
Stars* about it, though Jeremy was in fact in the 'wavy Navy'.
Immediately after the honeymoon, Jeremy was back in service
with Mountbatten's flotilla fleet. Peggy, having taken over from
Jessica Tandy as Miranda in an Old Vic *Tempest* that summer,
followed her marriage by appearing in an Anthony Asquith film
called, appropriately enough, *Quiet Wedding*.

One can hardly overestimate the importance of Peggy's third
marriage. The Thirties had for her been a time of career advance-
ment and considerable emotional strain, even profound unhappiness. Now, even with a husband on active service, her life had
a new-found stability. She was also marrying into an upper-
middle-class family of strong liberal convictions. Jeremy had
studied for the bar and, after wartime service, became a leading
QC and would-be Labour MP. His mother, Mary, was a well-
known Bloomsburyite, a great friend of the critic and theorist of
post-Impressionism Clive Bell, and herself very knowledgeable
about painting. Jeremy's sister, Barbara, was also a volatile, articulate figure with a passion for the visual arts. All this was to have
a strong influence on Peggy's political education and artistic tastes.

From 1940 onwards Peggy became a wife and eventually a
mother as well as an actress. But far from making her a less
dedicated or perfectionist performer, all the evidence suggests it
enhanced her qualities as an actress. Her technique improved, her
range of characterisation widened, her understanding of humanity
grew richer. This was partly due to the maturing process of time.
But, far from dwindling into a wife like Congreve's Millamant,
Peggy seemed to thrive in a state of settled matrimony. Her
friend, the designer Margaret Harris, puts it very succinctly:
'Before the war, Peggy was a delightful woman and actress. After
the war, she became a great woman and actress without sacrificing
any of her charm.'

CHAPTER EIGHT

Maturing into Greatness

IN PURELY CAREER TERMS the war years, inevitably, were something of a hiatus for Peggy. After her marriage, she resumed acting in January 1941 when she went on tour in George Devine's production of Daphne Du Maurier's imperishable romantic mystery, *Rebecca*, the *Jane Eyre* of its day. Peggy played the shy, nervous second Mrs De Winter and stepped with great aplomb into the shoes of Celia Johnson who had brought her own saucer-eyed magnetism to the role in the West End.

Because she was pregnant Peggy was forced to leave the tour before its end. But the final stages of the pregnancy were shadowed with doubt and uncertainty. On 21 May 1941 Peggy learnt that Mountbatten's ship HMS *Kelly* had been sunk in the Mediterranean. It was some time before she heard for sure that Jeremy was safe. But eventually a reassuring telegram arrived; and although Jeremy couldn't be home in time for the birth of his daughter Eliza on 14 June, he was given leave that enabled him to join his family in early August. Immediately after the birth, Peggy went to live in Tring in a folly belonging to her sister-in-law, Barbara, and her husband, Victor Rothschild. For fifteen months she didn't set foot on a stage – by far the longest gap in her career to date – but immersed herself in the role of motherhood. The only work she undertook consisted of three plays for radio and a quickie film for Carol Reed and the Army Kinematograph Service, *A New Lot*. When she did come back it was in October 1942 for a revival of Gielgud's production of *The Importance of Being Earnest* at the Phoenix. Little was changed except for the substitution of the etiolated, dandy-mincing revue star, Cyril Ritchard, in the role of Algy.

The year 1943 began badly. In January, Peggy was rehearsing a new production of Turgenev's *A Month in the Country* at the St James's when she broke her ankle getting into a taxi and had to retire hurt from the production. That meant rest and recuperation. More cheeringly, Jeremy got himself posted home to England by putting in for a Signals Course based in East Meon near Petersfield, which meant he was able to see his family.

Peggy's pioneering spirit also found another outlet when she helped to form the Apollo Society along with the pianist, Natasha Litvin. Peggy had realised in 1940, during the run of *Cousin Muriel*, that in wartime there was a huge public appetite for poetry readings: she and Edith Evans had given a number in the Globe Theatre in aid of a war fund and found, slightly to their surprise, that the theatre was jam-packed. In 1943 the Apollo Society was formed. It quickly found the support of people like Cecil Day Lewis, Jill Balcon, Maynard Keynes and Cambridge's spritely theatrical guru, George (Dadie) Rylands. It proved durable enough to last 40 years. 'The idea,' in the words of Dadie Rylands who became its first chairman, 'was to have recitals of poetry and make them more interesting by including pieces of music that were sympathetic. You could always doze during the music if you didn't like it. I'd done Sunday evening concerts at King's College of this kind. In later years they became the model for John Barton's *The Hollow Crown* which also started its life as a Sunday night college recital.'

The Apollo Society made its official début at the Arts Theatre, Cambridge, in the autumn of 1943 before a packed house and with the financial sponsorship of Maynard Keynes and the Council for the Encouragement of Music and Arts. The *Cambridge Review* recorded: 'The Poet Laureate made a moving and eloquent introductory speech. He explained that similar programmes will, it is hoped, be heard all over England in factories and camps as well as in theatres and that such an experiment may prove that English people are capable of enjoying the arts which are all instincts of delight ... Miss Peggy Ashcroft, Mr Robert Harris and Mr John Laurie brought to this experiment the advantage of their technical skill and yet avoided the dangers that beset the professional actor reading poetry.'

Peggy's work with the Apollo Society was of immense importance to her. It was a practical way of passing on her own delight in poetry. It was also in wartime a means of taking poetry and music to industrial areas, military camps, communities far from London rather than simply providing spiritual solace for the chosen few. And it provided a prototype for the kind of work Peggy was to do in later years when she allied her love of verse to her passion for causes. The Apollo began with a few friends putting ten quid each into the kitty. It proved both more durable and necessary than any of them ever envisaged.

In October 1943 Peggy returned to the stage in Rodney Ackland's *The Dark River* at the Whitehall. Ackland set the piece in a Thames backwater during the Spanish Civil War and then pitched a number of refugees from reality into this riverside Heartbreak House. Only one character, an ex-architect who designed air-raid shelters and who had been to Spain, was alert to the dangers ahead. Like the Communist poet, John Cornford, he realised that 'Our freedom's swaying in the scales'; but even he was unable to pierce the household's very English vein of nursery nostalgia and longing for times past. Seeing the play revived in 1984, I felt it had acquired an historical fascination as an attack on the ostrich-like attitudes of the English in the 1930s, and their dim awareness of events in Europe. But those living through a war in 1943 scarcely needed reminding of the culpable escapism that had preceded it. The public obviously thought so too, and it faded quickly. But Peggy gave a good, if totally out of character, performance as a former ballet dancer still living off her past triumphs. Frith Banbury, who saw it, rates it as one of her best. 'The character,' he says, 'is an unhappy woman who can't make up her mind and who is always harking back to past successes. It could be a very tiresome role unless played with enormous sympathy. Peggy made it real but also gave it that quality of poetic naturalism that is her forté.'

After *The Dark River* expired, Peggy had another long period away from the stage: nine months spent camp-following with Jeremy, doing the occasional radio play and Apollo Society recital and, above all, looking after Eliza. Motherhood was, and is, very important to Peggy. Rachel Kempson, Michael Redgrave's wife, recalls Peggy coming to see them in 1943 soon after the birth of their daughter Lynn:

'I was feeding Lynn and Peggy suddenly said "Oh God, why do we go on acting when there's all this?" In fact, I once asked her what it was that made her want to go on acting. She thought for a moment and then said "Well I think it's some kind of compulsion. I'm *compelled* to do it."'

The old compulsion returned in 1944 when Peggy was invited to play Ophelia, Titania and the Duchess of Malfi in a five-play classical season which Gielgud, backed by Binkie Beaumont, was setting up at the Haymarket. It was Gielgud's third attempt to create a company inside a commercial framework, though without many of the original pre-war 'family' who were on active service. A slightly older generation of West End actors, including Leslie Banks, Cecil Trouncer and Max Adrian took their place. This time there was no Saint-Denis or Komisarjevsky. Instead Gielgud and Beaumont relied on two theatrical magi from the older universities: George Rylands from Cambridge and Nevill Coghill from Oxford.

Rylands was, and happily still is, a Cambridge legend: a Fellow of King's, a friend of Forster, Eliot and Virginia Woolf, a guiding spirit behind the Marlowe Society (founded in 1907), a passionate believer in fine, clear verse-speaking and a redoubtable performer whose local triumphs included Cleopatra and the Duchess of Malfi in the days before the Marlowe admitted women. Nevill Coghill, with a profile once compared to a mixture of Owen Nares and the Apollo Belvedere, enjoyed a similar guru-like status at Oxford. But he differed from Rylands in one crucial respect. His chief talent lay less in fostering great verse-speaking than in creating stunning outdoor *coups de théâtre*: an early example came when he directed the medieval *Noah's Flood* beside the Thames at Pinkhill Lock and created the effect of the flood by opening the lock-gates.

George Rylands, who later in the season ran up against the obduracy of the hardened professional actor, was first in to bat at the Haymarket with his production of *Hamlet*. Gielgud was giving his fourth London Hamlet in 14 years, Leslie Banks was the King, Leon Quartermaine was the Ghost, Miles Malleson Polonius and Peggy Ophelia. But Peggy, desperately anxious to get back to the classical stage, suffered an appalling accident that kept her out of the early stages of the pre-London tour. Coming out of a rehearsal just by the Regent Palace, she was injured by one of the first V2 bombs to hit London: in the words of Eric Keown, she was 'blown straight into a barber's shop where she landed in the unresisting arms of a fat man who had asked only for a shave.' She got glass in her knee, which has troubled her ever since, and was immobilised for a week or two. It was a cruel twist of fate for an actress yearning to get back to work.

Peggy, at 36, was playing Ophelia for the first and only time in her career. George Rylands remembers her performance as 'genuine and true'. Her one problem was that she had no great singing voice, but she turned this to her advantage by making the mad scenes a touching extension of the earlier, betrayed Ophelia rather than, as so often, a self-contained neurasthenic cabaret or a twitching display of medical realism. Gielgud's Hamlet was also reckoned by many spectators to be his best: possessed of Irvingesque pathos, incisiveness, raillery and a quest-ing intellectual feverishness. A young actor playing Hamlet can give us the character's spiky alienation and moral disgust at his mother's o'er hasty marriage and Elsinore's decadence. It takes a mature actor (Gielgud was then 40) to catch the kaleidoscopic variety of Hamlet's moods and the breadth of his philosophical reflections on the nature of man, the art of acting, the ethos of suicide, the stoical acceptance of death. It is often thought to be a young man's part: in fact, it is a role that often only yields up its secrets to maturity.

George Rylands, who had been recruited by Gielgud and Binkie Beaumont on the strength of his work with the Marlowe Society, was content to unravel the play rather than to impose himself on it. For this he was much lauded by Ivor Brown in the *Observer*: 'No nonsense, no affectations, no stint of energy, no stunt of production. Every word is audible, every action visible. Mr George Rylands as director drives at lucidity. He wants the meaning and, now privileged to work with Mr Gielgud, he certainly gets it.' But for Brown's eventual successor, a stripling Kenneth Tynan then all of 17 and in love with a theatre of flamboyance and shock, Rylands's militant Cambridge classicism left a good deal to be desired: 'George Rylands's production,' Tynan wrote in *He that Plays the King*, 'was brown. I know that that is not nearly enough but neither was the production: dim, flatly-lit and snail-paced, it dragged its slow length along.' Clearly there was no overwhelming directorial viewpoint; equally obviously, with performers as powerful as Gielgud and Ashcroft on stage, it didn't greatly matter.

Peggy was delighted to be back in harness, and she followed her Ophelia with a remarkable Titania in Nevill Coghill's production of *A Midsummer Night's Dream* that opened in January 1945 (the season had already included *The Circle* and *Love for Love*). Coghill substituted Leslie Bridgewater's music for Mendelssohn's, directed the play in the style of a Jacobean court masque *circa* 1615, used sets suggesting Inigo Jones and kept the fairies to a bare minimum. His aim was to bring out the deep Englishness of Shakespeare's play. He was generally held to have been successful, except that Gielgud's Oberon, with a make-up like the ghost of Hamlet's father, was considered rather sinister and Max Adrian as Puck resembled a Greek satyr who had apparently got into Shakespeare's Athens while looking for the real one.

Peggy was obviously right for Titania. She has about her that quality of gravity and inexplicable sadness common to all first-rate actresses (Judi Dench, Maggie Smith, Vanessa Redgrave possess it) and vital for Shakespeare's fairy queen. One speech in particular, involving the dispute with Oberon about the little changeling boy, expresses a profound, internal melancholy:

> His mother was a vot'ress of my order
> And, in the Indian air, by night,
> Full often hath she gossip'd by my side;
> And sat with me on Neptune's yellow sands,
> Marking the embarked traders on the flood;
> When we have laughed to see the sails conceive
> And grow big-bellied with the wanton wind;
> Which she, with pretty and with swimming gait,

Following – her womb then rich with my young
  squire –
Would imitate; and sail upon the land,
To fetch me trifles and return again,
As from a voyage, rich with merchandise.
But she, being mortal, of that boy did die.

It is a brilliant passage filled with images of happiness, fertility and bounty suddenly punctured by that devastating last line in which Shakespeare sounds a death-knell and communicates an overpowering sense of loss. But it can of course be played in different ways. Maggie Smith at Stratford, Ontario, in 1977 – as an Elizabethan Virgin Queen Titania – suddenly brought us up against the reality of death. Peggy took a different line. 'To me,' she says, 'the speech expresses the non-mortality of Titania: the fact that dying was something she didn't quite comprehend. I tried to express the puzzlement and bewilderment of someone encountering the mortality of another world.'

As well as gravity, Peggy brought to the role a stillness and repose indicative of other-worldliness. J. C. Trewin rates her as his favourite Titania and even to this day can re-live that *Dream*: 'She wiped the stage with the rest of the company, including Gielgud, who for some reason was a very grim Oberon. He played him as a very tragic figure in green make-up that didn't really go. But Peggy's Titania was wonderful. The thing about her was that she didn't move. She didn't move at all. She spoke. The company made rings round her, in the physical sense, but she remained Queen. I don't think I'd ever been more aware of the musical quality of her speech. As Titania, the music was ceaseless. The night my wife Wendy and I went, she had the most terrific reception.' Alec Guinness also has a more private recollection of going to the performance with his wife Merula and their son Matthew, who was then barely five. When they went round to see her afterwards to congratulate her on a moving performance, Peggy – perhaps touched by Matthew Guinness's evident enjoyment of the play – wept with gratitude.

At its outset, Agate had dubbed Gielgud's Haymarket season 'unadventurous'. That hardly seemed the right epithet for a season that was to conclude in April 1945 with Webster's *The Duchess of Malfi*, much less common on the professional stage then than now. It had been a favourite of Peggy's and her brother's since adolescence. She had also seen the play directed by George Rylands with the Marlowe Society in 1943, and, when asked by Gielgud to choose a play she wanted to do in the Haymarket season, she had opted for Webster's dark masterpiece. Indeed she had taken on Ophelia largely in order to do the Duchess. But almost as soon as the play went into rehearsal, George Rylands found himself faced with a company mutiny:

'Some of the actors tried to stop me doing the play. I was rung up one morning before rehearsal by Binkie Beaumont and his assistant, John Perry, who asked to see me immediately. Some of the actors, led by Leon Quartermaine, thought that no-one would want to see *Malfi* and that the production would be a terrible failure. I was furious. The *Hamlet* had been a great success. I told Binkie and Perry that they could chuck me but they mustn't chuck the play because Peggy had agreed to do the season largely because of the Duchess. I told them they were cads, cowards and philistines and went at them with all guns blazing. The real trouble was that many of the actors didn't understand their parts and the versification of Webster. Many people can get away with Shakespeare; with Webster everything lies in the intensity of the poetry. Leon Quartermaine played the Cardinal like an eighteenth-century French abbé hoping that all the little girls would fall in love with him: he should be ice to his brother's fire. He had persuaded Gielgud that no-one would like the play and he, in turn, had taken the problem to Binkie. I think John was a bit feeble about this.'

Clearly the incident still hurts. But Dr Rylands, whose boundless charm conceals a strong will, went straight back into rehearsal and read the riot act to the company. It was as well he did, for the production turned out to be one of the triumphs of the Gielgud season with Cecil Trouncer's forthright Bosola, Gielgud's tortured, brainsickly, quasi-incestuous Ferdinand and Peggy's Duchess being garlanded with praise. Dr Rylands thinks it was Webster's intricate verse that put some of the actors off; Peggy thinks it was the horror of the mad scenes that shocked them. It certainly did take a wild courage to present this play at the end of a war that led to the perpetration of unprecedented horrors. The point struck two critics in entirely different ways. W. A. Darlington suggested in the *Daily Telegraph* that 'probably the only audience that would respond to this play today as Webster intended would be an audience of the Hitler Youth.' Conversely Ivor Brown pointed out in the *Observer* that 'the horrors seem almost trifling when matched with modern fact in Germany.' Brown had logic and history on his side: what the anti-Websterians overlook is the fact that lightning flashes of self-revelation and pure pathos illuminate the play's midnight darkness.

Having worked her way through the Shakespearean golden girls, Peggy was very keen to get to grips with the Duchess. As always, though, she was modest and insecure about her performance: never can there have been a great actress with less personal vanity. On the day of the first night she wrote a sweet and touching letter to her 'darling Dadie' which says: 'For the Duchess – I know I can never be the Duchess of your dreams any more than I can of my own – but I hope that during this week *something* of Webster's Duchess will come alive. If it does, I shall be enormously happy. You have been so patient – even when I know you have "chafed in the extreme" – and your patience has given me confidence. I still feel oppressed with the responsibilities of playing the Duchess. I love it so much I can *never* do it justice. Thank you for everything – I *am glad* we did it whatever "they" say.' She also included a little poem with the self-deprecating couplet: 'Peggy lacks the grander touches/Necessary for the Duchess?'

But 'they' – the critics – did not think so, with one notorious exception. Peggy got excellent notices, as did the production. *The Times* said that her wooing of the steward, Antonio, had ease and lightness; that the gossipings with her husband, her maid and the open-eared Bosola were full of sparkle and happiness assumed as a matter of course; that, at the climax, there was the resistant spirit of the doomed woman.

Agate, however, was waiting to pounce, and on the Sunday he came out in ferocious mood. Invoking A. B. Walkley's categorisation of actresses as either 'mousey-wousy' or 'roguey-poguey', he cast Peggy into the bracket of the 'teeny-weenies'. He claimed that the Duchess is a part for a Titan, not Titania: 'I say, with respect, that in the part of Webster's Duchess nothing but the grand manner will do. A contemporary critic wrote of Mrs Siddons that in Franklin's tragedy, *The Earl of Warwick*, she made her entry through a large archway "which she really seemed to fill." Any actress who is to present Webster's heroine must fill, and fill completely, the archway of the spectator's mind. And to do this she must have the tragic quality of voice. Something more than plaintiveness, however touching, is required if "I am Duchess of Malfi still" is not to sound like "I am Little Miss Muffet." '

Agate's words still rankle with Peggy. But the problem with this criticism is that it hinges on a notion of grand female acting as something Amazonian in scale, heroic of gesture and contralto of voice. Enthralled by the French classical tradition of acting, Agate clearly hungers for something rhetorical and extra-human. But this is the very reverse of Peggy's approach, which is to search for the abiding quintessence of humanity in classical characters and to deliver the poetry with unclouded directness and precision. Agate asks for the grand manner, which is something you consciously adopt: Peggy's style is to divest a tragic role of generalised suffering and go for the specific.

But did Peggy measure up to the diverse moods of Webster's Duchess? Her director, George Rylands, believes firmly that she did. 'Her performance,' he told me, 'was as good as it could possibly be. What Peggy has is a remarkable power of response to the literary in writing. Webster is an idiosyncratic stylist and his language has to be delivered by someone with the right instinct for it. The whole point about her cry of 'I am Duchess of Malfi still' is that it came out of the purity of her personality. I didn't ask her to do it in a great throbbing soprano voice. Webster also constantly shifts between the cosmic and the domestic and Peggy made you believe not only in the suffering heroine but in the mother who says to her waiting woman "I pray thee, look thou giv'st my little boy some syrup for his cold." Peggy got all that and the sense of a woman who was pure, true, genuine and in love with the steward."

Two radically different eye-witnesses of that performance also contest Agate's view. Peter Hall, then a 15-year-old Suffolk stationmaster's son making theatrical forays to London while staying with relatives in Lewisham, saw Peggy's art as based on a tug of war between visible order and invisible emotion: 'I saw her Ophelia and Malfi in the Gielgud season. What was striking was the way her English containment and decency contrasted with a wild passion that looked as if it would break the whole thing down. That has always been the extraordinary thing about her as an actress.'

Highly perceptive: as both actress and woman, Peggy has an intensity of feeling that belies her surface gentility. It is part of what makes her fascinating. J. C. Trewin claims that Agate took a thundering dislike to Peggy but would never explain why, beyond saying things like 'Very nice little girl, I suppose.' Trewin adds that he thought Agate was frightfully unfair: 'Her Duchess was not a splashy performance but the tragedy and the pathos were there.' Peggy bore with Agate's attacks, but one would love to have been a fly on the wall in C. B. Fry's box at Lord's for the Victory Test Match against Australia that summer, when the occupants included both the critic and the actress. Agate records in *Ego 8* that Clifford Bax put a finger to his lips, pointed to the Duchess and raised his eyebrows as if to say 'What about the gaffe now?' Agate writes: 'I replied, also in pantomime, "I am James Agate still."' Peggy says now that she didn't spot him in the crowded box and that it may have been just as well.

Gielgud's Haymarket season ended in June 1945, shortly after VE Day. It had restored the idea of a classical company in the West End and triumphed over the exigencies of wartime casting. It had also overlapped with the legendary Olivier-Richardson Old Vic seasons at the New which brought in *Peer Gynt*, *Richard III*, *Henry IV Parts One and Two*, *Oedipus Rex* and *The Critic*. Not only was London offered a feast of classical acting such as it had rarely seen this century, but a new generation was being given a glimpse of what could be achieved through star performers operating inside a repertory system. The teenage Peter Hall, trekking up from Suffolk, gazed in astonishment at the riches on display. Kenneth Tynan, already setting down his impressions in print as a boy critic, was sitting quivering in the dark at the New and the Haymarket. It would take another fifteen years for the company idea to take permanent, institutional form, but the torch had been lit.

Peggy, at the end of the war, had the more immediate matter

of a husband and a young daughter to think about, and for two years she took a break from stage acting. She was not, however, entirely claimed by domesticity. Upon being demobbed Jeremy, who had spent the last year of the war in Malta working with the Commander-in-Chief of the Mediterranean, immediately accepted an invitation to stand as a Labour candidate in the epoch-making General Election of July 1945 which saw the formation of the Attlee Government. Jeremy did so on the advice of his friend, Philip Noel-Baker, and he was adopted, without much difficulty, for the Abbey Division of Westminster. It was a safe Conservative seat but he managed to whittle the Tory majority down from 12,000 to 4,000 with the enthusiastic help of Peggy as a doorstep canvasser.

'Pimlico and Millbank was our area,' he explains, 'and on one occasion Peggy and I went canvassing at Number Ten Downing Street. We asked to see the staff and so a cook and two members of the household came to the door and one of them turned out to be a Labour supporter. We never asked to see the occupant. Though I'm no longer a member of the Labour Party, it was at the time a wonderful experience, and I think it's fair to say that Peggy's own very strong interest in politics stemmed from this period.' For the sake of the British theatre, it is perhaps as well that Jeremy Hutchinson never did become an MP: it is hard to imagine even Peggy managing to combine the role of a good constituency wife with those of Cleopatra and Hedda Gabler. But the happiest event of Peggy's two-year break from the stage was not canvassing at Number Ten – a story she has now grown tired of – but the birth in 1946 of her second child, Nicholas, and the realisation that motherhood was itself a fulfilling if demanding vocation.

The picture of family life neatly slotted into strenuous bouts of work makes it sound all too easy. According to Jeremy, Peggy always had a frightful struggle to balance the demands of the family with the pursuance of her career. By now the Hutchinsons were comfortably installed in their Hampstead home and there was an invaluable helpmate and housekeeper, Nan, to assist in running things and looking after the children. For her part, Peggy turned down job offers that would take her away from the family for extended periods and set her face against long runs: she invariably insisted on a get-out clause after six months.

The theatre to which she eventually returned in May 1947 was one that had very much reverted to a pre-war 'star' pattern. Donald Wolfit was playing Volpone at the Savoy, Noel Coward was coruscating through *Present Laughter* at the Haymarket and musicals, including *Oklahoma* at Drury Lane and *Bless the Bride* at the Adelphi, were reasserting their box-office power. The most hopeful portent was that Michel Saint-Denis, George Devine and Glen Byam Shaw were reunited in their creation of the Old Vic Centre which aimed to provide a school, a children's theatre and an experimental stage. At Stratford, Sir Barry Jackson had taken over as Director of the Shakespeare Memorial Theatre and brightened the whole image of the place by engaging directors of the calibre of Michael Benthall and Peter Brook: the latter's Watteauesque *Love's Labour's Lost* in 1946 and *Romeo and Juliet* in 1947, ablaze with heat and light, were not only astonishing personal calling-cards but intimations that Stratford was soon to become synonymous with the best in British theatre.

Peggy's return to the West End theatre in 1947 was sensational. If she had left two years previously still bearing marks of the *ingénue*, she came back very much a mature woman. But there was a double irony about her return. One was that it took an unashamed boulevard piece – *Edward, My Son*, adapted by Robert Morley and Noel Langley from a novel by the latter and providing, naturally enough, a huge star part for the former – to reveal new and unsuspected depths in her as a character actress. The other was that her acclaimed return was very nearly short-circuited by her own doubts both about the piece and her suitability for it.

The play is the story of a father who devotes himself to his son with ruthless single-mindedness. He burns down a shop for the sake of the insurance and in order to buy his small boy the best doctor available. He averts Edward's expulsion from a good school through the simple expedient of buying the school, rather in the style of an Arnold Bennett hero purchasing a grand hotel for himself in order to enjoy dinner there. He ascends to even greater rogueries and in the process ruinously spoils the unseen Edward, drives his wife to drink and his former partner to suicide. It offered a part 'to tear a cat in'; and Robert Morley, a far better actor than he is given credit for (not least by himself), held the piece together through the sheer abundance of his portrait of a self-made magnate: he even broke through the 'fourth wall' to address the audience with a rampageous glee.

The manager, Henry Sherek, had chosen Peggy for the role of the hero's neglected wife who starts out as a conventional lower-middle-class woman and who ends up rich, bitter, resentful and alcoholic. But Peggy soon found that she was out of her depth in a lavish boulevard piece where scenes were being re-written on the wing (or in the wings) and lines altered and re-shaped by the star and co-author, Robert Morley. He himself remembers the whole experience with a bemused tranquillity:

'Peggy was worried about the part and the play. She got herself into a state because of her capacity for self-criticism, something I may say I have never permitted myself. She used to stop and stare blankly in despair in rehearsal. I couldn't really understand what the problem was, but then I have never taken acting all that seriously. There was a general feeling that there wasn't enough for the wife to do in the later stages of the play so I went back to the Ritz, where I was staying during rehearsals, and very quickly wrote a drunk scene where the wife stumbles up the stairs counting them as she goes. But the crisis came when Peggy suggested it might be best if she dropped out of the show before we began our pre-West End tour in Leeds. I went to see her at her Hampstead home clutching an enormous and highly unsuitable plant. If Peggy did drop out, I had Ambrosine Philpotts lined up in reserve. I told Peggy that if she wanted to, she could chuck now and that she needn't reproach herself because we were covered. But I told her rather dramatically that if she gave up the part now, she would give up everything ever afterwards. It may not have been strictly true but there was something in it. Anyway, she retired upstairs to consult with Jeremy, came down and agreed. Shortly after, we opened in Leeds with a two o'clock matinée that ran for four hours. She came straight off stage and said she would do the play in London. The point is that, if they chuck it once, they chuck it again.'

It is as well Robert Morley's counsel prevailed, for *Edward, My Son* proved to be a new turning-point in Peggy's career. It proved that the delightful pre-war *ingénue* had ripened into a truly mature actress. It showed that Peggy was as much at home in modern drama as the classics. Above all, it demonstrated that she could invest even a lightish boulevard play with a Stanislavskyan truth. Alan Dent in the *News Chronicle* described it as 'a growing and glowing portrait of a woman totally unlike any other Ashcroft performance, a woman who in her ageing disillusionment drifts into drinking too much. This is the impersonative way of good acting whereas Mr Morley's is the self-expository way.' Audrey Williamson in *The Theatre of Two Decades*, describing it as 'one of the finest pieces of acting our stage has seen', also noticed that 'Its special quality is the manner in which, without over-emphasis, it revealed the woman's habits before even the text had drawn our attention to them.'

Williamson's point is very shrewd: it picks out Peggy's ability to create a character that lives not merely *through* the text but outside and beyond it. John Gielgud eloquently reinforces that observation:

'When she came downstairs in an apron at the beginning of *Edward, My Son,* she had so evidently been interrupted in giving her baby a bath that the child seemed more real than if it had actually appeared on the stage. And in the same play I remember two moments most distinctly. One in which she appeared in a Paris hotel room, fashionably dressed in a smart hat and furs, quite unlike her usual simple style; the other her glance at the butler when he came in with a tray of cocktails. In the final scene she was to become a hopeless alcoholic but the preparation for her disintegration was prepared with brilliant subtlety in the scene before.'

Peggy did not display drunkenness by staggers and slurred speech but by a succession of tiny gestures. So convincing was she that her friend, Fabia Drake, knowing how light a drinker Peggy was, thought someone must have given her a glass of champagne in the interval when she entered down a big staircase in the last act. Exactly like Gielgud watching *Cousin Muriel*, she found herself deceived by Peggy's total truth. In fact, it was Peggy's exit up those self-same stairs – counting them carefully as she went and suddenly saying 'That's the funny one' – that the critics seized on as a mark of her realism.

Edward, My Son, which opened in May 1947 at His Majesty's, did a lot for Peggy: it put her into a tremendous West End hit and earned her the Ellen Terry Award. One likes to think it also did something for her benefactor, Robert Morley. She remembers him saying to her at one point in tones of utter astonishment: 'I'm really looking at you now – I'm acting.'

To Peggy, the theatre is a temple; to Robert, it is a mixture of bank and fun-house. But, with this play, each gave the other something that they needed. Robert gave Peggy confidence; she gave his play a truthful study of progressive decline. In the autumn of 1948 she even went with the play to New York, but stayed for only six weeks in order to get back to her family. It is a measure of the jolly Morleyesque approach to the theatre that, during a New York photo-call, Robert pretended to a story-hunting journalist that the character he played strangled his wife halfway through the second act. A picture was duly taken of Robert with his hands round Peggy's throat. Had it appeared in print, there would have been some pretty surprised playgoers.

Although New York has never been Peggy's favourite city, the trip there proved useful in preparing her for her next major role in the London theatre: the plain-Jane Catherine Sloper in *The Heiress*, adapted by Ruth and Augustus Goetz from Henry James's *Washington Square*. On the boat out Peggy took with her the script of the play, which Binkie Beaumont had pressed on her. She found herself unable to get a clear picture of the play from reading it. While in New York she took the chance to see the Broadway production with Beatrice Straight playing Catherine. 'She was,' says Peggy, 'a beautiful actress and it suddenly struck me that it didn't make sense unless she was a plain girl. At that moment I knew I wanted to do it and I accepted Binkie's offer as soon as I got back to London.'

Peggy was undoubtedly wise, in career terms, to do the play, but that doesn't alter the fact that the Goetz adaptation 'theatres' down James's early novel, which is suffused with irony, wit and compassion. On the face of it, it is a melodramatic story about a heroine, Catherine Sloper, who is a victim twice over. A dull, plain, not particularly clever girl, she is jilted by a calculating lover, Morris Townsend, who fails to turn up for a midnight elopement when he discovers her fortune has evaporated. But she is also the victim of her cruel father, a widower living off the memory of his lovely, intelligent, companionable wife. Graham Greene once described the book as 'perhaps the only novel in which a man has successfully invaded the feminine field and produced work comparable to Jane Austen's.' What is remarkable is James's penetrating understanding of Catherine's psychology. For example, when Dr Sloper makes it clear that he does not regard Morris as a suitable son-in-law, Catherine consciously adopts the role of the good daughter. 'It was as if,' writes James, 'this other person who was both herself and not herself, had suddenly sprung into being, inspiring her with natural curiosity as to the performance of untested functions.' That pins down beautifully the obsessive self-scrutiny of the lonely.

But even if the play, which condenses the passage of time in the way that flaws all adaptations of novels, is not wholly Jamesian, it nevertheless manages to be what is known as good theatre. The production itself, however, underwent traumatic upheaval in the final weeks of rehearsal. Binkie Beaumont had entrusted the direction to John Burrell, a former BBC drama producer who had been, with Olivier and Richardson, co-director of the Old Vic Company during their triumphant seasons at the New; like them, he had been thanked with the brutal news that his contract would be terminated in July 1949. He was to receive an even greater shock during rehearsals of *The Heiress*: an event witnessed from the lower rungs of the company by Donald Sinden (playing Morris Townsend's cousin), who recalls the built-in hierarchy of the West End star-system:

'One was aware in those days of a gap between the leading players and the also-rans. You expected the leads to be paternal and maternal. If there was a Christmas party, they would give it because they were the stars. Though I have to say that while Ralph Richardson, who played Dr Sloper, was slightly aloof, Peggy warmed to the mother-role and always knew when anyone in the company was having any kind of family problem or was in any sort of trouble. But the significant thing is that there was a terrible problem with the production which we lesser mortals didn't get to know about. Ralph and Larry at the Old Vic would direct each other and John Burrell's job was to make sure that the extras didn't get in the way. Ralph was also perhaps less than enamoured of directors. Someone once asked him what he thought of them and he replied "I always say Good Morning to them and ask if they've had a good breakfast." Anyway on the Friday with a week to go before we opened in Brighton, John Burrell limped onto the stage and said "Ladies and gentlemen, I am sorry to tell you that I am leaving the production and on Monday morning John Gielgud will be taking over." This was the first most of us knew about the crisis. John came in on the Monday morning, asked us to run the play through, saying he didn't want to change anything and then proceeded to change absolutely everything. The scenery had been cream: it now became grey or green. All the furniture was made Empire furniture. It became a new production and, after its Brighton tour, a huge success.'

Peggy denies, however, that the stars were much better informed than the actors in the minor roles. She says that Burrell had great difficulty in simply moving people about the stage: 'We were hamstrung and couldn't get unknotted. Binkie rang me at home and asked me how I would feel if John took over rehearsals. I said I doubted if John could change the concept but Binkie promised he wouldn't change anything except the moves. He was wonderful. It was like somebody unlocking a puzzle. But it wasn't that the stars knew what was happening and the small parts didn't. It all happened suddenly.'

For Peggy the role of Catherine turned into another landmark success. She once again escaped the type-casting imposed by her own facial beauty and proved that she had the versatility of the *comédien* rather than the dominant personality trait of the *acteur*. It also reveals her native intelligence in the way she used James's novel as an aid to the creation of the character. She is normally guarded about how she achieves a performance, but she remarked to me, *à propos* this role: 'I think that any part that has its physical lineaments settled for you is a great help because it isolates and states certain things about a character that you might have to decide about one way or another. It gives you a physical framework with which to work.' In this case, James provides a beautifully clear biographical portrait of Catherine: a romp and a glutton in her earlier years, she is now possessed of 'a plain, dull, gentle countenance' and in character is 'affectionate, docile, obedient and much addicted to speaking the truth'. Pictures of

Peggy in the role show how the oval shape of her face is high-lighted by the swept-back, centre-parted hair and how she has assumed the look of a woman spiritually oppressed. But Peggy also used the novel in more direct, gestural ways. At one point, Catherine is described as sitting in a rocking-chair. Her aunt mentions casually that she has just seen her lover, Morris, in New York after a long absence. Nothing is said, but the rocking instantly stops. Peggy mentioned this to Gielgud in rehearsal. He sent straight away for a rocking-chair and the effect of its sudden cessation of movement is remembered by all who saw it.

A beautiful actress who assumes the mantle of a dowdy dullard is, of course, always praised. But there was much more to Peggy's performance than that. In the scene where she awaits impatiently the arrival of her lover, she was so alert to every sound that Donald Sinden, watching in the wings, says that it was as much as he could do to stop himself bursting onto the stage and saying 'Peggy, darling, it's only a play.' But she also caught every facet of Catherine's spiritual development from the dutiful daughter to the woman of incomparable coldness. Ibsen once said that the ultimate crime was to kill the love-life in a human heart; and, as Harold Hobson's breathless notice in the *Sunday Times* makes clear, that was the crime of which Catherine Sloper was the innocent victim.

'Of Miss Peggy Ashcroft's Catherine,' wrote Hobson, 'one hesitates to speak simply because anything one says must be inadequate. For her performance all superlatives are pale and feeble things. In her hands the exquisite tragedy of this unloved girl becomes one of the theatre's most moving experiences. I doubt if any line spoken on the stage has driven deeper than Miss Ashcroft's when, her match-making aunt accusing her of cruelty for her determination to send the young man to the right-about, she says: "Cruel? Of course I am cruel. I have been taught by masters." This is the real thing, this is the knock-out blow: the opposition, as was said of a larger matter, is utterly and at all points defeated and the tragedy is that the victor is defeated too.'

Great performances breed great criticism. And Hobson's words tell us that Peggy did not merely impersonate Catherine Sloper. She had, through the exercise of her creative intelligence, *understood* her to the very soul and then shown the process by which a fine woman is corrupted in spirit.

But though Peggy's immersion in the role was total, there is also a gay and mischievous side to her character which the public never sees. Donald Sinden caught a glimpse of it well into the Haymarket run: 'At the end of the play Peggy has gone upstairs to bed leaving Ralph alone on stage. He is a doctor, knows he is ill and that the worries of the world are upon him. He sounds his own heart and he knows that he is going to die and you see this dawn on him. He makes his final exit, goes upstairs clutching the banisters and the curtain slowly falls on this moving scene. On stage, the staircase is solid as a rock. Offstage there is a ladder down which you have to go. But the ladder creaked. So, out of deference to Ralph, Peggy would remain offstage at the top until the curtain-calls doing crochet. She'd been sitting there crocheting for six months and one night, as Ralph made his final exit up the stairs, Peggy – unseen by the audience – put her head round the corner of the flat and said "Boo". Ralph cried "Aaargh" and nearly fainted dead on the spot.'

It is nice to know that there was still something of the schoolgirl in Peggy, even as she reached mature greatness.

CHAPTER NINE

Infinite Variety

I HAVE USED THE word greatness to describe Peggy's post-war career. Perhaps a definition is in order. To me greatness in acting entails the ability to conquer, as G. H. Lewes said, the highest reaches of one's art; a sensibility that allows one to approach every role with a creative idea, which is slightly different from an intellectual concept; an expressive body and voice that enable one to give form and substance to that idea; an elusive personal quality that, as Henry James said, makes you speculate about the private character of the person on stage. Peggy is, I believe, a superb example of an actress who achieved greatness by her own driving perfectionism and application of the talents God had given her to the art of acting. But it was not really until the 1950s that she established her supremacy. In that astonishing decade she played Shakespeare, Sophocles, Ibsen, Brecht, Rattigan and Bagnold; and, in almost every case, she won.

It was her old friend, Anthony Quayle, who set her on the right path at the start of the decade. While she was still playing in *The Heiress*, he invited her to come to Stratford-on-Avon for the 1950 season to play Beatrice and Cordelia opposite John Gielgud. Quayle, whom Harry Andrews describes as 'a very good commander and a good team man with enormous enthusiasm and vitality like a head schoolboy', had taken over the directorship of the Shakespeare Memorial Theatre from Sir Barry Jackson in October 1948. Jackson had imported exciting young talent like that of Peter Brook and Paul Scofield. Quayle went much further in bringing to Stratford the glamour and excitement of stars. To do that, he relied at first on all his pre-war friends and contacts: 'I started out alone,' he says, 'but I immediately went to John and Peg and said "Here's the theatre – you've got to help me, come on." I also brought Tony Guthrie in and managed to pull the divergent, pre-war streams together. But what I remember is that I was nailed to the mast and said "Help me!" '

Help him they did, and the result (with Glen Byam Shaw joining him in 1952) was to rescue Stratford from its image of dowdy provincialism and to make it a centre of excellence. It was not, by a long stretch of the imagination, the kind of British Moscow Art Theatre that Peggy had always dreamed of. The company usually disbanded at the end of a season. Casting was as star-oriented as at H. M. Tennent's. With odd exceptions (such as the 1951 History Season) there was little attempt at stylistic consistency: as late as 1959 I remember an actor telling me that the wonderful thing about Stratford was that every production was different. What Stratford did achieve in the 1950s was to make the classic tradition seem inescapably thrilling and to pave the way – not least through the creation of strong financial reserves – for the establishment of the RSC in 1960. Even in the Quayle–Byam Shaw years, there was a dream of a London base and of a more permanent structure.

Given that Peggy became very much a part of Stratford in the Fifties, playing three seasons there, it is somewhat ironic that her first reaction to the theatre itself was one of horror. It seemed to her a terrifying space to have to conquer: 'I can remember that we rehearsed in the Conference Hall and when we first got onto the stage I burst into tears. I suddenly realised that there was really nowhere on the stage as it then was that you could hope to be heard in any reasonably realistic or intimate way. You had to get centre or downstage because you see it was very far back from the audience. There were those things called the "assemblies" [two side-entrances downstage of the proscenium arch] and you were always stuck behind them. It was a very difficult theatre to play in.' Harry Andrews, endowed by nature with a large voice, admits that there were vital marks on stage you had to hit to reach the whole theatre, as in a church or a cathedral. But it is possible that the very hazards of the Stratford stage obliged Peggy to develop both her vocal range and volume.

Her first appearance there in June 1950 was anyway slightly unnerving, in that she found herself stepping into the role previously occupied by her old schoolfellow and lifelong friend Diana Wynyard. Gielgud's production of *Much Ado About Nothing* had been the great hit of the 1949 season and now it was revived with Gielgud and Peggy as Benedick and Beatrice. It was an ornate, picturesque affair that belonged to the world of the High Renaissance: a world of opulent colours, formal gardens, lustrous statuary, ladies in rich dresses, men in nodding plumes. As so often, Gielgud's initial inspiration was visual, and Quayle remembers being sent off to Spain to find the specific designer, Mariano Andreu, whom Gielgud wanted.

Peggy may have been apprehensive about stepping into Diana Wynyard's shoes; she certainly drew the line at wearing her headgear. But that was because her own conception of the role was very different. 'Diana,' she says, 'had played Beatrice as witty and sophisticated and wore elaborately feathered head-dresses. I just think she is a natural. Instead of being a witty woman who can always say the smart thing, she just happens to say what comes into her head and it's spot on. She is merry, unpredictable, undisciplined, the poor relation who isn't a poor relation. I wanted to be dressed like Hero but slightly simpler if anything. I had my hair swept back and a simple headpiece with a halo so that I looked like a mixture of Beatrice Lillie and something out of Piero della Francesca.'

In rehearsal Peggy had been told by Gielgud, none too helpfully, 'You must come on with a lot of panache.' But her achievement, not instantly recognised by all the critics, was to rescue Beatrice from the glittering Restoration tradition of self-conscious wit and turn her into an instinctive girl who always speaks before she thinks. Philip Hope-Wallace in the *Manchester Guardian* felt that she was playing slightly against the grain in that 'Miss Ashcroft's best cards are those of a yielding and womanish pathos without the astringent manner of a natural Beatrice.' But Peggy was not after a spinsterish waspishness so much as a spontaneous mockery. And even if Gielgud as director was sometimes suspiciously vague, on stage his partnership with Peggy became one of the legends of high comedy. Eric Keown said that their banter became like listening to the finals in a championship of verbal badminton. Peggy compares their stage partnership to dancing: 'It was like following your partner so that you never quite knew which steps you were going to take but you could always respond since you were so in tune.' It is a highly apt metaphor since, to the Elizabethan mind, the dance was always an earthly image of heavenly harmony.

Much Ado opened in June. A month later came *King Lear*: Gielgud co-directed with Quayle and played Lear for the third time (the last had been in a famous Old Vic production of 1940 when he had been guided by Granville-Barker). This was vintage Gielgud. To some observers his performance seemed not so much *acting*, in the sense of something conscious and willed, as the actual *enacting* of events seen for the first and only time. At first, he was full of pettish arrogance, childishly nodding at Regan's protestations of love or sulkily refusing even to look at Cordelia when France accepts her. Later he used his violincello tones to give both terror and pathos to the recollection of his follies and his premonition of the future: 'O let me not be mad, not mad, sweet heaven, Keep me in temper, I would not be mad.'

But according to a sympathetic critic, T. C. Worsley, it was the recognition scene when Lear wakes to find Cordelia at his side that was the crowning glory of the production. This made nonsense of the old Charles Lamb remark that the *Lear* of Shakespeare cannot be acted. Here there was a genuine sense of *lacrimae rerum*. 'And,' wrote Worsley, 'beside Gielgud there is Miss Peggy Ashcroft to shed the tears for us. She has, more than any other actress, the power of touching us simply by her posture and the atmosphere she distils. The change from anxiety to a flooding relief is beautifully done. Her 'No cause, no cause' is marvellously dropped like two reassuring tears of forgiveness, and then again a shift into the feigned courtliness of "Will't please your highness walk?".'

More and more this note was to be sounded in any discussion of Peggy's acting, particularly in Shakespeare. It was not simply what she did that mattered. It was the moral character with which she invested the role, the atmosphere she distilled. At first, she seems a surprising choice for Cordelia. Peggy was then 42: Cordelia is Lear's youngest daughter. But, if the spirit is right, the age is irrelevant; and, as Ellen Terry pointed out, the essence of Cordelia is that there is so little to say, so much to feel. Shakespeare sets the actress playing Cordelia a damnably difficult problem in that almost everything has to be implied: one has to comprehend her love, affection, loyalty, goodness as much from her looks and deportment as from her actual words. I have seen productions of *King Lear* where Cordelia seems to have no emotional connection with her father and where you feel there is no iron-clad filial bond to be shattered in the first place. Peggy brought to the role her own particular blend of obduracy and breadth of sympathy.

Richard Findlater noted in the early scenes 'a sweet-sullen obstinacy in self-righteousness that is most convincing' though he regretted that the pathos of the reconciliation scene was drowned on the first night by booming music. Philip Hope-Wallace wrote: 'I call Peggy Ashcroft's Cordelia perfection. It is impossible to imagine the words "No cause, no cause" more movingly spoken (even, I believe, by Ellen Terry).' And J. C. Trewin wrote: 'Peggy Ashcroft's Cordelia is the best in my recollection. I am always afraid of a part which so many actresses have merely prettified but Miss Ashcroft's deep compassion will stay in my grateful mind.'

The 1950 Stratford season was a tumultuous success. It also included a notable *Julius Caesar* with Gielgud as a tough, soldierly Cassius (who had been advised by Quayle to study the hard-bitten faces of the men trained for action as they came out of the War Office) and Peter Brook's legendary production of *Measure for Measure* with Gielgud as an icily puritanical Angelo and a 19-year-old Barbara Jefford as Isabella. Stratford was still very much based on the star system. Harry Andrews, the indispensable backbone of British Shakespearean acting, recalls that around midsummer senior members of the company like himself might be offered a line of parts for the following year; the less experienced were always worried about whether they would be asked back and whether they would find themselves nudged a rung or two up the ladder. But Quayle deserves enormous credit for marrying the great stars to the great roles and for making Shakespeare big box-office. So popular was the 1950 season that it was extended for an extra month to 28 October, though both Peggy and Gielgud had to leave on 30 September: he to go to America to star in and direct *The Lady's not for Burning*, she to return to London in time for the historic re-opening of the Old Vic on 14 November with *Twelfth Night*.

Although Peggy left a Stratford buoyant with success, the Old Vic to which she returned was now a place riven by backstage politics and governed by a rather amateurish board. The building itself, badly damaged by bombs in 1941, had been handsomely restored – proud and white on the outside, grey, gold and dark red within – complete with a widened proscenium arch, designed by Pierre Sonrel, and a raisable forestage. The real problem lay behind the scenes.

The full story of the backstage politicking is told in fascinating detail by Irving Wardle in *The Theatres of George Devine*. From Peggy's point of view, the problem was that she had a strong emotional and intellectual commitment to the Three Boys, as they were called, who in 1946 had set up three linked organisations under the umbrella of the Old Vic and whose work was now under threat. They were, of course, Glen Byam Shaw who ran an acting school, Michel Saint-Denis who looked after the experimental theatre project and George Devine who ran the Young People's Theatre. In 1950 they formed an uneasy *ménage à quatre* with Hugh Hunt who a year before had been brought in as artistic director of the Old Vic Company at the New; now they had all joined forces in a quadruple directorship. Overseeing them was Llewellyn Rees who had been appointed as Administrator of the Old Vic after the wind-up of the Olivier regime and who was not sympathetic to the Vic's vital ancillary work ('I went into a class of Saint-Denis,' he told Wardle 'and these boys and girls were all being animals; it was like going into a lunatic asylum.') Periodically Vic Governors would also pay a visit to the classes: one group found them 'unwholesome'.

If the Old Vic was intended to be an embryonic National Theatre, it would seem, in retrospect, an ideal structure: a core acting company with a school, an experimental troupe and a young people's group to nourish and challenge it. And since the graduates of the Byam Shaw–Saint-Denis–Devine era include the nucleus of Manchester's Royal Exchange directorate, actors such as Joan Plowright, Denis Quilley and Prunella Scales, directors like Frank Dunlop and Christopher Morahan and designers such as Alan Tagg and Carl Toms, it is clear that in the long term their work had a profound influence. But in the 1950–1 Old Vic season it was apparent that an explosion was coming. Peggy herself says that 'There was unease in that Old Vic season because Hugh Hunt was cast as the Demon King working against the Three Boys.' Robert Eddison, who was a member of that Old Vic Company, also recalls that the season wasn't a very happy one because of the pressures upon the triumvirate: 'Peggy was very loyal to them and was unhappy with Hugh. She didn't approve of what was going on but, in a very professional way, she didn't let it show in performance.'

It was not the ideal context in which to re-launch London's most vital playhouse, but at least the grand re-opening of the Old Vic on 14 November 1950 was made memorable by the unexpected appearance of Edith Evans, direct from Broadway where a production of *Daphne Laureola* had prematurely collapsed, to speak Christopher Hassall's commemorative prologue.

The production of *Twelfth Night* that followed, directed by Hugh Hunt, was of the kind to reinforce the maxim that there is a perfect version of the play laid up for us in heaven. Hunt's production veered uncertainly between romping farce, centring round Roger Livesey's big-bellied Sir Toby and Paul Rogers's Robeyesque red-nosed Malvolio, and *commedia dell' arte* fussiness: there was a chorus of boys in beards and girls in urchin cuts rounding off each scene with skipping dances, clapping of hands, smacking of knees and lots of hurraying. When the *Kiss Me Kate* company, who were playing at the Coliseum, came to see it at an early matinée, Bill Johnson as spokesman for the group announced that they had enjoyed it. 'I'm so glad,' said Roger Livesey, 'because we got into a good deal of trouble for having all these people hanging around.' Bill Johnson rather tactlessly replied, 'Well take them away and hell what's left?'

What was left was Peggy's Viola, a part she had played eleven years before at the Phoenix. She was much praised for her rapt stillness in the scene where Orsino talks of love and Feste sings 'Come away Death', for her charming, unforced gentleness and for her ability to give key Shakespearean moments an unswerving truth. When Viola is confronted by her long-lost twin brother, Sebastian, and he asks 'What countryman? What name? What parentage?' there was a long, beautifully held pause before Peggy breathed 'Of Messaline'. But Peter Hall, seeing the production as a young Cambridge undergraduate, felt that 'she didn't have the melancholy that Viola needs.' This suggests that Hunt's Commedia del'Hearty approach missed the vital truth that this is a play of shifting, kaleidoscopic mood in which the tone of any one area constantly invades its neighbours, that there is Chekhovian pathos underlying the comedy just as there is an element of erotic farce in the mourning Olivia's sudden, violent affection for the messenger, Cesario. It was several years later that Hall himself and John Barton mounted productions which accurately caught the play's fragile, deliquescent spirit.

While *Twelfth Night* went on its rather strenuously merry way, the jockeying for position in the Old Vic power-struggle continued. According to Devine it was from this moment, with all the contending parties occupying the same building, that official policy changed and Llewellyn Rees assumed the role of boss. But Peggy, emotionally if not directly involved, threw herself wholeheartedly into the next production: a new version of Sophocles' *Electra* directed by Michel Saint-Denis and designed by Barbara Hepworth. 'Nothing,' Peggy says, 'could have distracted me from playing Electra. I had never much wanted to do Greek tragedy and it always filled me with horror when I saw things like Sybil doing *Medea* in the old Gilbert Murray translation. But some years before I had seen a production of *Electra* by Michel at the London Theatre School where there was a wonderful girl in the lead. It was so modern and accessible that I wanted to do it – it was like a female Hamlet.' The great academic critic, F. L. Lucas, has made a similar point. Sophocles's version of the story of Orestes' double-murder of his mother and her lover is, he says, a picture of vivid characters in action 'like, not *Hamlet*, but the original story of *Hamlet*'. Sophocles was also unusual in making Electra, Orestes' sister, the chief character. She urges her brother on to the end but is conscious that her obsessive hatred of her mother has debased her. She becomes the embodiment of a strong spirit in a body broken by physical and spiritual suffering.

Anxious as ever to avoid declamation and give the role reality, Peggy found herself up against several obstacles. One was the formalism of Saint-Denis's staging which placed the principals upstage on – in Peggy's words – 'a cruel rake' with the Chorus in front of them downstage. Then there was Barbara Hepworth's statue of Apollo which looked like the inside of an electric light-bulb with thick aluminium tubing. The day it arrived Saint-Denis greeted it with a cry of 'Don't put it on the stage yet because I don't know which way round it goes.' It was much mocked by the stage staff and eventually by the critics too, who compared it to 'a mangled parrot-cage' and 'the bindings of a champagne cork'. Barbara Hepworth herself wept when she came to rehearsals and found that her set representing the tall white pillars of the Palace of Mycenae was made of canvas rather than concrete as she had envisaged.

But the tears were not confined to the designer. Robert Eddison, who played Orestes, recalls that rehearsals were some-what fraught. 'I had this big recognition scene with Peggy and somehow whenever we got to it in rehearsal she burst into tears and we had to abandon it. I finally asked Saint-Denis if it were my fault and he said "No, No, Atavistic memories." I didn't quite know what he meant but there was clearly something in the scene that disturbed Peggy. It was extraordinary how often we stopped at my entrance and I thought she felt "I can't do it with this man." But she was so warm and affectionate off-stage that I realised I wasn't the problem.'

The cast struggled on and eventually the production was unveiled in March 1951. It was given a decidedly mixed reception. Hostile to all this modern-art nonsense at the Old Vic almost every critic had a swipe at the Hepworth statue. Saint-Denis also clearly failed to crack the eternal problem of the Chorus, who spoke in drilled unison and were variously described as 'a row of slightly paralysed debutantes' and 'this crocodile of perfect young ladies from the Argos High School for Girls who have paused while taking a walk in their best frocks to watch the local mur-derers at work'. Plonking them on Pierre Sonrel's new forestage, from which they watched the action taking place on an elevated platform, obviously didn't help.

No performance of Peggy's divided the critics more sharply

than her Electra. On the one hand, there were those who saw her as a miniaturist attempting a mural and lacking that final element of raw physical power needed for Greek tragedy. Harold Hobson, while praising her grave beauty of speech, added that 'she cannot undo the legacy of two millennia and make admirable this vengeful melancholic' (why, I wonder, should she be made admirable?).

On the other hand, there were those who saw the performance as a crucial extension of her range. Kenneth Tynan, who over the years was extremely equivocal in his attitude to her work, questioned whether the play was of more than anecdotal importance but wrote: 'Meanwhile Peggy Ashcroft is spanning some amazing arpeggios as Electra showing unsuspected vocal strength and variety.' But it was T. C. Worsley in the *New Statesman* who pulled out all the stops and saw that she had annexed new territory as an actress. It is worth quoting his response to her performance in full:

'From up on the main stage itself we receive a really terrific impact. Emotionally the drama simply wrings us out. Of course, it is a triumph for Miss Peggy Ashcroft, and all the more so because one might have supposed in advance that she was altogether too silvery an actress for the part. One imagined that she might have thrown over it just that shimmer of romanticism that is wrong for Greek drama, the kind of romantic shimmer which some of Gilbert Murray's translations give us. But in the event it was not so at all. From the first high wail on which she entered, it was clear that she was not going to go wrong in that direction. In fact, she never went wrong at all. She drives her way through the part with energy and resolution, and even a hardness which we might not have thought her to possess. She is, no doubt about it, on the grand scale. Her grief is a pure spring gushing from an unquenchable source: her hate is implacable: her love grows as strong as a tree. The assault on our feelings is just about as direct as it could possibly be, striking straight down on us, as it should, without haze or shadow. In Miss Ashcroft's performance we come as near to experiencing what Greek tragedy should give us as, at this distant date, we could expect.'

This is striking testimony that Peggy was tapping hitherto unused strengths and, as her rehearsal tears indicate, drawing on some vein of private emotion. She did not, however, go as far as the Greek actor, Polus, who originally played Electra: when the heroine delivers a lament over the urn supposedly containing the ashes of her dead brother he was said to have motivated his histrionic grief by placing his own dead son's ashes in the stage-urn. But, steering a precise course between that kind of Attic Method approach and the rhetoric that is the curse of Greek tragedy, she managed to give a performance that offered memorable images. At one point, she lifted her arms before her face and above her head in a way that reminded one observer, Audrey Williamson, of Kirsten Flagstad as Brünnhilde in *Götter-dämmerung*. In Greek tragedy a large part of the emotional impact derives from gesture: a case in point is Yukio Ninagawa's production of *Medea* where the male actor, Mikijiro Hira, advanced up the steps to murder his offspring with his sword raised menacingly and unequivocally above his head.

Whether Peggy's Electra is judged a resounding success or an honourable failure, it was a necessary stage in her artistic development. It proved that she could reach the peaks, that she could make a living woman out of a vessel of primitive emotion and that she could act in the highest register with total vocal control. As a box-office venture, *Electra* confirmed Llewellyn Rees's advance warnings that it would lose money. But for Peggy it was, she says now, 'a terrific adventure. It stretched me enormously. It's a short play but you never leave the stage. I think in a way it was something I drew on when I came to play Cleopatra in that I then knew how to pace myself and save myself for the peaks. It was also like Shakespeare in that one had to make heightened speech real. The one thing I didn't like was having the Chorus downstage. But when we toured the production to the Alexandra in Birmingham it was much better because they were placed at the side. It was as if a great barrier between me and the audience had been removed.'

Meanwhile the Old Vic's off-stage crisis was working towards its inevitable conclusion. Early in 1951 the Governors indicated that, because of the grave financial situation, it would be impossible to maintain more than three directors. In May George Devine wrote on behalf of himself and his two colleagues tendering their resignations. In June Tyrone Guthrie was brought in as a general manager with sweeping powers. He took the Three Boys out to dinner and delivered the *coup de grâce*. He told them that he had advised the Governors to close down both the School and the Young Vic. The latter was shut down in August 1951. The Drama School, in order to fulfil obligations to existing students, lingered on until 1952.

The three individuals who had founded the Old Vic Centre went on to other things. Michel Saint-Denis became the head of the Centre Dramatique de l'Est in Strasbourg. Glen Byam Shaw joined Anthony Quayle at the Shakespeare Memorial Theatre in 1952. George Devine also worked at Stratford before breaking away to become the founder of the English Stage Company. But the dream of an Old Vic Centre was abandoned and there was a huge outcry in the press about the way the Governors had behaved towards the distinguished trio: there was a flurry of news stories, letters to *The Times*, protests from politicians and writers.

Peggy was appalled by what had happened and she expressed her feelings powerfully in a private letter to George Rylands. What is striking is not simply her loyalty to three old friends but her passionate concern for the future of the Old Vic. Her letter reads, in part:

'As you can imagine I am deeply concerned about the recent events at the Old Vic. I am shocked more than words can say at the action of the Governors and I feel that it is a real disaster for the Old Vic that the three directors should be allowed to resign. A disaster not only for the immediate future of work at the Old Vic as it seems a wanton wrecking of something really important that had been built up during five years by three men of great talent and great integrity with absolute dedication and sacrifice of everything to their work but also a disaster because it *must* damage the reputation of the Vic in the eyes of the informed public. If it were not so tragic, it would be ludicrous.... I have never been so shocked and disillusioned by anything in my twenty-five years in the theatre.'

This is Peggy at her best: writing from the heart and voicing an ungovernable concern for the larger welfare of the British theatre. It was something she was to do ever more publicly as the years went by. As Anthony Quayle points out, her distress at the course of events at the Old Vic goes a long way to explain her distrust of Tyrone Guthrie. For his part, Quayle tried to get the

Stratford Governors to take over the Old Vic School and asked his Chairman, Sir Fordham Flower, to examine the prospects of a union with the Old Vic. Neither proposal came to anything; instead Quayle got Byam Shaw and Devine to work with him at Stratford. 'It was,' he says, 'as if the Old Vic had advanced up to a point and collapsed. The off-shoot became me pulling a lot of its strength over to Stratford.'

While the crisis was at its height, Peggy played Mistress Page in Hugh Hunt's production of *The Merry Wives of Windsor*, but she left the Vic that summer with some relief to spend more time with her family and to enjoy a short break from acting. The philistine sabotage of the Old Vic Centre only served to intensify her commitment to a theatrical ideal, and from then onwards she also became a much more vocal and partisan campaigner for causes in which she passionately believed.

One such was John Whiting's *Saint's Day*. In the early autumn of 1951 it won a £700 prize in the Arts Theatre Club play competition: the discerning judges were Alec Clunes, Christopher Fry and Peter Ustinov. But when it was produced on stage, it was received with that particular kind of savagery that British critics often keep in reserve for a major unclassifiable work (*The Birthday Party*, *Serjeant Musgrave's Dance* and *Saved* were later examples). After its critical mauling, a number of theatre people took up arms on its behalf, including Peggy and John Gielgud who wrote a joint letter to *The Times* which began: 'We are dismayed by the unanimous critical attack on the recent production of Mr Whiting's *Saint's Day* at the Arts Theatre. We found it beautiful, moving and fascinating – subtly directed and finely played. Is obscurity an unforgiveable crime in a playwright?' Certainly not; and on the two occasions I have seen Whiting's play on stage it held me by its atmospheric power and its strange haunting story of a reclusive literary grand old man who is visited first by a smooth-faced critic and then by three dangerous Army deserters who turn out to be the Eumenides in khaki. It is fascinating to find the newly militant Peggy campaigning on its behalf: even more significant to find her allying herself with a radical new work.

Peggy's alliance with the new took more practical form when she agreed – at Binkie Beaumont's behest and against her own instincts – to appear in Terence Rattigan's *The Deep Blue Sea*. Given Rattigan's posthumous reputation as a sleek Rolls Royce amongst dramatists and the work's high status as an emblem of the well-made play, it may seem in retrospect like a safe, inevitable choice. It was not so at the time. Peggy agonised long and hard over whether or not to play Rattigan's heroine, a Ladbroke Grove Emma Bovary: in the atmosphere of the West End in 1952 the idea of a female protagonist whose whole life revolves around sex was puzzling and even shocking.

The play itself – one of Rattigan's best – had had a chequered history. It had been triggered by the suicide of one of his lovers, Kenneth Morgan, an actor seven years his junior and ill at ease in the company of the dramatist's smart friends. Morgan had left Rattigan, taken another lover and then, after failing to kill himself with an overdose of sleeping tablets, gassed himself. Rattigan heard the news while on the pre-London tour of his play, *Adventure Story*. According to Anthony Curtis, he was shaken and stunned but instantly conceived the idea of a play built around a suicide attempt.

Rattigan – rather puncturing the idea of his supposed enthralment to the cosy values of his mythical middle-class spectator Aunt Edna – took his first version of the play, dealing with the tragic end of a homosexual affair, to Binkie Beaumont. Evidently Beaumont made it clear there was no question of the play being performed as written: not only was homosexuality still technically illegal, but censorship was still in force, and the West End was adjudged to be unready for an open treatment of masculine love. Mordaunt Sharp's *The Green Bay Tree* had in the 1930s darkly hinted at homosexuality, though nothing more suggestive occurred than the playing of a record featuring a boy soprano. And although Cicely Courtneidge was about to appear in Ivor Novello's *Gay's the Word*, it was then a word that didn't have the connotations it does now.

So Rattigan transmuted his material into heterosexual terms. The play became the story of Hester Collyer, a country parson's daughter and the wife of a High Court Judge who falls in love with a former test pilot whose passion is unequal to hers. Set in their dingy, furnished London flat, the play begins with a failed suicide bid by Hester, charts the course of her single-minded erotic attachment to a jovial barfly, Freddie Page, and, after he has left her, leads to what might be another suicide attempt. In fact, the play ends with a gesture on the side of life. Hester Collyer may, in her passion, resemble Flaubert's heroine: the crucial difference is that she does not finally opt for what Rattigan saw as the sentimental gesture of suicide.

Even though the protagonist underwent a sex-change, it remains a first-rate examination of Rattigan's abiding theme: the inequality of passion. Rattigan came to epitomise the gentlemanly code of English playwriting whose symbols were the fiercely buttoned lip and the well-polished understatement. But almost all of Rattigan's work is a heartfelt and implacable attack on the rooted Anglo-Saxon fear of passionate emotional commitment. From *French without Tears*, where the lads at a French crammer's retreat in terror before the sexually predatory Diana, to *Cause Célèbre*, with its dramatisation of the Alma Rattenbury case, he is preoccupied by the imbalance of passion and the emotional constipation of English men. For Hester Collyer, her lover, Freddie Page, is 'the whole of life'. To Freddie, an instantly recognisable overgrown schoolboy whose life stopped in 1940, she is a pleasing toy who makes emotional demands he can't fulfil. To her husband, Bill Collyer, she is a prized possession all the more valuable for having been stolen. Neither of them comprehends or can remotely satisfy her zealous and overpowering need for love.

Given that Hester was the best role written for an English actress since the war, why was Peggy so reluctant to play it? Her own explanation is clear-cut. 'I absolutely refused to do it at first and I was persuaded by the immortal Binkie Beaumont to take it on. I found her so unsympathetic that I said if I feel like that about the heroine, I can't possibly make an audience sympathise with her – which is what, of course, the audience has to do. I thought she was terribly selfish and cowardly to try and commit suicide just because her lover left her or was being neglectful. Binkie persuaded me that the fact that I didn't feel very sympathetic towards her would make my playing the role much more interesting. I don't know if he was right or not but it was a great success.'

Frith Banbury, a long-time Ashcroft watcher, was chosen to direct the production. He has directed no less than five actresses

as Hester and thinks that Peggy tops the lot because of her
formidable technique: he says astutely that she has a body and
voice that will do what her mind tells them to. But he believes
that Peggy drew back initially from Hester not from dislike of
the character but because it required a degree of self-revelation.
'She imagined,' he says, 'that it was something she was not. I
believe her reluctance to play it sprang from the fact that she
didn't want to undress spiritually in public.'

Utter nonsense, says Peggy. She felt she couldn't play a
character from whom she felt so emotionally distant. All the
same, Banbury's comment is interesting and reminds me of Peter
Hall's point that one of Peggy's key qualities is the combination
of a very English containment and decency with a hint of wild
passion fermenting underneath. Rattigan's role asked her to
exhibit just that without the comforting distance of period
costume: to play Hester to the full, she had to use something very
deep inside herself.

But that was not the only problem. Casting Freddie Page, the
carefree lover, was not easy. The first choice was Jimmy Hanley.
Then Kenneth More, a young actor who had worked at the
Windmill before the war and who had started to make his name
in films like *Morning Departure* and *Appointment with Venus*, was
brought to Binkie Beaumont's attention. More's early auditions
were none too good. And it was Peggy who suggested to Binkie
Beaumont that they give him a chance under more relaxed
conditions. So a reading of the play was arranged at Binkie's
house in Lord North Street and More walked off with the part.

Rehearsals in the winter of 1952 involved a good deal of
rewriting. Frith Banbury says Peggy was by now so good an
actress she could supply deficiencies in scripts. He kept throwing
lines out because he found Peggy was already indicating the
qualities required; when he came to direct the play in New York
with Margaret Sullavan he found himself reinstating the lines.

When *The Deep Blue Sea* opened at the Duchess Theatre on
6 March, there was a great shout of enthusiasm both for Rattigan's
craftsmanship and Peggy's. But there was also a certain puzzlement amongst older critics as to the source of Hester's problem.
Peter Fleming (whose wife, Celia Johnson, actually took over the
role of Hester later in the run) labelled her irresponsible and

inconsiderate, which didn't get one very far. But the most baffled review of all came from Ivor Brown in the *Observer*, who seemed totally unable to work out what was eating Hester. His review tested various theories. Boredom? Sensuality? The desire for somebody to mother? He came to the startling conclusion: 'Perhaps she just needs a good slap or a straight talk by a Marriage Guidance Expert.' One might as well say that Hamlet needed a cuff round the ears or that Phèdre needed a good talking-to from Nanny.

Other critics were more intuitively understanding. Harold Hobson -- both in his *Sunday Times* notice and in his longer study of the play in *The Theatre Now* – understood both that Hester was concerned with the total fulfilment of love and that Rattigan's achievement was to have written a play in which there were no villains. He sympathised with all his characters, showing Freddie as a kindly man unable to respond to the intensity of passion burning Hester's body and soul and Sir William Collyer as a compassionate husband who spoke without bitterness. Rattigan's comprehensive sympathy was for Hobson matched by that of the actors:

'I do not see how any acting in the quietest manner could well be more moving than that of Miss Ashcroft and Mr Culver. Their first scene together after the judge had been brought round to Ladbroke Grove by a telephone call telling him of his wife's illness was extraordinarily fine and played with that restraint which can on occasion suggest enormous tensions. They stood in the centre of the stage facing each other, Miss Ashcroft white and troubled but quite calm in misery, Mr Culver with piercing eyes watching her.... With a few simple words, a few indirect sentences, these players and their author created the entire relationship between Hester and her husband, its mutual respect and liking and even affection and the pitiable truth that respect, liking and affection, without passion, are not enough.'

The critic who best understood Ashcroft's potent combination of spirit and flesh was Kenneth Tynan. In later years he came to occupy in her private demonology the place vacated by James Agate: she rarely mentions his name, but when she does it is with an involuntary shudder. But the young Tynan, sending up nightly fireworks from the vantage-point of the *Evening Standard*, responded warmly to Peggy's Hester; and a year later, in a book entitled *Persona Grata*, he distilled her essence in shapely prose:

'Her quality, as we are most aware of it, is to be moon-lit and quietly plangent. Terence Rattigan, by writing *The Deep Blue Sea*, lured her out into the blaze of noon and she responded with a scorchingly realistic portrait of a woman in love beyond her lover's means. The play's shape is roughly analogous to that of *The Heiress*, her other recent triumph: deserted by her man at the end of Act Two, she rejects love itself at the end of Act Three. But its mood is quite different: seedy, frayed and suburban, whole worlds away from the poetic haven which Miss Ashcroft is popularly supposed to inhabit. Emotionally a slave, intellectually a fool, Hester Collyer is a character which lesser actresses would inevitably cheapen in performance. Miss Ashcroft filled in all the physical details – the chain-smoking, the pastiness, the generally unbuttoned look: and then by the simple device of not playing for sympathy overwhelmingly gained it. The correct metaphor for her performance is a melted candle, burned down and beautiful ... Miss Ashcroft can convey a serious, *raisonné* interest in sex, an ability which alone would be enough to set her apart from her English contemporaries.'

As usual, Peggy left the cast after six months to be with her family; she passed the baton on to Celia Johnson who then handed over to Googie Withers. In all, the play ran for 513 performances. What *The Deep Blue Sea* proved indisputably was that Peggy – in addition to being an admired classical actress – was also a West End star whose name above a title could bring customers into a theatre. It also cemented a strong relationship with Binkie Beaumont based on mutual loyalty and trust. Jeremy Hutchinson points out that Beaumont had a genius for getting people together and building up a production: such was Peggy's trust in Binkie that she never employed an agent but simply negotiated her contract with him direct. On the subject of money, Jeremy also observes that Peggy only earned substantial sums on her three big West End hits of the late 1940s and early 1950s. But the advantage of having another breadwinner in the family, as he says, was that it left her free to choose. Marriage has many pleasures: for an actress, one is that she is not always having to worry about the next job or landing the fattest contract. It is only with the faintest regret that Peggy herself points out that when films were made of her three biggest commercial hits, *Edward, My Son, The Heiress* and *The Deep Blue Sea*, her roles went to other actresses: Deborah Kerr, Olivia de Havilland and Vivien Leigh. 'I wasn't angry,' Peggy says, 'because I didn't want to be a film star. I was just a bit irked.'

Irked she may have been, but she had too much else to think about to dwell on might-have-beens. She was very much of the theatre and in the summer of 1952 watched with passionate concern the fortunes of her three friends from the Old Vic. George Devine was dividing his time between directing opera at Sadler's Wells (*Eugene Onegin*) and drama at Stratford-on-Avon (*Volpone* with Richardson and Quayle). Michel Saint-Denis was heading for Strasbourg after the final closure of the Old Vic School: Peggy, however, joined forces with John Gielgud, Edith Evans and Laurence Olivier to send a letter to *The Times* in July 1952 drawing attention to the brilliance of what he had achieved. Glen Byam Shaw, meanwhile, was installed at Stratford and busy planning the 1952 season while Quayle led a second company on a prestige-building, money-raising tour of Australia. It was Byam Shaw who, while Peggy was still at the Duchess, made her an offer she couldn't refuse but also found a little daunting: to return to Stratford for the '53 season to play Portia (no problem there) and Cleopatra. 'I was astonished,' says Peggy, 'when Glen asked me to play Cleopatra. I told him I thought he must be mad. But I trusted him, knew he had thought about the play a great deal during the war when he was wounded in India and said I was ready to have a go.'

Having a go has always been part of Peggy's philosophy, and in 1953 she found herself returning to a Stratford that was big business and hot news. Apart from herself the company was to include Michael Redgrave, Marius Goring, Harry Andrews, Tony Britton and Yvonne Mitchell doing a five-play season comprising *The Merchant of Venice, Richard III, Antony and Cleopatra, The Taming of the Shrew* and *King Lear*. The eight-month season was to prove a record-breaker, seen by over 360,000 people and taking nearly £180,000 at the gate. Press coverage was also enormous. As well as being Coronation Year, it was the 21st birthday of Elizabeth Scott's Memorial Theatre, which was often compared either to a jam factory (why jam?) or some great docked liner. It was a sign of Stratford's newsworthiness that on opening night the critic of the *Daily Mail*, Cecil Wilson, was expected to combine a review with a report about the Birmingham brass gleaming in the souvenir shops and the locals protesting about the lack of a through train to London. Indeed his piece was headed 'The Merchants of Venice and Stratford-on-Avon.'

Peggy opened the season in March playing Portia in Denis Carey's production of *The Merchant*. For her, this was familiar territory. She had been haunted by the play at school. She had first played Portia professionally in the very year, 1932, when the Memorial Theatre opened. She had done it again at the Queens. By now, her performance had ripened to perfection. As the lady of Belmont, in gowns of glowing blue and golden, daffodil yellow, she was witty, amused, subtle-sweet. 'She turns the preposterous Belmont fairy-tale,' wrote Ivor Brown, 'into something actual and the house pulses with true feeling.' In this, she was much aided by Tony Britton's Bassanio who was a serious, sensitive, Romeo-like figure rather than the conventional brassy adventurer.

But it was in the trial scene, where she donned German field-grey, that she came into her own. Partly this was because she had a Shylock genuinely worth fighting in the remarkable shape of Michael Redgrave, whose researches had led him into a study of Jewish culture and history, visits to the Amsterdam ghettoes and consultation with rabbis. Redgrave was a Stanislavsky actor on the heroic scale and his towering Shylock was variously described as a violent Piranesi Jew and an embryonic study for King Lear. But Peggy's success in the trial scene was also determined by the fact that she had plotted its progress with due care. Peggy says that when Portia comes on she knows exactly what the quibble will be and she has been told that she must try to let Shylock recant. She gives Shylock three opportunities or three loopholes in which to change his mind. He rejects them. She brings him to the point of admitting that he wants to murder Antonio. Then, having opened the trap for him, Portia strikes with 'Tarry a little, there is something else.' As Peggy remarks: 'There are those who think Portia is extremely cruel both to Shylock and Antonio, but I see her as an extraordinary mixture of legality and humanity.'

Redgrave's Shylock was controversial, Denis Carey's production was felt to make too little visual distinction between Venice and Belmont, but about Peggy's Portia there was little argument. Kenneth Tynan, still one of her eager champions, flung his cap in the air in the *Evening Standard*: 'The jewel of the evening is Peggy Ashcroft's Portia, a creature of exquisite breeding and uncommon sense. She speaks the poetry with the air of a woman who would never commit the social gaffe of reciting in public: with the result that the lines flow out new-minted, as unstrained as the quality of mercy itself. Her handling of the tiresome princelings who come to woo her is an object lesson in wit and good manners. Later, in the court-room, we wept at her compassion; and the last act, invariably an anti-climax, bloomed golden at her touch.' Peggy's Portia, uniting passion and intelligence, proved Olivier's point that acting is the art of persuasion.

The real challenge, however, lay in the third play of the season, *Antony and Cleopatra*, and Peggy knew it. After all, since the war she had specialised in playing suffering, passive victimised women living either in a state of sexual rejection (like Evelyn Holt and Catherine Sloper) or emotional unfulfilment (like Hester Collyer). But Cleopatra is sensually satisfied, emotionally aggressive, temperamentally mercurial, politically wily. She is regal, wanton, cruel, large-spirited, witty, wicked, filled with extremes of temperament and desire. Literary critics have tended to moralise about her with Coleridge writing of 'the criminality in her passion' and 'the habitual craving of a licentious nature'. But the essence of her character seems to me an emotional volatility full of split-second changes of mood. 'Let him forever go, let him stay.' This is Cleopatra.

Peggy may have seemed unlikely casting, but it is evident that the part was waiting for reclamation by a great actress. The play itself had certainly had a chequered history. In the eighteenth century, Dryden's temperate version of the same story, *All For Love*, dominated the stage. Garrick's dismembered version of Shakespeare's play lasted six nights in 1759. Lillie Langtry, expensively accoutred, had a shot at Cleopatra in 1890 and missed: a picture of her survives with knife poised as if about to plunge it into a steak at the Café Royal. Tree's production at His Majesty's in 1906 was dominated by scenic effects including processions through the streets of Alexandria with Cleopatra as the goddess Isis.

Later in the twentieth century the play found more favour but, apart from Dorothy Green who played the heroine at Stratford in 1927 and at the Old Vic in 1930, there was no volubly acclaimed Cleopatra. Edith Evans played the role twice: once at the Old Vic in 1925 when Agate declared 'she has not enough passion and vulgarity for Cleopatra' and again at the Piccadilly in 1946 when Tynan felt that Lady Bracknell had become involved in a low Alexandrian scandal. The biggest asp disaster of them all, however, was Komisarjevsky's short-lived version at the New in 1936, when Cleopatra was entrusted to an unintelligible Russian comédienne, Sophie Leontovich. Agate swore he heard her say: 'When you suet staying, Den was de time for Wurst.' Even Vivien Leigh's performance opposite Olivier at the St James's in 1951 was felt to be too kittenish, low-key and small-scale to reach the infinite variety of Cleopatra.

Peggy's doubts about her suitability for the role were widely shared. Margaret Harris, who designed the costumes, recalls that everyone said to Glen Byam Shaw that he was mad to cast her for the part, that she was too nice and middle-class to convey the requisite violence, but that she certainly managed to produce it. Harry Andrews adds: 'She must have felt it was against the grain. We felt that too. There was speculation that she didn't have the equipment to do it – that she would need to be supported in all sorts of ways by clothes and make-up. But she did achieve it in the most original way.'

As so often, Peggy's success lay in starting with a clear concept: in this case a very clear physical idea of the character. Wisely, she and her director decided to banish the serpent-of-old-Nile cliché and not present the audience with some bedizened harlot resembling Betty savagely deprived of Wilson and Keppel in the old music-hall sand-dance. Peggy was much influenced by a picture in the old Temple Edition that showed Cleopatra to be a Macedonian Greek, like Alexander, without a trace of Egyptian blood. The historian, R. H. Barrow, has pointed out that she was dominated by the passion for power and had inherited Alexander's dream of a fusion of East and West and of total conquest of the known world. So, instead of some voluptuous Egyptian dish, Peggy presented us with a pale-skinned figure in a red ponytail wig and in bright orange and purple robes. But doesn't this fly slightly in the face of the text? 'Think on me,' says Cleopatra, 'That am with Phoebus' amorous pinches black.' Peggy's retort is that you have to take the whole sense of the line which runs on 'And wrinkled deep in time'. In other words, she says, Cleopatra is middle-aged rather than violently sun-burned.

For Peggy, the four weeks of rehearsal flashed by. As she says, 'there wasn't time for fear: you just had to go in off the deep end and fish out what you could.' On top of rehearsals there were costume fittings, wig fittings, and nightly performances as Portia. 'She was very good at the *Antony* fittings,' says Margaret Harris. 'If you get an actor who doesn't react when you put the clothes on them, it's very difficult. If an actress just stands, one learns nothing. Peggy was very good in that she reacted in character to the costumes.'

When it came to the first night on 28 April, the Stratford air was giddy with expectation. Unusually for Peggy, there was even pre-publicity in the *Daily Express*. An interview with David Lewin reported that Peggy liked to paddle her own canoe from her house on the river 30 minutes upstream from the theatre, and told us that Peggy's costume revealed vital statistics of a bust of $36\frac{1}{2}$, a waist of 25 inches and hips of $37\frac{1}{2}$. Lewin also enticed from Peggy how she saw Cleopatra: 'As a vile woman – a wonderfully vile woman. But what a chance to be completely and fully feminine. In my last three plays, I ended as a drunk in one, I was an unattractive spinster in the other, and in *The Deep Blue Sea* I just had to suffer every night, twice on matinée days. And don't you dare say I suffered exquisitely. I hated it.'

Peggy is the first to admit that as Cleopatra she relied very heavily on her director, Glen Byam Shaw. Harry Andrews, who was a magnificent Enobarbus, has a clear memory of going into her dressing-room and finding Glen sitting at her table helping her with the make-up: at his behest, she even wore, for the first time in her career, false eye-lashes. The director and his designers, Motley, also gave the action maximum fluency and cleared the space for the actors. Transitions from Rome to Alexandria were done with cinematic speed and simple lighting-changes. A rope looped with canvas indicated Pompey's galley. Two purple poles suggested Octavius's court. Stratford's hydraulic lifts enabled the rear of the stage to rise and become Cleopatra's monument. I saw the production as a schoolboy – my first sight of Peggy on stage – and it remains clear to this day in my mind's eye. My only regret is that in giving the production pace Byam Shaw cut the vital scene between Seleucus and Cleopatra at the end of the play when the former admits to Octavius that he has gone through Cleopatra's inventory of treasure and it is incomplete. This shows that, right to the last, Cleopatra is wily and deceitful.

But, given all the initial doubts, did Peggy succeed with Cleopatra? My own recollection, from 35 years ago, is that she did. I remember still her running entrance with Redgrave's Antony: he was tethered to her by a long rope of water-lilies and she pulled him towards her on 'If it be love indeed, tell me how much.' I remember the sparky wit of the scenes with the eunuch and Cleopatra's attendants. Above all, I remember what J. C. Squire called 'the long adagio of Cleopatra's end.' Shakespeare sets the actress – and the audience – an almost insuperable problem in following the death of Antony in Act IV with the death of Cleopatra in Act V. But I recall Peggy, throned in splendour with eagles' wings behind her and torches blazing at her side, crying 'Give me my robe; put on my crown; I have immortal longings in me' and expiring in a state of lulled rapture. Whether this was great acting, I don't know. I can only record that it seemed so at the time.

The newspaper critics virtually all made the point that Peggy was working against her natural grain. A. V. Cookman in *The Times* thought she was still 'an exquisite miniaturist'. But the general feeling was that Peggy had conquered against the odds. Philip Hope-Wallace in the *Manchester Guardian* expressed well the general mood: 'For real emotional impact it was to Miss Ashcroft alone that we could look. And it was sheer acting on her part which carried the evening, once we had got over the initial surprise at seeing this tender actress essaying the serpent of Old Nile – which indeed seemed at first to have in it something rather of Marie Corelli of Old Avon. But she soon completely silenced criticism by the sheer sincerity and passion and skill of her acting, alike in varying moods of scorn and elation. . . . Taken as a whole this was a noble and elegiac Cleopatra which at the end transcended all limitations and became the "fire and air" she claims to be.'

The majority verdict was that Peggy had triumphed over her own temperamental and physical limitations to become the Cleopatra of her generation. But, of all the critics, the one who really burnt his boats – or perhaps his barges – was Alan Dent, who both in his overnight notice for the *News Chronicle* and in a follow-up piece the next Friday reached for the ultimate word in the critical vocabulary: great. In his back-up piece he also made a vital point that eluded most of his critical colleagues: that Peggy was a past mistress of roles requiring ecstasy and fulfilment. He reminded readers of Peggy's prowess in playing hauntingly unhappy women, adding Sophocles' Electra to the now familiar litany. But he shrewdly noted that in the same post-war period as Peggy was becoming the mistress of sorrow and frustration, she had also portrayed radiant happiness in women such as Beatrice, Viola and Portia. 'And now,' he added, 'at Stratford-upon-Avon she plays Cleopatra, a creation of earth and air and fire which is all happy and unhappy women rolled into one. And fulfilling the character as well as she does, she automatically raises herself into the position of being rightly and justly called a great actress.'

There, it had been said. Hobson had been the first to spy greatness in Peggy, but it was Dent who greeted its manifestation. The one strenuous critic of Peggy's performance was Kenneth Tynan in the *Evening Standard*. He started from the premise that an English Cleopatra was a contradiction in terms and that the only role native actresses were equipped to play was Octavia, Caesar's docile sister. Once he had played that card, the rest of his notice was predictable. He objected to Peggy's Sloane Square vowels and Chelsea hairdo. 'I missed too,' he went on, 'the infinite variety. To play Cleopatra, as to play Shylock, you need the Continental actor's ability to juggle with seemingly contradictory emotions; you have to leap from majesty to bawdiness in mid-sentence. For this fitful blaze, Miss Ashcroft substituted a steady glow. A nice, intense woman, you nearly murmured: such a pity she took up with the head gamekeeper.'

Peggy is English middle-class, it is true. But not unchangeably or irredeemably so; and, unless my teenage memory is hopelessly at fault, there was far more to her Cleopatra than a Lady Chatterley in a ponytail wig or an SW3 cocktail-party hostess. My memory is of volatility and passion. Peggy also reclaimed a role that had been long been deemed to be virtually unplayable and showed that it could be conquered through a comprehensive femininity. It was tough work. Peggy's co-star, Michael Redgrave, whom I remember as a ruined Titan, began to suffer the first symptoms of debilitating illness and some nights had to be discreetly prompted by his Cleopatra. But Peggy's real triumph was that she reached the summit through application, intelligence, emotional dynamism and shrewd husbandry. Since 1953 virtually every major British actress (including Judi Dench, Maggie Smith, Vanessa Redgrave, Glenda Jackson, Diana Rigg, Helen Mirren, Janet Suzman and Barbara Jefford) has played the role. A few have reached the lonely peak. Others have got within sight of the summit. But all, I believe, are indebted to Peggy. It was she who finally proved that Cleopatra was not the unattainable K2 of English acting it had seemed but a role that could be conquered through forethought, planning and the support of a first-rate team.

CHAPTER TEN

Taking a Hedda

ONCE *ANTONY AND CLEOPATRA* was on, there was at least the chance to enjoy a Stratford summer: picnics, parties, boating on the river, cricket matches. Peggy was often the organiser, not just because of her role at the head of the company but because of her sense of fun. Cricket has always been one of her passions and Harry Andrews remembers captaining a side against a women's team led by Peggy. The gentlemen batted left-handed and bowled under-arm and the pre-arranged plan was that scores would finish level. The highly competitive Robert Shaw, then making his mark in the company, would have none of this and swiped endless sixes. But, in the end, the Ian Botham of English acting was caught in the deep by Angela Baddeley. 'I didn't,' says Harry Andrews laconically, 'put Bob Shaw on to bowl.'

At the close of the Stratford season, *Antony and Cleopatra* did a London season at the Princes and then in January 1954 went off on a short European tour to The Hague, Amsterdam, Antwerp, Brussels and Paris. It was a triumph everywhere except Paris where Peggy and Michael Redgrave were disconcerted to find themselves being greeted on the first night by distant chuckles. Why the laughter? A French actress explained over dinner: 'It's very simple. In France, in tragedy, *on ne court jamais*. You *never* run.' Trained in classical tragedy, the French could take neither

151

the running entrance of hero and heroine nor the play's quicksilver comedy: the best audience on the tour was a sixth-form one in Amsterdam.

After nearly nine months away from home, Peggy was more than grateful to revert to being a Hampstead barrister's wife and a busy, attentive mother for most of 1954. The part that drew her back to the stage, at the invitation of Tennent productions, was Hedda Gabler: her first Ibsen and a role that we now think of, rather like Cleopatra, as one of those hoops through which every major actress must jump. But, if we think that, it is once again partly because of Peggy's success in redefining its contours and proving it playable.

Before Peggy there had been striking Heddas. But reading contemporary accounts of them you are struck by how often the role was invested with humourless heaviness or romantic bids for sympathy. Eleanora Duse in 1903 was spiritual and statuesque and it took the beady satirical eye of Max Beerbohm to understand that 'Hedda ought to be played with a sense of humour, with a comedic understanding between the player and the audience.' There was evidently not much of that in Mrs Patrick Campbell whose Heddas of 1907 and 1922 swathed the role in tragic beauty and imperious grandeur. Ivor Brown said she seemed to be the daughter not only of General Gabler but of the entire Norwegian Post Office. Jean Forbes-Robertson played the role three times with some success. The one English actress who seemed to have caught something of Hedda's mockery and cruelty was Pamela Brown, but she played the part only briefly in a wartime production at the Oxford Playhouse.

Peggy herself approached Hedda with an awareness of theatrical history and a determination to rescue the character either from somnambulistic severity or romantic grandeur:

'I'd never played Ibsen and I'd often questioned myself, thought I ought to be wanting to play Ibsen because, after all, Shaw was my guide and mentor when I was growing up and he was a great Ibsenite. But I used to read the plays and I funked them. They aren't easy. I think Ibsen's texts have to be dug very, very deep to get at them. But during the war, when I was in the country with my baby daughter, I was reading William Archer. He has a fascinating essay in which he says "Of course, Hedda

1 William Worsley Ashcroft, Peggy Ashcroft's father

2 Violet Maud Ashcroft (née Bernheim), her mother

3 With brother Edward
on a tiger rug

4 With her mother

5 Desdemona in *Othello* with Paul Robeson (Othello)
Savoy Theatre: 1930

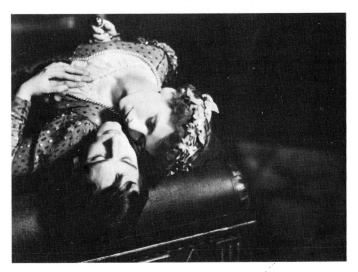

6 Juliet on the Capulet tomb in *Romeo and Juliet*
with Laurence Olivier (Romeo), New Theatre: 1935

7 Cleopatra in *Antony and Cleopatra*,
Shakespeare Memorial Theatre: 1953

8 Hedda Gabler in *Hedda Gabler* with Rachel Kempson
(Mrs Elvsted), Lyric Hammersmith: 1954

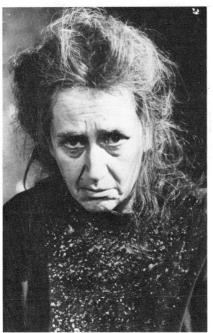

9 Margaret of Anjou in *The Wars of the Roses* with William Squire (Suffolk), Royal Shakespeare Theatre: 1963

10 Margaret of Anjou in later years

11
Claire Lannes
in *The Lovers
of Viorne*,
Royal Court:
1971

12
Winnie in
Happy Days
directed by
Peter Hall,
Old Vic:
1975

13 *The Jewel in the Crown*: 1984

14 *A Passage to India*: 1984

15 With John Gielgud
and Ralph Richardson

16 Peggy Ashcroft

Gabler is the sort of woman one takes down to dinner every night" and I thought "Oh, that's interesting because that's not how I'd imagined her." Mrs Pat and many other actresses had played Hedda and I felt she was a sacred monster and ought to be very different from the everyday characters I played. But Archer intrigued me and then reading Ibsen's description of Hedda's very thin hair fascinated me further and I became deeply involved in the play.'

It says a lot about Peggy that she found her way into the character through a tiny detail: the thin hair that symbolises her jealousy of Mrs Elvsted and, in a way, her own raging self-dislike. Other actresses looked for big effects. George Rylands saw Mrs Pat play Hedda complete with a grand piano draped with a shawl. 'By the time you had that and Mrs Pat,' he says, 'there was not much room for anything else on stage. With Peggy, you realised Hedda was a character of considerable complexity and with conflicting feelings she would never resolve. Her own self was to her insoluble.'

Rehearsals began in London in the summer of 1954 with a formidably strong cast: George Devine as Tesman, Micheál MacLiammóir as Judge Brack, Rachel Kempson as Mrs Elvsted and Alan Badel as Lovborg (a role Michael Warre later took over). The director was Peter Ashmore who had refereed *Edward, My Son*. The designer was Motley (in the person of Margaret Harris) who came up with a set that was light, pleasant and baked in a blinding sun. There was a general agreement on the line to be taken, which was to rescue Ibsen from an atmosphere of sexless, penitential gloom where, as Guthrie once pointed out, high thinking takes place in a world of dark crimson serge tablecloths and huge intellectual women in raincoats and boots. With only three weeks' rehearsal, the intention was to bring out Ibsen's satiric, comedic side, and it succeeded all too well. The production opened in Dublin and was greeted by the audience as if it were *The Importance of Being Earnest*. 'They thought,' said Peggy, 'it was the greatest, wittiest, funniest play ever and when it came to the end and we had a rapturous reception we all knew that we had got it entirely wrong.' So for the remaining six weeks of the tour the cast, minus their director, dug up the play and sorted it out amongst themselves.

Peggy adored the intellectual sleuthing that went into playing Ibsen. She and Devine even had a phrase for it: 'digging potatoes'. They would meet each other at rehearsal each morning and say delightedly that they had dug another potato last night. What Peggy discovered in the course of rehearsal may, after a multiplicity of Heddas, seem self-evident: that the character is a self-obsessed egoist, a snob, more her father's daughter than her husband's wife, frantically jealous and without the courage of her own inclinations. Dr Rylands says Peggy's Hedda had feelings she couldn't resolve. Peggy herself puts it very differently: 'She was a hypocrite and she was onto herself.' It is that self-knowledge that makes life insufferable. Judge Brack, for instance, suggests she might find some vocation in life that would attract her. 'Heaven knows,' she replies, 'what sort of vocation that would be.' She realises, all too clearly, that her only talent is for 'boring herself to death'.

It is one thing to understand Hedda; quite another to translate one's discoveries into theatrical terms. Peggy did it in a number of ways:

In the cruel play of her whiplash mouth.

In the amusement of her eyes as she snubbed Aunt Julia and made a fool of George.

In the snake-like way she caressed Mrs Elvsted's hair.

In the controlled hysteria of her repeated laughter.

She even found herself on stage doing things spontaneously but totally in character: at one moment, she picked up Tesman's smelly pipe with a rancid disgust that she herself hadn't even noticed. Frith Banbury and Binkie Beaumont motored down to Cardiff to see the production on its pre-London tour. Banbury was very impressed at the way Peggy brought out the comicality of Hedda's social pretensions and said he thought the production was very good. Glen Byam Shaw, one of Peggy's oldest friends, also caught the Cardiff version and was less sure it was on the right lines. Says Peggy: 'Glen told me that Hedda should be much more passionate and violent in her feeling. This disturbed me. I saw I must do the very opposite of what Glen suggested and freeze Hedda. That was my final note to myself: that Hedda must be like an iceberg with fire underneath.'

When the production opened at the Lyric Hammersmith on

8 September 1954, the critics were not merely full-throated in their acclaim. They seemed to have divined exactly what Peggy was after. Kenneth Tynan – who had none too kindly compared Peggy's Cleopatra the year before to the firm-willed governess taming a barbaric court in *The King and I* – drove straight to the point: 'The centrepiece is Miss Peggy Ashcroft's Hedda, a flinty, marvellously impartial performance. How many temptations this actress resists. She makes no play for sympathy; nor does she imply that she despises the woman she is impersonating. Her vocal mannerisms, teaspoons twirled in china cups, are exactly fitted to Hedda's malice; and the whole display is a monument to *nymphomanie de tête* which might be roughly translated as the nymphomania of Hedda.'

That precisely pins down Peggy's achievement: she captured the truth of Hedda without the moral comment or play for sympathy that is often the vice of English acting. What is more Peggy, who is often prey to self-doubt and insecurity, knew in herself she had got it right – a fact confirmed by a curious anecdote related by Sir Alec Guinness:

'One of the most interesting little insights I had into her came when I went round to see her afterwards at the Lyric Hammersmith. I thought she was marvellous but various people had said Peggy could never play Hedda: they thought she would emotionalise it. In fact, she was wonderful. But usually after a performance she is drained of vitality and everything has gone. She will try and disguise it but if you asked her out to supper, she would say No or maybe finally Yes. After *Hedda Gabler*, I didn't suggest going out for a meal but I was astonished to find her as bright as a button in her dressing-room. I congratulated her and said "It's very unlike you to be so up at the end of a performance." She said "Oh, it's wonderful. It's such a relief because there is absolutely nothing in Hedda at all, there is no feeling. She's a woman of no feelings, everything is calculated. It makes no demands on me at all. I come on, I say the lines, I do what I think is the right thing and I feel years younger doing it." What particularly came over in Peggy's performance was Hedda's callousness and indifference: I always remember the comedy of the incident over the aunt's hat where she deliberately makes rude remarks about it. It was superbly done but so unlike Peg.'

After almost three months in Hammersmith, the production moved into the Westminster in late November for a further eight weeks. Then early in 1955 it took off for a tour of Holland, Denmark and Germany. Rachel Kempson remembers that the first leg of the tour was a real treat. The company were based in Amsterdam and the Hague and each day they would set off in a huge car to play one-night-stands. She, Peggy and George Devine all took turns behind the wheel while Micheál MacLiammóir in the back seat would keep them amused with an endless flow of Irish anecdote. The pattern was the same each day: lunch in a country restaurant, a short rest, a drive to the theatre for the performance and then a post-play supper. 'It was all simple, enormous fun,' says Rachel Kempson, 'and Peggy was always at the heart of it in spite of the travelling and her immensely taxing performance. She was an ideal team leader and enchanting company.' But the off-stage charmer transformed herself on stage: to this day, Rachel Kempson remembers the cold shivers that ran down her back when Peggy's Hedda got hold of her head and threatened to burn her hair.

The real test came in Oslo where a local production of *Hedda Gabler* was already installed. Pre-first night nerves were not helped when an interviewer suggested to Peggy that Hedda was frigid. Peggy's warm eyes allegedly became dark as she replied: 'I would rather characterise her as frozen fire.'

The performance, however, was a triumph; and the critic of the leading Oslo newspaper, *Aftenposten*, perceived Peggy's achievement: 'It is curious to have to register the fact that an English actress has shown the Norwegian public how Hedda should be played. After only a few minutes we realised that she had that rare combination of emotional receptivity and intellectual capacity that characterises actresses of the first order. There is the most intimate connection between the Hedda Gabler of Peggy Ashcroft and the intentions of Ibsen himself.'

The one unnerving moment for Peggy came one night when there was a knock at her dressing-room door after the performance and a booming, sepulchral voice announced itself as belonging to 'Mr Ibsen'. For a second, Peggy thought the sage of Skien himself had returned from the grave. Happily it turned out to be the great man's grandson, Tankred, who had come to add his compliments to the many. Peggy also had an audience with King Haakon of Norway who, in recognition of her performance, awarded her the King's Gold Medal, telling her, 'I think you were very brave walking into the lion's mouth.' He also recalled as a young man meeting the venerable Ibsen and rather rashly asking him about the meaning of *The Master Builder*. Ibsen simply turned on his heel and walked away. As well he might.

The Fifties was a golden decade for Peggy. Apart from doing work that was well within her compass, such as Portia and Beatrice, she also constantly surprised both the doubters and herself by succeeding in roles that seemed to run against the natural grain. Greek tragedy? She hadn't the big guns it needed. Except that she pulled off an astonishing Electra. Cleopatra? She hadn't the sexiness or passion. But, of course, she had. Hedda Gabler? Oh, Peg's far too nice a lady to convey bitchy viciousness. But, my God, she did. As Margaret Harris says: 'Her compassion is amazing. She seems to understand everything. Being what she is, she is able to put what she understands into her performance. You never get the feeling that Peggy will never understand that, never feel that. Because she will understand most things – good and evil.'

But although the Fifties was a decade in which she was constantly pushing the frontiers of her art outwards, even she drew in her horns and retreated into a skilful obduracy when asked to wear tubes of felt as Cordelia in a production of *King Lear* designed by Isamu Noguchi and directed by George Devine.

The background was this. In 1955 the Shakespeare Memorial Theatre Company split into two halves. Laurence Olivier and Vivien Leigh led the home team in a famous season that included *Macbeth* and *Titus Andronicus*. Meanwhile Gielgud and Peggy were at the head of an equally distinguished away team scheduled to do a gruelling six-month tour that would take in eleven European cities, six British provincial cities, play a summer season at the Palace in London and end up in Stratford just before Christmas. There were two productions. One was a revival of the famous Gielgud *Much Ado* with Peggy once again lending Beatrice her unique combination of featherweight lightness and attack. The other was the notorious Noguchi *King Lear* that attempted to divest Shakespeare's tragedy of 'Historical and decorative associations' but instead invested it with costumes that provoked ridicule and derision – not least from the actors.

The designer, Isamu Noguchi, was an American-born Japanese sculptor and furniture designer who also worked in theatre and who had done sets for Balanchine's *Orpheus* and Martha Graham's *Appalachian Spring*. Devine and Gielgud were united in wanting him, and his sets certainly fulfilled the brief of avoiding realism. I remember being impressed with them at the time. Even today, looking at a photograph of his Act One design, one has the sense of something mythic, timeless and oriental. Downstage, left and right, are two vast armorial shields. Centre stage is a two-level plinth on which is a jagged, triangular throne ('the seat of a golden and metaphysical lavatory' suggested Harold Hobson). Above it is suspended what might be the disembodied beard of a Kabuki actor. To its left, above Cordelia's stool, is a beautiful, blue diamond-shaped object. But the essence of the Noguchi designs was their mobility and association with particular aspects of character.

It was the costumes that caused the problem. Noguchi had never designed costumes before. He sent to Devine from New York paper maquettes painted and cut to scale. When the actors finally put them on at a dress parade at the Scala Theatre, the general reaction was one of horror. Lear himself appeared in a gown full of holes that made him look like a Gruyère cheese, his face was surrounded by a mane of white horsehair and on his head he wore a crown unkindly compared to an inverted hatstand. Honest Kent wore a leather jerkin surrounded by rubber rings that suggested a slightly depleted Michelin man. Goneril and Regan were swathed from collar to toe in Minoan dresses. Peggy was asked to wear a tubular structure but shrewdly managed to change it for a plain, straightforward dress before the first night. 'If you'd seen the company doing the play without the Noguchi costumes,' says Peggy, 'it would have come off magnificently. George Devine's throwing away of rhetorical attitudes to Shakespeare was all in line with how he was thinking. It was tragic that somehow Noguchi got in the way of it. I think Noguchi's intentions failed because what he did was to illustrate the characters rather than to free them of specific associations.'

The European press, when they saw the production, were puzzled but respectful. By the time it reached London in July – with Peggy handing over the role of Cordelia to Claire Bloom in order to spend the summer holidays with her family – respect had given way to mocking irony. Few critics in the popular papers could resist quoting Lear's 'I do not like the fashion of your garments.' Space-travel serials were frequently invoked. With heavy irony, Harold Hobson suggested that Noguchi as a child had come under the influence of a Far Eastern magician 'who probably worked under some outlandish, mysterious name like Robertson.'

To a young theatregoer the production seemed by no means the total disaster that it was labelled. Noguchi's sets did have a strange unearthly grandeur. There were some momentous effects such as, in the scenes on the heath, the obtrusion from the skies of a monstrous, forbidding black torpedo. And Gielgud's Lear surmounted the costuming to appear as a great oak struck by lightning. It is also worth recalling that when Peter Brook was working on his famous Beckettian *Lear* seven years later at Stratford one of the first things he did was to consult the Noguchi set-designs.

Even if *King Lear* was not exactly Peggy's happiest experience in the theatre, it did nothing to dent her friendship with George Devine. Far from it. Devine in 1955 was hard at work on his plans to turn the Royal Court into a centre of new British, Continental and American writing, and even before setting out on the European tour (in which he played Gloucester and Dogberry) he asked Peggy if she would be interested in playing the lead in Bertolt Brecht's *The Good Woman of Setzuan*. This was long before Brecht had gained a foothold in the British theatre and even before the first historic visit by the Berliner Ensemble. Peggy unhesitatingly said yes. And, while the Stratford company was on tour to the Berlin Festival in September, Peggy and Devine met Brecht and Helene Weigel after a matinée of *Much Ado* for beer and sausages. Peggy remembers Brecht as 'physically a little bit like Sean O'Casey, terrific sense of fun and humour, very delightful.' Out of that meeting came an agreement by Brecht that Devine and Peggy could do his play: an agreement that later ran into severe complications.

The seven-month tour of *Lear* and *Much Ado*, even with a short sabbatical in the middle, was extremely gruelling. But in the sixteen months after that tour finished, Peggy threw herself wholeheartedly into a period of unparalleled activity that, more than anything, demonstrated her kaleidoscopic range. In April 1956 she was back under the Binkie Beaumont banner playing Miss Madrigal in Enid Bagnold's *The Chalk Garden* at the Theatre Royal, Haymarket. Six months later she made her début with the newly founded English Stage Company at the Royal Court playing the dual roles of Shen Te, the golden-hearted prostitute, and Shui Ta, her bestial cousin, in Brecht's *The Good Woman of Setzuan*. And six months after that she was back in Stratford-on-Avon to play Rosalind in Glen Byam Shaw's production of *As You Like It*. It is impossible to think of any other British actress at that time who could have leapt with such confidence from Bagnold to Brecht to Shakespeare. More significantly, it is hard to think of another actress who would have even wanted to.

Versatility alone does not make for greatness in acting. Stark Young says that 'mimicry is to acting what memory can be to culture or education': a quality not to be despised, but one that of itself does not make someone an artist. Max Beerbohm also once said of Eleanora Duse that she never 'stoops to impersonation'. My own belief is that, as performers get older, acting becomes increasingly a judgement of character: that it is who or what they are as human beings that determines the quality of their art. In their early or middle years, there is often a frank delight in the chameleon aspect of acting. Peggy once told me of a revealing conversation she had with Olivier during the 1935 *Romeo and Juliet* when he said, in what she thought was an irritatingly lordly way, that he felt awfully sorry for actresses because they didn't have the chance to change themselves from one character to another. 'I thought,' says Peggy, still bridling quietly, 'well really that can't be so. I mean my approach is one of change. I may not change but I know I try to see a character as outside myself and there is always that horrible moment when you come to put on your make-up and your costume and you are confronted with the same face. There is nothing you can do about it.'

Peggy's remarkable line of parts through 1956–7 is proof of something more than her range. It also shows the tenacity of her friendships and her determination to be where the action is. At this time the English theatre was going through a period of artistic upheaval. The year before *The Chalk Garden* opened, Joan Littlewood's Theatre Workshop, while still struggling for recognition at home, had been the surprise hit of the Paris Festival. Also in 1955 Beckett's *Waiting for Godot*, directed by Peter Hall, had detonated a sizeable explosion at London's Arts Theatre. In May 1956 John Osborne's *Look Back in Anger*, while formally a very traditional piece of work, introduced the voice of the dispossessed young into British theatre and released a head of steam in native playwriting. And in August of that year the Berliner Ensemble's visit to the Palace Theatre had a profound impact on our own direction and design and showed what permanent companies could achieve. Peggy was the first member of the so-called theatrical Establishment (even before Olivier) to ally herself with the new movement by simultaneously appearing at the Court and doing a play by Brecht.

Seen in this context, *The Chalk Garden*, produced by Binkie Beaumont, directed by Gielgud and co-starring Edith Evans, may look like a last glorious display by the old brigade; and indeed, a month before the noisy advent of Osborne, Kenneth Tynan wrote in imperial terms that at least the West End cavalry 'went out with a flourish, its banners resplendent in the last rays of the sun.' In fact, the West End style was much more tenacious than he assumed. And although Enid Bagnold's play was 'mannered to the point of affectation in its phraseology' (Peggy's own phrase), it also had greater substance than many at first assumed.

On one level, Miss Bagnold's play works like a murder mystery: Agatha Christie rewritten with studied wit. Miss Madrigal is engaged as lady companion, precisely because she has no references, by the richly eccentric Mrs St. Maugham. At the beginning of the second act she is recognised by a judge who has come to lunch as the woman he sentenced to death fifteen years ago for the murder of her stepsister.

This is woman-with-a-past territory, but the real action concerns Miss Madrigal's relationship with her employer's granddaughter, Laurel, to whom she has been appointed governess.

Miss Madrigal indicates that the murder charge against her had plausibility but not truth; yet, because she was a habitual liar, when she eventually told the truth she wasn't believed. Laurel too is a congenital liar who claims that she was raped in Hyde Park at the age of 12 and that she hates her mother. Miss Madrigal extends to the girl the pity and charity she herself was denied. She goes into battle to rescue her from the symbolic sterility of her grandmother's chalk garden and the awful reality of her own neurosis. She teaches Laurel, who has a surprising hardiness, that truth is more interesting than fiction.

Under the drawing-room surface lay a play that, as Eric Bentley pointed out when reviewing the New York production, was more or less Pirandellian: the meaning of life, it argued, was to be discovered not in fact-finding but in compassion and regard for the domestic pieties. In class terms, it also showed a young girl being saved from the aridity of a wealthy irresponsible life. But Peggy cut an astonishing path through Miss Bagnold's mannered, oblique, neo-Firbankian style to create a real character in the dumpy shape of Miss Madrigal. J. C. Trewin pregnantly observed to me of Peggy that 'She always makes you aware of the past of any character she has played.' He cited the example of her Viola, where the prolonged pause before the revelation of her ancestry made the whole of her life appear in a single moment. But he could equally well have cited the scene at the lunch-table in *The Chalk Garden* where Peggy, slightly flushed with the wine she has gulped down, releases the pent-up frustrations of fifteen lonely years and allows real emotion to penetrate the light, easy, amusing banter like a knife going through silk.

Even now the pictures of Peggy give a vivid impression of the character she created. The hands clutch the little black handbag for security, a trim, belted, governessy sort of hat perches on her head, the white blouse is secured by a chaste brooch at the neck. Every physical detail is right. Ivor Brown accurately described Peggy as 'at first tight-lipped and jerkily moving, like a wibbly-wobbly pudding on its plate, then emerging as the woman with a will and mind as well as with a past.' But the key to the performance was the way Peggy grew from being the shy, stubborn, incalculable spinster into the woman who had known suffering and who was determined to pass on a lesson about self-destructive mendacity.

To Edith Evans went the showy part of the elderly eccentric swooping into drawing-rooms with exasperated complaints about 'this *mule* of a garden'. But critics were quick to understand that it was Peggy's Miss Madrigal that gave the play its emotional dynamic. J. C. Trewin saw the play on the first night of its pre-London tour in Birmingham and remembers Edith Evans flapping about and Peggy controlling her with the utmost tact. And, after the Haymarket opening, A. V. Cookman wrote in *The Times*: 'The play is an actor's play and in a special sense it is Miss Ashcroft's play. It is her business to make good a slightly comic but genuine reality in the midst of artificiality, a business which she carries through without a single false touch.'

Although *The Chalk Garden* may not have been the highest reaches of her art, it demonstrated that she never rested on her laurels but invested commercial work with the same poignant truth as Shakespeare or Chekhov. In the course of the Haymarket run, she was created a Dame of the British Empire: from now on she was Dame Peggy. The same honour had been accorded to Sybil Thorndike at 49 and Edith Evans at 58. Peggy was 48. But while she received her accolade with gratitude, she has never made any great fuss about it. The same might be said for her *Evening Standard* Award (in only the second year of that institution) for Best Performance by an Actress which she gained for her Miss Madrigal. While delighted at the recognition of her work, she is very philosophical about being publicly garlanded: 'You do realise,' she says, 'it's the luck of the draw.'

Anyway, by the time she was on the podium being hymned for her Miss Madrigal she was busy elsewhere. She was, in fact, working at the Royal Court, where she was partially vindicating Binkie Beaumont's new nickname for her, the Red Dame, and doing her bit to make the post-war theatrical revolution a living reality.

CHAPTER ELEVEN

Red Nights

SWITCHING FROM THE GILDED elegance of the Haymarket to the puritan plainness of the Royal Court was, in theatrical terms, a bit like travelling from West to East Berlin: a journey from the capitalist heartland to a centre of missionary fervour. In September 1956 Peggy started rehearsing Brecht's *The Good Woman of Setzuan* while finishing her allotted six-month run in *The Chalk Garden*, but the story behind this move was more complicated than a simple transition from the commercial to the subsidised sector.

Peggy had been asked by George Devine to play the dual role of Shen Te/Shui Ta in the summer of 1955. Brecht had given his full approval. But, very shortly after, Binkie Beaumont rang Peggy to say 'Darling, I've got a marvellous play for you which I think you'll be very interested in. *The Good Woman of Setzuan* by Brecht.' Peggy told him, 'I'm terribly sorry, Binkie, I've already said I'll do it at the Royal Court.' 'Oh dear,' said Binkie, 'missed the boat.' End of conversation.

'But then,' says Peggy, 'what happened was that between our meeting with the Brechts in Berlin and our doing it at the Royal Court, Brecht himself died and his agents played the Royal Court up rotten, because they had tumbled to the fact that they had got a West End manager after the play. Binkie behaved extremely

164

honourably both towards them and towards us. He told the Brecht estate: "No, the Royal Court have asked for it first, I have no interest in it now, that's gone." But the Brecht estate were very difficult and in the end reluctantly had to accept the contract with the Royal Court.' So much for the notion that West End managers are exclusively interested in money and Marxist estates solely motivated by art.

For Peggy, playing Brecht was a learning experience. It required her to act part of the time in a half-mask, to sing, to find new ways of looking at a character without jettisoning traditional acting techniques. At its most basic level, Brecht's play is the story of Shen Te, a good-hearted prostitute, who invents a tight-fisted capitalist male cousin, Shui Ta, to protect her tobacconist's shop from parasites: she cannot remain good and survive. But, within the framework, there are numerous ironies. Shen Te's lover earns promotion in Shui Ta's sweatshop by refusing to accept more money than is his due and is therefore regarded as an ideal worker. And there is a great scene when Shui Ta is accused of murdering the prostitute and is told 'You were her greatest enemy.' To which he replies 'I was her only friend.' Of course, the play is a Marxist parable about the power of ruthlessness and the impotence of virtue. But, as Eric Bentley whose translation was used at the Court, has pointed out, it also dramatises the divided nature of Brecht himself, and perhaps of humanity in general. As Bentley once wrote, the characters 'express such a division for all of us and the tendency thereto which exists *in* all of us.'

It is easy to forget how little Brecht had been seen in Britain at this time. There had been fleeting amateur productions. Joan Littlewood had staged (and played) *Mother Courage* in Barnstaple in 1955, Sam Wanamaker had directed *The Threepenny Opera* at the Court itself in 1956, and the Berliner Ensemble had imported three productions to the Palace Theatre that summer. But, to all intents and purposes, Devine, Peggy and the whole Company (including Joan Plowright, John Osborne, Rachel Kempson, Robert Stephens and John Moffatt) were making a leap in the dark in that autumn of 1956. What they did have to go on were Brecht's copious theories and his much-discussed and much-misunderstood *Verfremdungseffekt* (alienation effect). Historically,

this was a corrective to the tendency towards a rhetorical romanticism in German acting. Intellectually, it was based on the idea
of encouraging the spectator to adopt an attitude of enquiry and
criticism in his approach to a play. Brecht didn't want the actors
to plunge the audience into a world of false illusion or to sweep
them away by displays of temperament. Writing in 1940, he
put it this way: 'The actor does not allow himself to become
completely transformed on the stage into the character he is
portraying. He is not Lear, Harpagon, Schweik: he shows them.
He reproduces their remarks as authentically as he can; he puts
forward their way of behaving to the best of his abilities and
knowledge of men; but he never tries to persuade himself (and
thereby others) that this amounts to a complete transformation.'
That is the essence of Brecht's 'alienation effect.'

This was contrary to everything Peggy had been taught as an
actress and to thirty years of practice. Except that it wasn't. For
what Peggy grasped intuitively is what many actors and actresses
have discovered since: that even in Brecht the actor or actress still
has to comprehend the character's governing purpose and project
his or her emotions with maximum truth. Sam Wanamaker
astutely remarked of Helene Weigel's great performance in
Mother Courage that she was indistinguishable from a superb
Stanislavsky-trained actress. Peggy quickly learned whilst
working on Brecht that he does the alienation for you.

She recalls: 'I did actually put this question to Helene Weigel
because she came over in our last week of rehearsal at the Court
to see if she could be of any assistance which was wonderful for
us. I said please tell me, am I right in thinking that we've really
got to be as totally three-dimensional as we possibly can, that one
doesn't do alienation on one's own, that it is done by the writing
of the play and presentation. She said in her view that is so. And
if you think of her Mother Courage it was totally human. By the
end you knew all about that woman.'

Jocelyn Herbert, who worked on the designs for the production with the East German Teo Otto, and who has become a
close friend of Peggy's, believes it was less the Brechtian method
than the ideology which sometimes fazed her: 'I remember she
was very nervous about the whole thing. But once she accepts
something she does it whole-heartedly. She believes totally in the

humanity of the play but I think she drew back slightly when it became politically dogmatic. Shen Te, for instance, sings The Song of Defencelessness when she puts on Shui Ta's mask and cries "You can only help one of your luckless brothers by trampling down dozens of others." I remember the composer Paul Dessau coming to the dress rehearsal and saying to her "No, No, you must get it over" and Peggy got so angry that she put it across with real vigour and it was electrifying. It was very funny but she hardly ever did it like that again. She was brilliant in the play. But there was something in Brecht's message that was alien to her. I've often noticed that. Humanly, she is always for the underdog and the oppressed. But when things are too overtly political in a doctrinaire way, she withdraws.'

Devine's production, after a ludicrously short period of rehearsal by European standards, opened at the Royal Court on 1 November 1956. It did respectable business: 59 per cent of financial capacity which, for the Court's first season, was fair going. But the production had the misfortune to coincide with the Hungarian Revolution, which was not the best time to be putting on the work of a Marxist dramatist. It also had to contend with some brutally patronising and dismissive reviews. The critics' strictures on Devine's production were doubtless justified: it was, if anything, too slavishly Brechtian, following the rule-book rather than the natural impulses of the English style. But the attitude to Brecht himself was dismally condescending, with one critic explaining that Brecht had to write for an audience of 'overgrown children incapable of consecutive thought', which might have come as news to the patrons of the Zurich Schauspielhaus where the play was first presented in 1943.

Kenneth Tynan in the *Observer* was virtually alone in understanding what Brecht was driving at ('A fallacy has been exposed: that of seeking to be perfect in an imperfect society'). He also raised the fascinating point that Brecht's famous alienation effect was a dam constructed to keep his own violent human sympathies in check. But even he was politely dismayed by the dawdling production and his attitude to Peggy's performance was basically one of 'Liked him – hated her.' He wrote: 'Peggy Ashcroft in the taxing central role is only half-way fine. As Shui Ta, flattened by a tight half-mask which helps her to produce a grinding nasal voice, she is superb: nothing tougher has been heard since Montgomery last harangued the troops. Yet her Shen Te won't do: sexily though she blinks, all hints of whorishness are expunged by those tell-tale, prim Kensingtonian vowels. What remains is a portrait of Aladdin as it might be sketched by Princess Badroulbador.'

Jocelyn Herbert concedes that Tynan's review had an element of truth: Peggy doesn't naturally play anyone vulgar and she was better as the man because she found herself liberated by the half-mask. In Miss Herbert's experience, this often happens. Eight years later she worked on Tony Richardson's production of *Saint Joan of the Stockyards* and found that the final chorus only took off when the cast were put into masks; they relaxed and felt they weren't being seen. Regarding *The Good Woman*, she says astutely: 'There is always something of Peggy in everything she plays. When she put on the mask, she was totally brilliant. When she was a woman, she was still a little bit Peggy.' For Peggy herself, the role was 'an adventure' worth undertaking. She also, by the force of her example, established a vital bridge between the West End and the pioneer work at the Court, one over which Olivier was shortly to tiptoe with dazzling finesse in *The Entertainer*. But, as so often, Peggy was in at the beginning.

Given that Peggy is a natural pioneer, it may seem a sign of retreat that almost as soon as she finished her stint at the Court she set about preparing for the 1957 season at Stratford (now under the sole direction of Glen Byam Shaw) where she was to play Rosalind and Imogen. Wasn't she, at 49, a bit mature to be playing two of the golden girls she had first tackled at the Old Vic a quarter of a century previously? And wasn't the Glen Byam Shaw period at Stratford what Sally Beauman in her book, *The Royal Shakespeare Company*, harshly calls 'a caretaker regime'?

These criticisms overlook several things. One is the enormous affection in which Peggy was held by the Stratford public. I was present at the last night of the 1956 Stratford season when the late Emlyn Williams made an elegant verse speech in which he held out the promise of 'an Ashcroft spring'. There was a delighted intake of breath followed by a huge burst of applause.

As for the eternal question of whether or not age is relevant in Shakespeare, the only truthful answer is that there is no inflexible rule in the matter. Gielgud was 41 when he gave his last Hamlet. Redgrave was 50 when he played the role at Stratford the following year and encompassed more of the character than any actor I have seen before or since. In contrast, I have seen young players fresh out of drama school who lacked the inner vitality and vocal resonance to measure up to the great parts. Peggy's own view is that weight is more of a handicap than age, and she still winces at the recollection of the first Portia she saw who looked like an upended Chesterfield and who couldn't convince her that 'My little body is a-weary of this great world.' Costume is also a great camouflage. As Rosalind, Peggy was cunningly accoutred by Margaret Harris in leather jacket, breeches and boots to disguise the fact that slim boyishness was not perhaps her first attribute. Peggy sanely argues that if a role is within your 'imaginative compass' then an audience will accept you.

To those who suggest that Glen Byam Shaw from 1957 to 1959 was just carrying out a holding operation and that productions were marked by increasing lifelessness, predictability of design and lack of company playing, I can only report that that is not how it seemed at the time. Those were the seasons of Peter Hall's productions of *Cymbeline* and *Twelfth Night*, of Tony Richardson's *Pericles*, of Tyrone Guthrie's *All's Well that Ends Well*, of Peter Brook's *Tempest* and of great performances such as Peggy's Imogen, Gielgud's Prospero, Redgrave's Hamlet and Benedick, Olivier's Coriolanus. It is true that the company disbanded at the end of each season, though there were occasional London transfers or foreign tours. But when one looks back at the programmes for the 1957 season what is impressive is the all-round strength: Richard Johnson, Alec Clunes, Robert Harris, Clive Revill, Patrick Wymark and Mark Dignam were amongst the lead players while names like Julian Glover, Eileen Atkins and Toby Robertson crop up amongst the Lords and Ladies. The foundation of the Royal Shakespeare Company had a certain artistic and historic inevitability, but it would be foolish to write off the years that preceded it as a mere time-filling interlude.

Glen Byam Shaw's own virtues as a director were clarity, lucidity and narrative drive. Partly that was conditioned by external factors: the Stratford curtain in those days had to come down by 10.30 because of the curfew imposed by public transport. But Mark Dignam remembers him as a man who did meticulous preparation and who used every minute of the four-week rehearsal period to the full. Peggy passionately believes that he was a very fine director and infinitely more than a caretaker. 'He would always at the first reading start off with a statement about the play and then elaborate on every single character and then take us off to look at the set and costumes.' It was, if you like, a traditional way of working, but the complexity of staging a Shakespeare play in a month allowed little time for introspective analysis. Perhaps his greatest virtue was that he saw himself as the 'pre-audience' for the play: hence his capacity to tell a story quickly.

Rosalind, whom Peggy played in Byam Shaw's opening production of *As You Like It*, has never been one of her favourite Shakespeare parts. It is amusing to find her writing to George Rylands in the course of rehearsal: 'Rosalind is a wonderful girl but I wish she didn't talk *quite* so much.' But what she brought to the role – and she was admirably partnered by Richard Johnson as a virile Orlando – was a passionate sincerity. When she cried, 'But what talk we of fathers when there is such a man as Orlando?' it was with the moonstruck rapture of one fathoms-deep in love.

This seems to me the crucial test of any Rosalind. Do you actually believe she is smitten by Orlando? I have seen Rosalinds lately who look as if they would much rather have a good natter with Celia about the works of Betty Friedan or Kate Millett than waste their time in the arduous business of wooing. There is also the Restoration Rosalind who enjoys raillery for its own sake and the hoydenish thigh-slapper who looks as if she is awaiting the arrival of Dick Whittington's Cat. Peggy had the feverish vivacity of the woman in love. Derek Granger put it eloquently in the *Financial Times*: 'The shades of fancy and wonder which cross her face at the moment of falling in love are as sweetly defined as the light and shower of April weather; and, even in between the lines, her little starts and hesitations as her heart sways her carry the charming import of a woman becoming joyfully enslaved.' Only Kenneth Tynan was less than enchanted; he found her too 'daughter-of-the-late colonel-ish', which somehow suggests Hedda Gabler down in the Forest of Arden.

On 28 April – two weeks after the opening of *As You Like It* – Peggy and John Gielgud with Natasha Litvin at the piano were scheduled to do an Apollo Society recital of poetry and music. It is fascinating how eagerly Peggy threw herself into these recitals even while she was busy grappling with Rosalind. In a letter to George Rylands in early April, she outlines the shape of the programme: dialogues from Milton, Webster, Dryden and Fry in the first half, a mixture of Shakespeare and Beethoven in the second half. But what Shakespeare to choose? 'I'm unable to make a selection,' Peggy writes. 'I read your book and want to do it all but as my old brain is rather creaking under the pressure of Rosalind I'm feeling rather anxious about it. I go home on Saturday and then have four days in London in which to hatch the music with Natasha and then present John with the programme.' But typically, on top of the desire to get the recital right there is also the hope that 'darling Dadie' will come to Stratford and play some croquet and talk to her about *Cymbeline*.

In addition to all this, in 1957 Peggy was asked to serve on the artistic committee of the English Stage Company at the Royal Court, which meant frequent meetings in London. But she was – and is – a great enthusiast. She also likes to see her enthusiasm shared by others. That summer the Queen and Prince Philip paid one of their relatively rare visits to Stratford to see *As You Like It*. Mark Dignam recalls: 'Glen introduced us all. I was on the extreme left and they made their entrance on the side of the stage we hadn't expected so Duke Frederick and the Banished Duke were the first people spoken to. The last were Peggy and Richard Johnson. When they'd finally finished their conversations, Peggy cried out, "Well come again, won't you", which had just the faintest undertone of "I probably don't think you will."'

They didn't, as far as I know, come back later in the season to see Peggy playing Imogen in *Cymbeline*. More's the pity. Shaw may have called the play 'stagey trash', Dr Johnson may have dubbed it a tale of 'unresisting imbecility', but Peggy's performance, instinct with impetuosity and grace and the very embodiment of a heartfelt fidelity, was one of the finest I have ever seen her give.

In many ways, the real significance of that *Cymbeline* for Peggy was that it marked the start of a personal friendship and a working relationship that was to dominate the next twenty-five years of her career. The production was directed by Peter Hall, a chubby-featured, 25-year-old visionary – half his leading actress's age – who already had a remarkable track-record. His production of *Waiting for Godot* had not only introduced Beckett to London but also defined the outline of that play for a generation to come: he treated the two major characters as itinerant *clochards* though there is nothing in the text that specifies that. He had also worked in the West End (*Gigi* and *The Waltz of the Toreadors*), directed his first opera (*The Moon and Sixpence*), formed the International Playwrights Theatre (for whom he directed *Camino Real*) and made his Stratford début (with a rather chilly, formal *Love's Labour's Lost*). Even in 1955 when he first met Anthony Quayle and Glen Byam Shaw, at the end of lunch Quayle turned to his colleague and said 'That's the next director of the Stratford theatre.' At the time, however, that was a well-kept secret. To Peggy, at the time of *Cymbeline*, Hall was the new generation whom she was eager to work with. To him, she was faintly awesome but also a decisive influence on his working methods as a young director, as he reveals:

'She was the first of the great actors I worked with. I approached her with enormous trepidation. I talked to her a lot before we began. It doesn't alter the fact I was very scared. But I have to tell you a long, boring story. When I came into the theatre directors were supposed to block the moves in the privacy of their own room with a model of the set and some tin soldiers they moved around. The test of being a director was whether you could block the play in the first week of rehearsals. That was thought to be professional. You gave the moves and the actors took them down and did them. It's a way of saving time and it means the director has done his homework. But it's the most arbitrary and deadening way of working because it means the actors are being put into a revival that was originally created in the director's head. I may think my tin soldier looks very nice moving in a certain line and making a certain shape on the stage but a human being is very different. One of my main quarrels with opera is that a director is there to give the moves. But a move done by one person is quite different to the same move done by someone else.

'Anyway, I'd done my homework. By Friday afternoon of the first week I was on the last scene. The last scene in *Cymbeline* has 17 anagnorises: discoveries not known before. Shakespeare obviously delighted in this but it's a beast to stage. There was a moment when I said "Dame Peggy, on this line you should move right across the stage." She moved across the stage, wrote it down and I thought at the end of the week I shall have got through it. I'd just started on the next move when she said "Pete" (I may say she's the only person who calls me Pete – I can't bear being called Pete except by Peggy Ashcroft) "Pete, that move is wrong, I can't do it." I said "But you've got to be over there because this is a terribly difficult scene and if you're not over there, the whole of the next 15 pages is going to be wrong." She said "But it's the wrong move – I can't do that." I remember thinking do I say from the height of my 25 years that you've got to do it, otherwise the whole thing is in chaos. Or do I say all right, let's tear up the whole thing and go back to the beginning. In fact, I tore the whole thing up and started again.

'She was right. It was arbitrary. It was a pattern. When I say I never block a play, I have to know what the physical life of a scene will be and I have to know that the exits and entrances are right and that the furniture's right. I have to have a basic structure. But nowadays I never give moves. I just watch the actors and suggest something and say I like that or I don't like that. But actors must always feel they've invented it. Peggy would say there is nothing worse than a director who doesn't know what he wants and can't stage a scene. It's a case of having enough confidence to work on the actors and use their responses that she taught me. It started a whole new method for me.'

Peggy changed Hall's working methods. But his production also had the advantage of a strong visual concept. He took a play that was normally seen (when it was seen at all) as a hodge-podge and turned it into an adult and sophisticated fairy-story. Lila de Nobili's romantic, stage-filling set comprised three huge trees (based on existing Stratford oaks), a Gothic palace, an eroding grotto, an Italianate banqueting-hall, ivy-hung turrets and distant woodlands. But within this fairy-tale world – where staircases curled in enticing cracks – serious emotions were on display. Imogen became the epitome of all the virtues. Iachimo (Geoffrey

Keen) and Cloten (Clive Revill) symbolised different aspects of lust: Iachimo's lust was the embodiment of sex in the head, while Cloten was a Jacobean angry young man whose lust was bestial and horrifying.

Peggy's Imogen, as Maurice Baring once wrote of Catullus, combined the three great lyrical factors: passion, pathos and grace. When she cried 'Oh, for a horse with wings', the ecstasy of her passion seemed to linger in the air. As T. C. Worsley noted in the *New Statesman*, she also revealed her capacity to do some things better than any actress living 'like her little run forward to reveal herself to her husband in the final recognition scene.' She even surmounted such difficulties as the scene where Imogen wakes up next to the headless corpse of Cloten and a costume as Fidele that aroused memories of Little Lord Fauntleroy and the Earl of Dorincourt.

The production itself received mixed notices. Not so Peggy's Imogen. Alan Dent said, 'She moves with the moon's soft pace.' J. C. Trewin described her as 'a rapturous creature taking the verse in quick ecstatic rushes.' The one raspberry came from Kenneth Tynan, who wrote in the *Observer*: 'I was prepared to be entranced by Peggy Ashcroft's Imogen until I began to be obsessed by this actress's ocular mannerisms. We all know that she blinks: it was my misfortune to discover that her blinks coincide with the words she intends to emphasise. Having spotted this trick, I watched only for her blinking and am thus in no position to assess her performance.' It was a cruelly cavalier dismissal of a performance that seemed the spirit of beauty and truth. But Simon Callow makes a shrewd point in his biography of Charles Laughton when he says that Tynan was always looking for an interpretation. Laughton, he remarks, was never able to satisfy him, 'just as Tynan could never appreciate the great genius of Peggy Ashcroft, stemming as it did from an overflowing radiance of soul.'

I saw her performance three times that summer at Stratford. To me her Imogen not only defined the way the character should be played but seemed the exemplar of female constancy. Proof that I am not alone came when Ian McKellen described in the *Observer* in 1986 some of the performances that had shaped his career. 'In 1957,' he wrote, 'I saw Peggy Ashcroft in *Cymbeline*.

The beauty and grace of her Imogen was so overpowering that I fancied it was all for my benefit alone. I had seen Dame Peggy up close when I got her autograph and knew that she was, in life, old enough to be Imogen's mother. But from the back of the stalls, she was essential youth in voice and gesture: "Accessible is none but Milford way" – the tune still plays in my ear as it hung in the air when she floated off upstage left. I think I realised that Imogen is a great part – but how did Ashcroft do it? This divinity was beyond what I knew of acting. It made no connection with my own clod-hopping efforts.'

How she did it, as McKellen says, is hard to define. But her Imogen was proof of the transubstantiation of great acting in which the performer simply becomes the character.

On-stage Peggy was caught up in enchanted worlds: the forest of Arden or Lila de Nobili's fairy grotto. Off-stage, she was very much involved in good theatrical causes, nipping up to London for meetings at the Royal Court or organising a letter from members of the Stratford company protesting at the demolition of the St James's Theatre and pointing out that since the war between 80 and 90 theatres in Britain had either been demolished or put to other uses. In rehearsal Peggy is a doer, not a talker. The same might be said of her work in the public sphere. She is not one of those actors who sits around in pubs moaning into their beer about the state of things in the theatre and the world at large. Wherever possible, she gets up and does something.

One bonus of returning to Stratford in 1957 had been the chance to work with Peter Hall. The following year she was thrilled to receive from him the script of a documentary drama by Robert Ardrey, *Shadow of Heroes*, that dealt with events leading to the Hungarian uprising of 1956. It gave Peggy the chance to combine a major role, as Julia Rajk, with some feeling of contributing to public understanding of recent events. 'It was,' as she says, 'of the moment. Here we were being given the chance to do a play about recent events and existing people: in my case, a woman in prison and an exile.'

Ardrey's play dealt with Hungary's political plight from 1944 to 1956. It showed the Communist underground leader, Lazlo Rajk, and his wife Júlia being arrested by the Nazis and imprisoned. It developed the theme of the post-war conflict between

Rajk and his opponent, Janos Kadar, portrayed as a Stalinist Party functionary, which culminated in the former's arrest and execution. It went on to show Julia Rajk's speech to the Petofi Club in October 1956 that helped to initiate the revolution and led to her arrest and imprisonment by the Soviet authorities after the Russian tanks had moved in.

Shadow of Heroes was not great drama. But it was a significant link in an important theatrical movement. In its treatment of real events, it harked back to the Living Newspaper Unit that flourished briefly in New York from 1935 to 1939 as part of the Federal Theatre Project. It also anticipated the Theatre of Fact that was to gain ground in England in the 1960s and that brought plays about Vietnam, J. Robert Oppenheimer and the House Un-American Activities Committee to our stages. It was an exciting and vigorous movement. But Kenneth Tynan – one of its chief champions – raised two crucial qualifying points in his sympathetic notice for Ardrey's play: that the invented dialogue must ring as true as the known facts and that facts in the theatre 'come to be equated with truth' because of our customary willing suspension of disbelief. The durability of these doubts was proved by the row surrounding the Royal Court's projected production in 1987 of Jim Allen's *Perdition*, which alleged that Hungarian Zionists acted in collusion with the Nazis over the despatch of Jews to the concentration camps.

Ardrey's play circumvented many of the problems inherent in documentary theatre by using a narrator (Emlyn Williams in tweed overcoat and muffler) to spell out which events were authenticated and which were not. He also used a very Brechtian distancing device. Thus Peggy was said to 'speak for' Julia Rajk, Moegens Wieth to 'speak for' Lazlo Rajk and Alan Webb for Janos Kadar. But, as in her experience of Brecht at the Royal Court, Peggy still found one had to give the character as much reality as possible. She made contact with a friend of Julia Rajk's who lent her some of Mrs Rajk's clothing. She also studied a photograph in which Mrs Rajk held her son in her arms, enfolding him in an oilskin: Peggy copied the gesture on stage. Peggy's great fear was that the presentation of the play would jeopardise Mrs Rajk's life; she only went ahead when assured that Mrs Rajk wanted her story told through the play.

For Peggy, an increasingly *engagé* actress, there was an edge of excitement about doing a play that dealt with fact rather than fiction. But there was also the awesome responsibility of playing a living, suffering woman and periodic reminders of the reality of events depicted on stage. Two weeks into the run at the Piccadilly Theatre there was a special performance attended by 20 Hungarian freedom fighters who had fled the country after the abortive uprising. Also present was Dr Edith Bone, who for more than seven years had occupied the basement prison reconstructed on stage. At the end of the performance, the Hungarian émigrés went backstage and presented Peggy with a wreath. It was all she could do to withhold her tears.

Critical opinion was divided about Peggy's performance and her handling of the vital speech at the Petofi Club on 23 October 1956 that helped to inspire the uprising. Kenneth Tynan felt 'there is not that iron in her soul that must have existed in Julia Rajk's.' Conversely Kenneth Hurren in *What's on in London* claimed that she conveyed 'much, if not all, of the hard passion and wearied desperation of Rajk's wife and widow.' But it seems bogus to award points for and against her performance. What was remarkable was that Peggy Ashcroft – a Dame of the British Empire – was giving what I suspect was the first ever sympathetic portrayal of a Communist heroine on the West End stage. She was also participating in a production, directed with Brechtian spareness and simplicity by Peter Hall, that presented a conflict between those who saw the Communist party as an instrument of progress and those who used it as a band wagon to which they must cling for personal motives. Ardrey's play may not have been great drama. But it at least forced audiences and critics to address a matter of historical substance and find out more for themselves. That is the perennial challenge presented by the Theatre of Fact.

Shadow of Heroes enjoyed only a brief run at the Piccadilly. But in the last year of what for Peggy was an amazing decade, her passion for worthwhile causes, both theatrical and humanist, manifested itself more strongly than ever.

In February 1959 she joined the leaders of the theatrical profession in writing a letter to *The Times* forcefully urging the government to implement the 1949 National Theatre Act. The letter also backed up a highly original suggestion made in the Commons by Sir Hamilton Kerr, 'that the £750,000 set aside for cultural purposes in the Television Act of 1954 and which it is understood the Independent Television Authority has never called upon' be diverted either to the building of the National Theatre or its running costs. This anticipated the 1986 Cork Report's radical proposal that a levy be imposed on television companies and their profits to subsidise the theatres on which they depended for talent. Why shouldn't those who live off the theatre put something back into it? In March Peggy was a signatory to an ad in *The Times* urging support for Christian Action's Defence and Aid Fund to safeguard freedom and dignity in Southern Africa in connection with the South African treason trial. She was in good company: Benjamin Britten, Canon Collins, Trevor Huddleston, Henry Moore, J. B. Priestley, Stanley Spencer and Arnold Toynbee were amongst her co-signatories. Peggy now likes to play down her increasingly public role. She says that it is only alphabetical accident that ensures her name usually appears at the top of letters of protest thus making her appear the chief begetter. But the fact is that over the next three decades Peggy increasingly gave her support to any cause she deemed worthy.

She also did some acting in 1959. She went out on the road together with Eric Porter in a play by J. M. Sadler, *The Coast of Coromandel*, that never came to London – wisely, in the view of one observer, who found Peggy's portrayal of a lower-middle-class woman none too convincing. She was teamed with Porter again in November in a Royal Court revival of Ibsen's knottiest play, *Rosmersholm*. Somewhat ironically, in view of her own increasing commitment, Peggy found herself playing the heroine, Rebecca West, in the work where Ibsen forgoes his battle for social good and closes his account with political radicalism. That did not stop her capturing the 'controlled power' and 'quiet determination' that Ibsen called for in the actress playing Rebecca even if she missed, maybe due to the production, that final hint of triumphant irrationality required by the extraordinary conclusion.

Peggy and Devine had talked in *Hedda Gabler* rehearsals of 'digging potatoes.' In *Rosmersholm*, they found a whole field of them waiting to be ploughed up. Essentially, the play is about the power of the past over the present. Rebecca is the young housekeeper for John Rosmer, an idealistic, widowed Norwegian pastor. She loves him and he her. She actively encourages his democratic plans and his dream of liberating the minds of his fellow-countrymen. But halfway through the play he discovers that Rebecca has driven his first wife, Beata, to drown herself by hinting untruthfully that she was pregnant by him. The ruthless Rebecca is undeterred. Then she learns that the man whom she had assumed to be her guardian and with whom she once had an affair was, in fact, her father. She refuses Rosmer's offer of marriage. Unable to be united physically, they join forces spiritually by throwing themselves into the mill-race while the old housekeeper, looking on, says 'The dead woman has taken them.'

That is the bald outline. But where to find the essential key to Rebecca's character? For Peggy the answer lay partly outside the text itself. 'I discovered that Ibsen had been much influenced by the psychological theories of a man called Jensen who was a precursor of Freud. But it was Leonard Woolf who gave me a copy of Freud's famous essay about the play, *Character Types*. I immediately discussed it with George and said I wanted to make it the centre of my interpretation. Rebecca has loved Rosmer as a free woman. Then she discovers that Dr West, with whom she had an affair, was her father. She can't reconcile her ideas about freedom and her love of Rosmer with what she has done in the past. I think it's guilt that leads her and Rosmer to the mill-race. They are expiating their sins.'

On a first reading of the play Peggy had not spotted the incest-motif, and George Devine apparently didn't know the Freud essay until Peggy introduced him to it. They fell upon it with delight. And Mark Dignam, who played the conservative bigot Kroll, remembers an early read-through of the play at Peggy's house in Frognal where Devine read the Freud essay out to the assembled company. But not even Freud's brilliant perception – that Rebecca's daydream of replacing the mistress of the house at Rosmer has been preceded in childhood by a precisely corresponding reality – can ever explain the whole of this baffling play. What also dooms Rebecca is the crushing spiritual inheritance of Rosmersholm itself: 'The Rosmer way of life,' she claims, 'has *infected* me.' And how does one interpret the famous suicidal death-leap? Is it motivated by guilt, as Peggy says? Or is it a sign of Rebecca and Rosmer's new-found moral courage, lifting the play into a different poetic dimension?

It is a fiendishly difficult play to get right. But when Devine's production opened at the Royal Court in late November, in the midst of a particularly mindless London season, the critics treated it as manna from heaven. T. C. Worsley thought it was as near perfection as one was likely to see. Harold Hobson even found a religious message in it with Rebecca, in freeing Rosmer from the shackles of his conscience, acquiring a Christian conscience of her own. But the most thoughtful notice came from Alan Pryce-Jones in the *Observer*. He was one of the few critics to make reference to Freud's essay. He also, while praising Peggy's unfailing intelligence, suggested her performance was too discreetly naturalistic:

'At the very end when she and Rosmer go to their death in the millrace, there is a disordered poetry which eludes her. For if Mrs Rosmer, whom we have never seen, was mad at the moment of her own death, so Rosmer and Rebecca, in their last hour, are mad too. Their death has to be given a cathartic quality in order to make sense of it. In this production, it seems more like the upshot of another calculation rather than an action as poetically right as the drowning of Valhalla at the end of *Götterdämmerung*.'

That articulates my own reaction when I saw the play on its transfer to the Comedy early in 1960. I missed the vital sense of sexual chemistry between Rebecca and Rosmer. I admired Peggy's steely determination without finding in her performance that element of the young witch-wife from near Lapland lit by an internal fire. And the ending seemed, frankly, implausible. Shaw said that the actors in *Rosmersholm* must be able to 'sustain the deep black flood of feeling from the first moment to the last.' But Devine's production struck me as a sane, low-key rational account of a play that ascends into a wild romanticism. In pinning so much on the Freudian explanation of Rebecca's female Oedipus complex, Peggy and her director had missed the character's craving for the razor's edge of excitement. As the theatrical magazine *Encore* irreverently asked: is it true that someone died of boredom during *Rosmersholm* but the relatives hushed it up?

To me, it was one of the rare occasions when Peggy's naturalism seemed insufficient. But that in no way diminishes her astounding track-record in the Fifties. She had played Shakespeare, Sophocles, Ibsen, Brecht, Rattigan, Bagnold and Ardrey. She had moved easily between the West End, Stratford and the Royal Court. She had shaken hands with greatness. But maybe there was a daemonism and ferocity inside her still waiting to be unleashed. As the decade headed towards its close and she headed nightly towards the millrace, she was buoyed up by the knowledge that she was about to take part in an artistic adventure towards which she had been steadily working all her life.

CHAPTER TWELVE

In Comes Company

IN JULY 1958 THE 27-year-old Peter Hall was officially invited to succeed Glen Byam Shaw as the director of the Shakespeare Memorial Theatre. The appointment became public knowledge in November. But it was not until the following month that Hall and Sir Fordham Flower, the Chairman of the Governors, thrashed out a radical plan of action that would drastically change the face of British theatre.

The setting for their meeting was the slightly incongruous one of the Hotel Astoria in Leningrad where the Stratford 1958 company was in the midst of a triumphant Russian tour. The two men talked into the early hours of the morning. They met in an old-fashioned, pre-Revolutionary room filled with dusty Edwardian furniture: somewhat ironically, in view of the fact that their plans were revolutionary rather than evolutionary. The project involved securing a London base for the Stratford company, combining Shakespeare in Stratford with revivals and new plays in London and putting actors, directors and designers under long-term contract. Stratford would be self-supporting. The London theatre would be financed from the reserves built up during the Quayle–Byam Shaw years. When those were depleted, application would be made for state subsidy. But the important point was the creation of a permanent company such as the English theatre, in all its fitful glory, had never seen.

As soon as he got back to London, Hall made his first move towards creating a company. He took Peggy out to dinner after a performance of *Shadow of Heroes*. 'Throughout the meal,' he recalls 'we talked about plays we'd seen and this and that. I didn't dare say what was on my mind. Afterwards I drove her to her car, which she'd parked somewhere else, in my little Ford Prefect. We were driving round Trafalgar Square, and I explained to her the idea of the new company and the three-year contract. I said to her "If you will be the first, that will make it work. Will you do it?" She didn't blink an eyelid. She said "Yes, I'll do it." The fact that we had one of the undisputed leaders of the profession endorsing the whole scheme meant that other actors, other directors followed. The creation of the RSC owes a great deal to her presence. Not just because of the superlative work she did, but because of her moral example. What one forgets is that it was an extremely refusable invitation in that she had played most of the great Shakespeare parts at Stratford already and certainly didn't need Stratford or me. She just believed in the idea.'

From Peggy's point of view, it was certainly an invitation not to be refused: in fact, no proposal from any nervous suitor was more welcome to a willing bride. Her whole professional life – from reading about the Moscow Art Theatre to working with Gielgud at the New, the Queen's and the Haymarket – had been one long quest for a permanent company. Now, at last, it was about to happen. But it would be romantic myth-making to suggest that Peter Hall simply waved a wand and overnight a magical being called the Royal Shakespeare Company came into existence. He did achieve certain things very swiftly. He re-designed the Stratford stage giving it a rake and an apron stage that jutted 15 feet into the auditorium. He initiated the idea of three-year contracts. He secured a lease on the Aldwych Theatre in London. He commissioned new plays on a large scale from Whiting, Bolt, Shaffer and Arden.

But Hall's plans were given anything but a universal welcome. There was considerable opposition from West End managers nervous of his expansionist plans, from audiences in love with Stratford's star-laden Fifties and from actors who took exception to his criticism of existing verse-speaking standards. I recall John

Neville telling an audience at the 1960 National Student Drama Festival that Hall's comments on the speaking of verse 'would be patronising if they weren't so bloody insulting.'

The growth of a company also takes time. Hall's first season at Stratford in 1960, showing the range of Shakespearean comedy through six productions, was marked more by arresting performances and striking directorial concepts than by any sense that we were watching the kind of ensemble that the Duke of Saxe-Meiningnen would have recognised. Hall's own opening production of *The Two Gentlemen of Verona* was pretty to look at but a stylistic hotch-potch in terms of acting, with nothing much uniting such diverse players as Denholm Elliott (fresh from the movies), Derek Godfrey (late of the Old Vic), Frances Cuka (a Shelagh Delaney heroine) and Jack McGowran (exuding Irish wit and charm).

The most radical casting of the season was the pairing of Peggy as Katherina with Peter O'Toole as Petruchio in *The Taming of the Shrew*. She was a 52-year-old classical actress; he was an intemperately exciting 26-year-old with a wild-man reputation and a big London success behind him in *The Long and the Short and the Tall*. On top of this the production was to be directed by a former Fellow of King's College, Cambridge, John Barton, who was making his professional directorial début. It was a combination that could lead either to fireworks or disaster. It also had to overcome an initial stumbling-block: Peggy's instinctive hesitancy about playing Kate.

'The initial casting,' says John Barton, 'was Peter Hall's idea. But Peggy at first said she was much too old and it was a stupid notion. The only way we got her to do it was by agreeing to her idea that she must audition with Peter O'Toole. Peter Hall and I went with the two of them to a London theatre late at night to do a work-out after the curtain was down. It was a wonderful occasion. She flung herself into it. She asked O'Toole which bit of Shakespeare he knew best and they settled on doing the quarrel scene from *Julius Caesar* because Peggy had played it at school with herself and Diana Wynyard as Cassius and Brutus. At the end of it, Peter Hall and I both said "Come on – of course you're not too old." I was struck then, as I always have been, by her liveliness and humanity. She can get very nervous about something. She then has a go and flings herself into it and breaks through that way.'

The production also went through traumas in rehearsal. John Barton, perfectly understandably in view of his inexperience, was not used to the business of getting a show onto the Stratford stage in a matter of four or five weeks. Peter Hall took over rehearsals at a late stage, something that allegedly left him with a guilt-complex about his relationship with his old friend whom he had imported from Cambridge. Be that as it may, the production turned into one of the durable hits of Hall's first season. It also bore what came to be seen later as the hallmarks of Barton's approach to Shakespearean comedy: a blend of wideawake scholarship and unmistakable Englishness. Barton, incorporating lines from the earlier non-Shakespearean source-play *The Taming of a Shrew*, kept Christopher Sly on stage throughout. The whole action took place in the courtyard and snuggery of a thatched-roof country inn. Brian Priestman's music was freely adapted from sixteenth-century airs. Robert Speaight, writing in *Tablet*, sent his heart to the right place when he said: 'The centuries roll back to reveal an England that really was merry; and when Mr McGowran as Sly wandered off after the actors at the end one would not have been surprised to meet him on the road to Canterbury. Here was the world of Chaucer still intact before the virtue of Malvolio had raised its forbidding countenance against cakes and ale.'

Peggy, who knew she was not natural casting for Kate, also vindicated Hall's selection. There was a real rapport between her and O'Toole's knockabout Petruchio. As so often, she also caught the precise gradations of change within a character. At first, in her flame-coloured dress and auburn curls, she was all rampageous anger as she brandished a three-legged stool at her tamer. On the return journey to Padua, she was bright-eyed and humorous as if she had seen the point of Petruchio's tactics: the famous moment when Kate looks to Petruchio to confirm that it is indeed the sun and not the moon that is shining set the house on a roar. And in the final scene she was not so much cowed and acquiescent as liberated from the demon that had first possessed her.

Today virtually every production of *The Shrew* we see is based on this notion: that once Kate has been shown the mirror-image of her own violence by Petruchio she falls headily and madly in love with him and that her final speech of submission is an act of ironic homage rather than literal obeisance. But the stock approach of the 1980s was still something of a novelty in 1960. And it was Kenneth Tynan in the *Observer* who pointed out Peggy's success in re-defining the central role: 'Peggy Ashcroft, in prospect an impossible Kate, confounds prophecy by demonstrating herself ideal for the part; it was her predecessors who were impossible. This is no striding virago, no Lady Macbeth *manquée*; instead we have a sulky, loutish girl who has developed into a school bully and a family scold in order to spite Bianca, the pretty younger sister who has displaced her as father's favourite daughter. Her fury is the product of neglect; Petruchio's violence, however extreme, is at least attentive. He cares, though he cares cruelly, and to this she cautiously responds blossoming until she becomes what he wants her to be. The process is surprisingly touching and Dame Peggy plays the last scene, in which the rival husbands lay bets on their wives' obedience, with an eager, sensible radiance that almost prompts one to regret the triumph of the suffragette movement.'

Almost every critic made the point that Peggy was cast against the grain but had triumphed over the fact; the same point had been made about her Cleopatra and even her Hedda Gabler. But this raises the question of what that grain is. Presumably people meant a certain gracious quietude, plangent pathos and middle-class Englishness. Time and again, however, Peggy has proved that there is no such thing as an 'Ashcroft' type or role. Her whole career is one of confounded expectations in which she proves that she can bend her body and mind to her will or wherever, in the depths of her imagination, the spark of acting genius lies. She doesn't always succeed, as her Shen Te and her Rebecca West showed, and elements of her own personality are invariably present. But she has a wide-ranging imaginative sympathy that allows her to enter into the spirit of all sorts and conditions of people. It is the very quality singled out by her mentor Ellen Terry when she wrote:

'My experience convinced me that the actor must imagine first and observe afterwards. It is no good observing life and bringing the result to the stage without selection, without a definite idea. The idea must come first, the realism afterwards.'

That, in the end, is the seed of all artistic production: the idea must come first.

But if Peggy had to shed years in order to play Kate, she had to put them on for her other role in Peter Hall's first Stratford season, Paulina in Peter Wood's production of *The Winter's Tale*.

At first, the casting came as something of a shock. Here was a star actress playing what is, in effect, a supporting role; and here was the perennially youthful Peggy moving away from the gallery of Shakespearean golden girls into the mature character roles. But then wasn't this what companies were all about? The salutary surprise was to find a character who can all too easily seem a terrible old scold and barking harridan ('old hag', 'mankind witch', 'Dame Partlet' is how Leontes in his madness describes her) endowed by Peggy with profound common sense and practical humanity. It is, I believe, one of her most under-rated performances, maybe because the production opened in late summer and never transferred to London.

Peggy brought to Paulina ferocity, pride, a stiff-backed regal bearing. But there was also a most touching and exquisite pathos in the scene where she shows Leontes his new-born daughter: 'Behold, my lords, although the print be little, the whole matter and copy of the father.' And, in the reconciliation scene between Leontes and Hermione sixteen years on, Peggy epitomised the generosity and sadness of age. She became a kindly fairy godmother in mauve leaning on a ballet-mistress's stick and awaiting her end with a moving resignation: 'I, an old turtle, Will wing me to some withered bough and there My mate, that's never to be found again, Lament till I am lost.' For the second time in the season Peggy had taken a character often played as a ranting virago and found her essential humanity. 'Her age as a woman,' Richard Findlater wrote of Peggy in *Time and Tide*, 'is irrelevant; only her age as an actress counts. Her Paulina is admirably free from the stock granny routines into which middle-aged character actresses stiffen so arthritically when required to wear a few years more. Dame Peggy grows old, as she grows young, to the right point of the right life; projects that life with the authority of the seasoned star; and, what is so important in Shakespeare, projects the *words* as well (which is something that seasoned stars all too often find impossible). To have Dame Peggy in the company is of immense value not only for the plays but for the actors.'

It is worth adding that Wood's production came nearer than any that season to approaching the cool, dry, witty approach to verse-speaking that Peter Hall was after. It owed much to the presence of Eric Porter, stepping in for Harry Andrews as Leontes, who carried the verse with the seemingly effortless ease of a champion weight-lifter. He proved that speaking Shakespeare's lines is often a matter of intelligent stress. 'I charged thee that she should not come about me,' he cried of Paulina, 'I *knew* she would' – finding an unexpected laugh purely through delicate pressure on the active verb.

And that would normally have been that. At the end of a Stratford season the company would annually disperse to seek their fortunes on the open market. But Hall's plan was to keep the basic company together to form the nucleus of the team that would move into the Aldwych in December 1960. The production chosen to launch that historic Aldwych season was Webster's *The Duchess of Malfi* with Donald McWhinnie directing, Peggy recreating the role of the Duchess, Eric Porter as the lycanthropic Ferdinand, Max Adrian as the Cardinal, Patrick Wymark as Bosola and such now distinguished names as Diana Rigg, Roy Dotrice, and Philip Voss amongst the ladies, peasants, madmen and executioners. Once again when a new venture was starting Peggy was there: a permanent creator of landmarks.

At Peter Hall's request, Peggy had no hesitation in going back to a role she had played for George Rylands in 1945. Those in a position to know reckoned she had gained in pathos over the intervening years. My own recollection, seeing the production when it played a preliminary week in Stratford in early December, is that she was tremendous but that McWhinnie's production was a thing of fits and starts and never quite discovered the smoky horror of this disordered Italy. I saw some fine classical playing but little of what Rupert Brooke found in Webster: 'The feverish and ghastly turmoil of a nest of maggots ... Human beings are writhing grubs in an immense night.' But there was always Peggy: poignant, touchingly in love with her steward (Derek Godfrey) and gaining, in her final moments, an extraordinary religious peace. Agate had looked for thunder in her

Duchess and found a not very resounding tinkle. I was struck by the quiet nobility of her performance and the touching awareness of mortality on 'Heaven's gates are not so highly arched as princes' palaces; they that enter there must go upon their knees.' Whoever said that progress in art is progress towards simplicity was speaking the truth.

On 15 December the production opened at the Aldwych, to tumultuous cheers, launching a season that included the Stratford *Twelfth Night*, Giraudoux's *Ondine*, John Whiting's *The Devils*, Anouilh's *Becket*. It was billed initially as the Stratford-on-Avon Company but it established a pattern that in expanded form is still with us today, one that has survived persistent under-funding, government indifference, the hostility of West End managers and quite often that of the Arts Council too (why can't they go back to Stratford where they belong? was often the unspoken cry). What Anthony Quayle had long dreamed of, Hall had made a reality within a year of taking over Stratford.

In her book, *The Royal Shakespeare Company*, Sally Beauman has unravelled the complex theatrical politics of that period and the plans hatched at Olivier's home at Notley Abbey for the whole Stratford operation and the Old Vic to be part of a National Theatre federation. But, as the Stratford company moved to the Aldwych, these plans were being discussed with surprising openness. The morning after *The Duchess of Malfi* opened, the *Daily Telegraph* carried a report from its Theatre Correspondent announcing that the Aldwych had advance bookings of nearly £30,000 and had done a deal of £250,000 with the Keith Prowse organisation, giving it a secure financial base. Peter Hall's response, when asked if the Aldwych experiment would end if the National Theatre were built or well-advanced by the end of the three-year Aldwych lease, now seems surprising: 'Yes, it would. At the Aldwych Theatre we would become part of the National Theatre. We are prepared to give ourselves over to it.' He went on to explain that the Shakespeare Memorial Theatre itself would also come under the National Theatre umbrella and would act as its Midlands centre. The idea – explained in a confidential memorandum from the Joint Council of the National Theatre to the Chancellor of the Exchequer on 9 December 1960 – was in fact to have a National Theatre company that would be divided into three groups: one at a new building on the South Bank, another at Stratford, a third on tour.

It was an unwieldy, bureaucratic scheme and in the end Stratford pulled out of it. It didn't want to sacrifice its autonomy; Fordham Flower and Peter Hall also angrily felt that future subsidy for the Stratford company was being made conditional upon its being part of any National Theatre scheme. But it is fascinating to realise just how much the whole Aldwych operation hung in the balance in December 1960. It is also fortunate that the National and Stratford went their separate ways: this created a climate of competition that has lasted to this day. But the period also produced its minor ironies. As the Aldwych opened, Collie Knox of *Woman's Own* went to interview Peter Hall. 'I see no escape for you,' he said to the young director. 'You must end up Sir Peter Hall.' There was a pause. 'The dark young man,' he continued, 'turned pale but rallied.'

For all the behind-the-scenes uncertainty about the Aldwych's role in future National Theatre plans, the London opening of Webster's play was greeted with huzzahs in the daily papers and raspberries in the two quality Sundays. In the daily press, no-one could resist pointing out that Webster's horror-comic was occupying the stage once given over to Aldwych farces but the significance of the occasion was fully grasped and splashed all over the reviews. On Sunday came a douche of cold water. Kenneth Tynan compared Webster's play unfavourably to Hitchcock's *Psycho* as a catalogue of horror, dismissed the production as noisy and melodramatic and reserved his few words of praise for Peggy, saying that her Duchess 'was more ripely moving than her Haymarket performance of fifteen years ago'. Harold Hobson spent most of his column criticising Hall's choice of play, saying that Webster was dead as a dodo, suggested that Mr McWhinnie deserved 'a few kicks in the stomach' and compared Humphrey Searle's music to 'an unsuccessful effort to break wind'. As for Peggy's Duchess, it was 'at first radiant and later patient but she does not give us the grandeur that Webster doubtless thought was in this woman's soul.'

Naturally enough, Peggy herself believed passionately in the enterprise and in the ongoing vitality of Webster's play. As everyone testifies, she goes through a familiar, recurrent cycle in her approach to an enterprise. Initial doubt; total immersion; last-minute *crise*; protective loyalty towards the role, the company and the play itself. Shortly after the *Duchess* opened, she wrote a friendly, faintly pained letter to George Rylands who had clearly not been overwhelmed by the production but who had singled out a particular speech for praise. '*Hoped* you would have liked more than that,' she writes, 'for I *feel* the part has grown in size as it should having had its earlier production. I would *like* you to see it again when it has all settled but I think you would not want to.' She respected her friend's doubts but felt that maturity had lent weight to her interpretation.

She was also not exactly gruntled by Rupert Hart-Davis's reaction, which he recorded in a letter to George Lyttelton: 'We didn't care greatly for *The Duchess of Malfi*: indeed we were thankful when the last two characters simultaneously stabbed each other and we could escape. Peggy Ashcroft was lovely and the staging superb (some of the best I've ever seen) but the other performers were moderate and the play! The idiocy of Shakespeare's plots is masked and redeemed by the poetry but, except for three or four lines, there is nothing here but rhetoric and wind. Bloodshed and horrors get steadily funnier and more absurd as they multiply. I'm quite glad to have seen it once but please never again.' At the time, she was not aware of the intensity of his reaction. When she read his published letter, she was momentarily furious at his put-down of a play in which she passionately believed.

Peggy's only other engagement in that first momentous Aldwych season was in John Barton's anthology about English monarchs, *The Hollow Crown*. What had started as a private King's College entertainment and a one-off Sunday special for the Stratford company soon blossomed – with the help of ecstatic reviews – into a staple feature of the Aldwych programme. For Peggy, who took over from Dorothy Tutin, the show was a familiar and welcome return to the form of Apollo Society recitals. For John Barton, who over the years slotted 70 actors and actresses into the constantly changing cast, it eventually became something of a nightmare. But it also taught him a certain humility about directorial influence: 'What works for actor A is not necessarily right for Actor B. Peggy and Dotty Tutin were the people who did it most often. Because Dotty went into it first, I couldn't help hearing it through her. But Peggy had, quite rightly, to find her own idiom, her own comedy, her own wit. It made me realise that if you say the same thing to two different actors, the results will be entirely different. I learned that later when I directed *Richard II* with Dicky Pasco and Ian Richardson. I think a director can kid himself how much he influences or moulds actors because one is dealing with that impalpable thing of what makes an actor tick.'

The way Peggy instantly responded to the company idea with no star nonsense is impressive. She took over in *The Hollow Crown* when available. In the autumn of 1961 she also returned to Stratford (where the officially designated Royal Shakespeare Company was now appearing at the Royal Shakespeare Theatre) to play Emilia in Franco Zeffirelli's production of *Othello*. She claims, rightly, that Emilia is not a secondary part, but nor is it the play's central female role. Peggy was happy to play as cast.

Unfortunately, the Zeffirelli *Othello* turned out to be a spectacular disaster. The first night was, as Peggy says, the kind that actors have nightmares about. It ran for over four hours. It had thunderously operatic sets, evoking not only Veronese and Titian but Shakespearean productions of the previous century, which took ages to set up. It had some strange misinformation about the plot, with Ian Bannen's Iago announcing late in the evening that 'Cassio is dead' which he then amended to 'I mean Cassio is almost dead'. It had Sir John Gielgud as Othello with, at one point, some crucial facial hair coming adrift. One reflected that if *Hamlet* was the tragedy of a man who could not make up his mind, *Othello* was here the tragedy of a man who could not make up his beard. In this sad farrago Peggy's Emilia, full of coarse honesty and sharp wit, shone out like a beacon.

Surprisingly, the nature of the impending disaster did not hit the company until they moved out of the rehearsal room onto the Stratford stage. 'John,' Peggy swears, 'was about to give one of the great performances of his life. We rehearsed in the Conference Hall in a very detailed, naturalistic manner treating the play as a domestic tragedy. It was one of the most exciting rehearsal periods I remember in that we were preoccupied with truth and reality. Having been led in one direction, we got on to the stage and then found that we were in the midst of operatic sets that had to be changed in black-outs and that fell over. Also one realised in horror that John in dark brown make-up was going to be seen against a dark brown background. He could have been a superb Othello, bringing out all of the character's nobility. But in the circumstances he had no choice but to succumb to rhetoric. If in 1961 we had had a venue like The Other Place in Stratford, it could have been a tremendous production.'

Zeffirelli in his autobiography gives no hint of the production's potential greatness. He simply relives the experience with amused detachment. He recalls the lack of any real contact between himself, Gielgud and Bannen. He remembers how on the first night one of the huge columns he had set up swung loose on its cable and came perilously to rest against another. He describes the high comedy of the second act where a wall on which someone was sitting suddenly rose unbidden, carrying him aloft like something in a Mack Sennett movie. He adds that he needn't recount what the critics said, but their gentlemanly restraint is surprising. *The Times* headlined its review 'Remarkable Leading Performance'. Somewhat less full-throated was the *Daily Telegraph* heading: 'Gielgud Tries Othello for First Time – Part Unsuited' which was no match for the one they allegedly ran on another production 'Negro Murders Italian Girl'. The *Sunday Telegraph* was nearer the mark with 'Stratford's Black Night'.

The failure of a single production was less disquieting, however, than the fact that in the whole 1961 Stratford season there was only one production – Michael Elliott's famous version of *As You Like It* with Vanessa Redgrave – that lived up to the expectations aroused by the words Royal Shakespeare Company. Peter Hall's great dream – one to which Peggy lent all her authority and style – was beginning to look a little fragile at the end of the 1961 season. Where was the company style? Where was the directorial cohesion? Where was the exemplary verse-speaking for which we had all been looking? Certainly not by the Avon that year.

In the commercial theatre a string of failures spells disaster. The essence of a company system, however, is permanence: you are not thrown onto the street simply because you don't always strike gold. Three months after the *Othello* fiasco, the RSC began to show the form of which it was capable with a production of *The Cherry Orchard* at the Aldwych directed by Michel Saint-Denis. It had been ten years since Saint-Denis had been rudely exiled from the British theatre after the demise of the Old Vic Centre. Hall shrewdly invited the ruminative, pipe-smoking Saint-Denis (perfect casting for Maigret) back to direct the Chekhov play on which he had been working for Binkie Beaumont at the outbreak of war. Then Peggy had been cast as Anya. Now she graduated to the role of the feckless landowner, Madame Ranevsky. Once again, she was also part of a remarkable cast in which the RSC brought together two different generations of players: John Gielgud as Gaev and Patience Collier as Charlotta alongside Judi Dench as Anya, Dorothy Tutin as Varya, Ian Holm as Trofimov.

Opinions differ wildly about the quality of Saint-Denis's production. Many of the original cast speak of it in tones tinged with disappointment, as if they got less from Saint-Denis than they had hoped: others remember it as one of the best post-war English Chekhov productions. Alec Guinness told me that Ian Holm's Trofimov – intense, urgent, on the brink of neurosis – was very much the kind of performance he would like to have given in 1939. And, as I write, moments from the production rise up before me clear as daylight. I see Peggy's wilful, irresponsible, charming, selfish Ranevsky sitting languorously back in her chair totally oblivious to the arthritically aged Firs massaging her foot; Gielgud's sublime Gaev drifting around in a dandified dream apostrophising a bookcase and muttering to himself like a Russian Walter Mitty ('I'm a financier ... pot the red'); and the tears in the eyes of Dorothy Tutin's Varya as she knelt downstage waiting for the proposal from Lopakhin that never comes and then busying herself with domestic chores to hide her emotional desolation.

The reviewers were totally divided about the production. Some thought it sombre and insufficiently funny; others thought too much attention was given to the comedy. Some called it Marxist (presumably because Trofimov was taken seriously); others thought it was rooted in the middle-class Englishness of Torquay. My recollection is that Saint-Denis caught the essential point about Chekhov, which is that his plays are a collision of solitudes in which people marooned in their own private worlds are brought into social contact. People also act out their inner lives in a way that is both farcical and sad. The gigantic Pischik believes he is descended from Caligula's horse; he calls out, astonished at himself, in the middle of a dance that he has had two strokes; he cries like a baby when he says goodbye to his friends. He leaves himself utterly exposed.

What of Peggy's Ranevsky? Too cool, too English, too gracious, as some suggested? I don't think so. She had seen the famous Moscow Art Theatre production when it visited Sadler's Wells in 1958 and, though she had befriended the company, had disliked their Ranevsky: too old-fashioned, mannered and monotonous. Her own performance was marked by that emotional volatility that Tynan had found singularly lacking in her earlier work. Maybe V. S. Pritchett, who wrote a brilliant notice in the *New Statesman*, had a point when he said that Western productions of Chekhov nearly always treated his characters as if they were upper-class Russians out of Turgenev. Maybe Peggy missed something of the character's lethargy. But Pritchett caught her changeability very well: 'The First Act passed off beautifully. It was lovely to watch the players. The tears rose to our eyes and Dame Peggy Ashcroft brought the whole life of an impulsive, shallow, tiresome and feckless woman to the scene. She was nervous and changeable. When she fought back in the speech that derides Trofimov for his chastity and his failure to understand that to love may be to have a genius for unhappiness, she showed great resource. She is an actress in whom intelligence, irritability and sensibility nag – but with great art. When one is almost to be driven mad, she turns and charms.'

What one tends to forget about Peggy, because her public life is so full, is that the hard-working actress always dashing from one role to the next is also the busy Hampstead wife and mother. At one point early in 1962 she writes to George Rylands that she is having to cope with the fact the children are in bed with flu, with her own laryngitis and with two performances of *The Cherry Orchard* that day. The doctor has told her that she must have three days silent and solitary confinement if her voice is to be fit for a television recording of the Chekhov play. There could hardly have been a greater contrast than that between the sentimental indolent muddler Peggy was playing on stage and the practical private woman chafing at her confinement and furious at having to cancel appointments.

In fact, by her own restless standards, Peggy had a relatively quiet year in 1962. She finished the run of the Chekhov at the Aldwych. In June she went to Paris with *The Hollow Crown* where she won the Best Actress Award at the *Théâtres des Nations* international festival. She also took part in another Barton anthology, *The Vagaries of Love* at the Belgrade, Coventry. And, of course, she was active on committees. In addition to her work with the English Stage Company she became a member of the Arts Council: the panel that makes crucial decisions about the principles and practice of funding. She was also busy with myriad smaller activities. Lord Kilbracken, interviewing her in *The Tatler* – a rare event – noted that she had just come from opening a new comprehensive school, appropriately called the Sarah Siddons, at Paddington Green.

But one of her sharpest critics, Kenneth Tynan, had a point when he said of her Madame Ranevsky that she should perhaps for a number of years refuse any part of which graciousness was an essential ingredient. In her mid-fifties, she could easily have settled into a comfortable career playing great ladies. But Peggy has always risen to the challenge of the impossible. Give her something that looks slightly beyond her grasp and she is off and away tearing into it with relish and confounding her critics. Peter Hall late in 1962 was cooking up just such a project: one that was not only to confirm the RSC's world-class credentials but also to tap a new side of Peggy's talent and set her the toughest task of her whole career.

CHAPTER THIRTEEN

In the Wars

THE GENESIS OF *The Wars of the Roses* – in which Peggy might be said to have enjoyed her finest ten hours upon the English stage – really dates back to 1950. Two young men were both reading English at Cambridge: Peter Hall at St Catharine's, John Barton at King's. They knew each other well, acted in each other's productions and shared a common conviction that there was something to be done with Shakespeare's early History plays, for all their bombast and rhetoric. In fact, something was done with them: Douglas Seale staged the *Henry VI* trilogy at Birmingham Rep in the early 1950s and later at the Old Vic. It was a fine but now largely forgotten production.

Hall and Barton went their separate ways in the 1950s. Then at the end of the decade Hall went to see a Cambridge student production of *Three Sisters* (with a cast that included Derek Jacobi and Ian McKellen) directed by Barton: he thought it was one of the finest Chekhovs he had ever seen. He persuaded Barton to abandon the sequestered security of Cambridge and join him at Stratford as Assistant Director, resident scholar and dramaturge. He also suggested to the Governors that Barton should be given a production in his first season: *The Taming of the Shrew* which Hall took over in the last weeks of rehearsal.

That cast a shadow over their relationship. But still the

dream of resurrecting Shakespeare's early History plays from the 1590s persisted. Twice Peter Hall suggested to his co-director at the RSC, Peter Brook, that he tackle the project. Twice Brook refused, saying that it was three years' work. Brook suggested that Hall himself might do them. Hall discussed the idea with John Barton and late in 1962 commissioned his colleague to produce a workable text conflating the three parts of *Henry VI* into two plays ultimately to become *Henry VI* and *Edward IV*. They would be followed, in performance, by *Richard III*.

'The whole of *The Wars of the Roses* came about,' says Barton, 'from the purely practical consideration that the box office wouldn't sustain the complete *Henry VI* trilogy. But when you compress three plays into two, you have to re-shape them to make them two complete works. I felt you had to have a different curve and climax so that people would see Play One and a Half as a complete entity. The further I got into it, the more I found I had to change. There are twenty battle scenes in the whole trilogy and it became obvious that two or three could be telescoped into one. Then in rehearsal major inventions occurred, such as staging the initial scenes at the Council table. I think that was my idea in order to get away from ranting, roaring barons. But, in my opinion, it's how an awful lot of adaptations happen: from a practical theatrical need rather than any lofty aesthetic reason'.

Late in 1962 Barton set to work, with certain pieces of casting clear in his head: Peggy, for instance, had already agreed to play Queen Margaret. But work was delayed when he went to New York with *The Hollow Crown* in 1963 and also suffered an acute attack of bronchitis. Back in London Barton worked from eight in the morning till eight at night slashing, re-writing, adapting. Each evening he and Hall would meet to study the work so far. Barton would write a speech for a dying cardinal ('A man's a dog and dogs do crave a master') three-and-a-half pages long: Hall would take it out. Work continued until early June when rehearsals were due to start in Stratford. Barton delivered the newly titled second part, *Edward IV*, just as the show was about to go into rehearsal. But at the moment when this huge project that would occupy twelve weeks of rehearsal was about to crank into operation, Hall collapsed from a combination of overwork and personal stress. It was Peggy, with the aid of Peter Brook and John Barton, who helped to bring Peter Hall back from the brink and ensure that the show got on the road.

'She's seen me,' says Peter Hall, 'through a lot of terrible crises both personal and professional. The most important one was during *The Wars of the Roses*. I'd been overworking to such a ludicrous extent that I collapsed. My marriage was also breaking up and I was terribly overtired. I was just about to embark on the longest piece of work I'd ever done and the doctor said I must have six months' rest. It was Peggy's doing more than anyone's that Peter Brook came over from Paris and the two of them told me to get back to work. They knew one had to get back on the horse and just do it. Peggy not only had to cope with an enormous part but in the early part of rehearsal had to support me as well. She was amazing – as was John Barton.'

Barton and a young assistant, Frank Evans, kicked off the twelve-week rehearsal process. Hall joined as soon as possible, suffering from desperate lassitude and often conducting proceedings from a couch with a doctor in attendance. For everyone it was a huge undertaking, but Peggy carried one of the biggest burdens of all: moving in the course of three plays from the wilful, alluring, 25-year-old Margaret of Anjou to a wrinkled septuagenarian witch haunting the court of Richard III like a dark chorus.

Peggy is not without a certain obduracy and the directors were hard put to convince her that they were doing an adaptation rather than pure Shakespeare. John Barton recalls that for the first week she carried around her Temple Edition of *Henry VI Part One* and would only say lines that had been written by the Bard himself. Then one day Barton smuggled in a speech he had written, pretending it was by Shakespeare, and convinced her to include it.

'After a week or so,' claims Barton, 'she totally changed. She chucked the Temple Edition away and said "Christ, this is what we're doing, let's have a go at it and let's make it work." That was characteristic. My memory of her is of her being worried about putting her foot in the swimming-pool and then taking the plunge and flinging herself in.'

Another key question was how Margaret should sound. Peggy was convinced that the essential point about Margaret was that she was a Frenchwoman by birth and therefore an outsider in the English court. So to establish her foreignness she adopted a French 'r' sound. Peter Hall, willing to let actors try anything, allowed her to use it all the way through the rehearsal process and then at the dress rehearsal suggested it might go, as it was now unnecessary. Peggy dug her heels in. So it stayed and came to seem a vital symbol of Margaret's permanent sense of alienation. Peter Hall's argument was that if Shakespeare meant people to have foreign accents he invariably wrote them in. And if Margaret has a French accent, then why not Joan la Pucelle? Logic may have been on Hall's side, but he concedes now that Peggy's distinctive 'r' sound was fully assimilated into the characterisation. 'What I think it proves,' he says, 'is that the sound of things is terribly important to Peggy.'

Peggy heard Margaret in her head from the beginning, and never for a single solitary second sounded, as she might have done, like Yvonne Arnaud caught up in unseemly broils between York and Lancaster. But the great mystery of her performance lay not in the transition from youth to age, startling though that was, but in the excavation of hitherto untapped reserves of hate and venom. Up till now Peggy had demonstrated just about every quality in her acting except that of raging, demonic fury. But it had to be there in Margaret; most famously, in the scene in *Edward IV* where the temporarily victorious Margaret captures her foe, the Duke of York, on the plains near Sandal Castle. She insults and humiliates him. She places a paper crown on his head. She then daubs his face in the blood of his dead child with a paper napkin before finally stabbing him. York calls her 'She-Wolf-of-France.' He enquires in genuine perplexity:

Oh Tiger's heart, wrapp'd in a Woman's hide,
How couldst thou drain the life-blood of the Child
To bid the Father wipe his eyes withal,
And yet be seen to bear a Woman's face?
Women are soft, mild, pitiful and flexible;
Thou stern, obdurate, flinty, rough, remorseless.

The scene is horrendous in its cruelty. But where exactly, in an actress renowned for her kindliness and compassion, did the requisite barbarism come from?

Two insights are provided: one by Donald Sinden who played the Duke of York, the other by Peggy herself. When I asked Sinden about that scene he recalled: 'However well you know someone, there comes a moment when you're rehearsing when something changes. One moment it's "Donald would you be awfully sweet and do this?" And then there comes a point when you're not Donald but the character. We do it to each other. So in the death scene of the Duke of York – though we were getting on like a house on fire off-stage – suddenly I could see genuine hate in her eyes. I thought she can't hate me – we've just had a cup of tea together. But the character has completely taken over. So often you don't see it in the eyes. You simply see it in an attitude, a face, a voice. With Peggy you see it in furious close-up.'

Sinden's remark is revealing: it suggests the transformation of an actress through the alchemy of imagination. It doesn't explain *how* it is done. But it suggests there comes a moment in rehearsal when Dame Peggy Ashcroft – a middle-aged Hampstead house-wife and mother – loses the sense of self and mentally and physically becomes Margaret of Anjou *in extremis*. As Ellen Terry said, the actor must imagine first and observe afterwards. The crucial difference between the great and the good actor is that the former always has that transcendent power of imagination.

But Peggy herself explains how the clue to the playing of the scene was intellectual as well as imaginative: that it derived in fact from a vital insight of Peter Hall's.

'Margaret,' says Peggy, 'is a tough cookie. Unscrupulous, devious, unfaithful, a liar, etc. But the daubing of the Duke of York's face with the blood of his son is going pretty far. I didn't justify it, but I understood the ability of a woman who has had the head of her lover, Suffolk, sent to her in a parcel to have a sense of violent grievance which explained many of her actions. One of the most revealing pieces of direction that Peter gave me when we were rehearsing that scene – and of course it's difficult to arrive at the climax – was that the thing to remember is that Margaret is the weak one and that York is the power in that scene. He has the strength of endurance and she does what she does out of hysteria, hatred and violence.'

Peggy discovered the emotional resources; Peter Hall provided the intellectual insight. John Barton, in rehearsal, also made the technical point that if you strike twelve too early in Margaret's long opening harangue to York, it becomes boring and repetitive: the key is not to peak early on but to give the speech light and shade. Clearly it worked. Donald Sinden remembers that, at the first dress rehearsal, he and Peggy gave the scene all they had got, then staggered off the stage and simply collapsed onto a bench. Peggy, emotionally drained in heavy armour, gasped out 'You were best.' Sinden instantly replied 'But you were funniest.' From that moment on, there was an indissoluble bond between them.

Even if that one scene took off, there was little confidence amongst the company at the time that they were in a guaranteed success. The production had been faced with many problems such as the last-minute arrival of the final script and Peter Hall's crisis. The company had been working flat out ten hours a day seven days a week. They were at the point of exhaustion and, after a fiasco of a final dress rehearsal, Peter Hall had to rally his tired troops like Henry V. Would the public take to over six hours of unremitting political gangsterdom? Would the critics accept Shakespeare rewritten and reordered?

The first two parts of the trilogy, *Henry VI* and *Edward IV*, opened at Stratford over a matinée and evening performance on 17 July 1963 (it was not untypical of the RSC to have offered *The Beggar's Opera* at the Aldwych the night before). The company drew on every ounce of reserve energy and the cheering at the end told them that they had a huge success on their hands. The notices the next day confirmed the fact. Bernard Levin in the *Daily Mail* spoke for the majority when he described the production as 'a landmark and beacon in the post-war English theatre and a triumphant vindication of Mr Hall's policy as well as of his power as a producer.'

It was, in every sense, a corporate triumph. If I spotlight on Peggy's Margaret, it was because her performance was marked by an extraordinary growth and development. She began as the auburn-haired French bride of incredible sexiness brushing aside with girlish gestures the embarrassment of her dowry-less arrival in England. From that she moved into the foreign queen, alone and isolated at a remote corner of her husband's council table. She became in the great battle scenes the maddened she-wolf displacing her saintly, ineffectual husband. But perhaps she was at her finest in defeat, encouraging her dispirited followers in their last stand like a lioness while making you feel that the beast inside her was already dead. Here was an actress often associated with the quiet virtues of pathos and grace proving that she had in her the animalism that betokens greatness.

Philip Hope-Wallace came back to the plays in the *Guardian* a few days after he had phoned a breathless overnight piece from a box somewhere on Edgehill. He caught, in his own impressionist style, the sense of a character evolving and changing before our very eyes:

'It is a most marvellous performance by an actress about whom some people now, I notice, voice reservations. None from me. The energy of it for a start: things fairly began to *buzz* every time she came on. It was as if the whole play and everyone on stage took a charge of electricity. Then, the sheer protean range. Gifted with a wonderfully flexible voice (the weakness of the present Henry, the strength of the future Richard III), this actress also has great expressive skill of movement. She first appears as a girl, light of step, looking not a day over 15; wigs and costumes as innumerable as Mary Clare's in *Cavalcade*, lead her on to an old age where the termagant rallies her troops (still with a finely suggested French accent but lesser now in old age), keeping herself alive, one felt, by sheer passion of inner hate. It is one of the most gradually "growing" performances I have seen.'

The success of the productions owed a lot to Peggy – but also to David Warner's lean, gangling, Dostoyevskyan holy fool of a king; to the massive, overbearing pride of Brewster Mason's Warwick the Kingmaker; to the nobility in humiliation of Donald Sinden's Duke of York; to the virtuosity of the staging and the way the huge, iron-clad doors of John Bury's set swung into action like the cruel jaws of a vice; to the sheer *sound* of the two-handed, six-foot long swords scraping the surface of the wire-mesh covered stage; to the brilliant device of the vast diamond-shaped council-table where decisions cooked up in private were publicly ratified. If the productions struck a chord with the public, it was, however, due to something more than the dynamic expressiveness of the staging. It was because at a time of ever-increasing cynicism about the political process (we were, of course, into the twelfth successive year of Tory government in Britain), Shakespeare seemed to anticipate and echo our own disenchantment. He showed us not merely that power corrupts but that you have to corrupt yourself in order to be politically powerful.

But the RSC was not yet out of the wars. On 21 August they completed the cycle with *Richard III*, staging all three parts of *The Wars of the Roses* on a single day. It was the first of five occasions on which they were to do this during the season and it was Peggy herself who was partly behind the idea. When Peter Hall had first broached the idea of the trilogy to her in the autumn of 1962, she jokingly assumed they would be played together occasionally as an Oberammergau-style epic. Hall leapt at the idea and put it into practice. So began the RSC's habit of staging orgiastic theatrical marathons which continued with Terry Hands's production of the *Henry VI* plays in 1977, *The Greeks* and *Nicholas Nickleby*. We have Peggy to thank for setting the marathon business in motion.

Peggy's own performance in *Richard III* was a magnificent extension of what had gone before. This was not the usual, faintly tedious mad Margaret whose moans and curses we barely comprehend. Instead we saw an old, dismayed, barely tolerated figure, her very fingers gnarled with loathing, haunting the court she had once entered as a young, beautiful bride. It was the pathos of this bedraggled figure with her mane of wiredrawn hair that struck us, rather than the cursing insanity. But the character made sense because we had been given the dynastic context. And the same argument applied to Ian Holm's Richard III. Instead of being a solo portrait of ironic villainy, like Olivier's matchless performance, it was a development of what had been seen earlier. Holm grew from the cunning whelp of *Edward IV* into a debauched, snickering psychopath and midget Hitler backed by the tramping iron guards of Catesby. It was a performance that grew steadily in power and that made fullest sense the following year when Stratford presented the whole historical cycle from *Richard II* to *Richard III*: it then became the palpable embodiment of a curse laid upon England ever since the deposition of Bolingbroke, the climax of a cycle of crime and punishment comparable to Greek tragedy.

The Wars of the Roses was a landmark for Peggy as an actress, in that it called upon an untapped demonism and showed that now anything was possible for her. It also required a large-scale gestural acting that made nonsense of the condescending claim that she was simply an exquisite miniaturist. Even for her friends it was something of a shock. Fabia Drake went to see it and came away astonished: 'In my view, it was her finest performance. That Margaret was astonishing. Especially to anyone who knew her gentleness and docility, it was a revelation. One had never seen this passion in her before except in that little girl who dashed in front of the curtain in *Before Sunset* in 1933 and shouted "Go Away". You can use that kind of power and passion in your work and channel it into a vitriolic area. What Peggy showed in this production is that it is the actor's job to advance and expand and never stop.'

Harold Pinter, who had yet to begin a very productive working relationship with Peggy, also saw her Margaret and found it 'pretty staggering'. Describing what makes her special, he says: 'It is her combination of ferocity and tenderness that is singular. Ferocity seems quite an accurate word: it hadn't occurred to me till I said it. But it's to do with an absolute focus and concentration and a kind of immediate insistence on excavation of the moment: a refusal to let it out of her grasp. I think one also detects a very definite vulnerability in her personality on stage: allied to the ferocity, there is a kind of panic that the image will elude her, that it needs a further grasp to sustain the moment.'

But if *The War of the Roses* was a landmark for Peggy, it was also one for the theatre at large. It defined Hall's ideas about the vitality of the company principle and proved the indispensability of the RSC at the very moment, in August 1963, when Sir Fordham Flower was announcing to the Governors an overall deficit of £47,000. In its examination of the nature of violence (someone counted over 40 corpses in the course of the three plays) it paved the way for Peter Brook's Theatre of Cruelty experiments which were to prove so controversial in 1964. And, not least, it restored critical and academic interest in a neglected group of plays.

Peggy herself became one of their most articulate champions. Four years later she wrote an introduction to the Folio Society edition of the original *Henry VI* plays which is full of the practical wisdom of the committed player. She briskly despatches Hazlitt's point that they do little more than show England as a perfect bear-garden. As she says, they reveal Shakespeare's detestation of war, his concept of the Divine Right of Kings and of the curse on all who murder God's anointed and his ambivalent attitude to power. On the question of disputed authorship, she points to the thematic unity of Shakespeare's Histories and suggests that he could not have achieved the mastery of the later Histories without the prentice work of *Henry VI*.

But the voice of the working actress really comes through when she highlights the power of individual scenes and the way they play:

'The scene (Act V, Scene 2) in which Margaret meets Suffolk and in which, through his sudden infatuation, he conceives the idea of making her Henry's wife and his own mistress, is the only scene in which Margaret appears in Part 1. It comes immediately after the brutal capture of Joan and is a marvellous dramatic contrast. It has, I believe, been singled out as one particularly unlikely to be by Shakespeare but to me the daringly contrived scene, witty, sensual and comic, could only be his and is a small glimpse of what is in store with Katherina the Shrew and Beatrice; just as in Part 2 (Act III, Scene 2), in the farewell between Margaret and Suffolk, there is suddenly a spark that will later burn into Antony and Cleopatra.'

All Peggy's devotion to Shakespeare comes out in this 3000-word essay. But if the plays are as good as she persuasively claims, was the RSC right to present them in such a ruthlessly edited form? In later years Peter Hall, taking on the role of militant classicist, has expressed doubts. John Barton remains unrepentant, arguing that if something doesn't quite work, then it is legitimate to alter it because the work will always be done again. *The Wars of the Roses* was invaluable in directing our attention to neglected plays. But only when Terry Hands presented the complete cycle in 1977 did one realise that locked inside it was a panoramic

English masterpiece, traversing all aspects of society, in *Henry VI, Part 2*.

The only problem with *The Wars of the Roses* from the point of view of Peggy and other cricket-buffs within the company was that it clashed with an enthralling Test series between England and the West Indies. Stratford legend has it that she solved the problem at one performance (in pre-Sony Walkman days) by wedging a tiny transistor under Margaret's battle-helmet so that she could hear the score and replay it, at appropriate moments, to her army.

Cricket also provided some necessary relief to the nightly battles of York and Lancaster. Neville Cardus once described a famous Roses match as 'a rack of torture upon which we were stretched hour by hour.' The season must have felt a bit like that at times to the company. So, ten days after all three productions had been safely installed in the repertoire, Peggy fixed up a cricket match between the rival factions of York and Lancaster at Stratford's Manor Road ground. It was in aid of the World Freedom from Hunger Campaign. Cyril Washbrook was invited to captain the Lancastrians, Sir Leonard Hutton the Yorkists. Peggy opened the batting for her side, Janet Suzman went in first for the opposition while John Barton umpired with a couple of coronets perched on his head and J. B. Priestley, Neville Cardus and Robert Robinson supplied the commentary.

It was a light-hearted affair, but Peggy to this day proudly recalls that she once opened the batting with Cyril Washbrook of Lancashire and England before being bowled out by Len Hutton for 16. In terms of achievement, it may not quite rank in the history books with her performance as Margaret of Anjou, which many of us would argue was the greatest of her career, but it says a lot about this extraordinarily reticent and modest woman that it's about the one thing in her whole life I've ever known her to boast of. On the other hand, perhaps it just proves Harold Pinter's point that cricket is God's greatest invention.

CHAPTER FOURTEEN

Modern Times

PEGGY WAS NOW 56: a dangerous time for any actress, when the prospect ahead might seem to contain Ladies Bracknell and Wishfort, the Nurse in *Romeo and Juliet* and a nice revival of N. C. Hunter at the Haymarket. But the startling fact is that, after the palpable triumph of her Queen Margaret, Peggy became *more* adventurous, not less; ever hungrier for new experiences rather than content to rest on her laurels. In the latter half of the 1960s one finds her playing not just in Shakespeare, Chekhov and Ibsen as one might expect, but in Duras, Pinter and Albee, which one might not.

But while applauding her private enterprise, one should remember that it was the existence of the RSC which enabled her to ally herself with new writers, new directors, a younger theatrical generation. Today it has become dismally fashionable to pooh-pooh our twin national companies, regarding them as mammoth whales that devour everything in their path. But in the Sixties they themselves were a rallying point for idealists. Without an organisation like the RSC, an actress of Peggy's vintage would never have enjoyed such a rich harvest of roles. If before the war she epitomised the intelligent *ingénue* and immediately post-war conveyed better than anyone the ecstasy of desolation, from 1964 on she became a *radical* actress, exploring the desperation of women of violently different classes, cultures, temperaments and backgrounds.

Her appetite for work also remained ravenous. The first three months of 1964 saw her back at the Aldwych for a London season of *The Wars of the Roses*, which kicked off, with a somewhat bloodstained toe-cap, the Shakespeare Quatercentenary celebrations. Critics, wiping the dust of sleep from their eyes, were invited to view the trilogy as a whole on Saturday, 11 January, entering the theatre at 10.30 a.m. and finally quitting it just over twelve hours later. One, Philip Hope-Wallace, now found it cumulatively deadening to the senses and starved of spiritual uplift such as you find in Wagner. Others pointed to the increased spontaneity of the playing, the extraordinary sense of ensemble and the overpowering total design showing the work as a divine comedy of God's revenges.

In Peggy's case there was universal praise for her transformation from gingery-locked sub-bitch of the morning to the bedraggled, glittering-eyed crone of the evening. One writer, Roger Gellert in the *New Statesman*, picked out particularly well the meaningful detail of her performance as well as its curvilinear sweep: 'The scornful, impatient brutality of her battling prime can encompass a moment when, haranguing her army, her voice suddenly cracks with tears; and, as the cursing revenant to Richard's court, the play of her demented spidery fingers round wrists red, one feels, with the sleepless rash of neurosis, is more frightening than her cruellest words and pitiful too.'

While reincarnating Margaret of Anjou nightly (sometimes daily) at the Aldwych, Peggy went into rehearsal for a production of *The Seagull* that opened at the Queen's on 12 March. This united two loves of her life: Chekhov and the English Stage Company. While the Royal Court was closed for six months of necessary repairs, the ESC launched a three-play West End season. Tony Richardson was in charge, Vanessa Redgrave was to be the central member of the acting team and *The Seagull* was to be followed by Brecht's *St Joan of the Stockyards* and Michael Hastings's *The World's Baby*. In the event, the season folded half-way through when Vanessa Redgrave's pregnancy supervened and the Brecht got appalling notices.

The Chekhov's cast-list was impressive: Peggy as Arkadina,

Vanessa Redgrave as Nina, Peter Finch as Trigorin and Peter McEnery as Konstantin with George Devine as Dorn, Paul Rogers as Sorin, Mark Dignam as Shamrayev and Rachel Kempson as Polina. Here were many of the best of the Gielgud generation (except the maestro himself) united with a rising generation of star talent, and, in Finch, an actor rescued from the movies. But my memory is of a patchy, muted affair in which a few brilliant performances were accompanied by others of unrealised potential. In Caryl Brahms's phrase, referring to English productions in general, this was Chekhov with the gloves on.

Peggy's Arkadina was, however, very fine. This was a precise account of an ageing beauty used to getting her way not through imperiousness of manner but through pouts, flirtiness and coy wheedles of the voice. The detail was right, down to the tetchy fidgeting of her bare shoulders as she was obliged to watch Konstantin's play or the calculated clutching of Trigorin's knees in a desperate attempt to hold on to him. Peggy, the least actressy of women, is very good at depicting that quality in others. George Devine's Dorn, a detached figure in a panama hat, was the perfect embodiment of the retired lady-killer. Ann Beach's plump, fluffy Masha also seemed ineradicably marked by sorrow.

But if Richardson failed to find all the sub-textual resonance Chekhov needs, the cast certainly enjoyed themselves. Jocelyn Herbert, whose design had a light, poetic quality with the slatted house and garden beyond, says the cast were nearly all old friends and had great fun during the off-stage dinner-party in the last act. George Devine determined that while Nina and Konstantin were alone on stage, the family party should be as realistic as possible. Mark Dignam recalls it vividly: 'Peter Finch, Ann Beach, Peggy, Rachel and I were all sitting together off-stage. George decided to turn it into an acting exercise. When a light came on, Peter Finch and I had to tell an anecdote about the lives of the characters and make everyone laugh. We could easily have recorded something and been sitting up in our dressing-rooms. I used to spend the whole evening wondering what I was going to say over the supper-party. I invented something one night about the bailiff having been an atheist in his youth and Peggy reacted with shock just as Arkadina would have. Then someone suggested we should get Peggy a bit tiddly so we went to an off-licence in

Shaftesbury Avenue for some wine and George provided grapes and brown bread. Eventually we got sick of that so people started bringing ever more outlandish drinks. It certainly made that off-stage supper-party into a real event.' Listening to this account of life in the wings, one feels that if Devine had directed the whole production, it might have had a fuller sense of lived experience.

No sooner had *The Seagull* finished its run at the start of the summer than Peggy was back in Stratford where *The Wars of the Roses* was fitted into a momentous cycle of all Shakespeare's History plays from *Richard II* to *Richard III*. It was momentous not simply in that it was the first time the whole cycle had ever been presented chronologically but in that you became aware of the thematic unity of the plays. The theme was England. What one saw – for anyone lucky enough to witness the whole cycle in a single week – was something akin to the retributive pattern of Greek drama in which the curse pronounced upon Bolingbroke's usurpation of Richard II took more than 100 years to work itself through. The critics reviewed individual productions but never the whole sequence: a pity since there is no permanent record of one of the RSC's greatest achievements.

But if Stratford had a great season with the Histories in 1964, there were ructions at the RSC's London base in which Peggy ultimately got involved. Following on from its 1964 Theatre of Cruelty season at LAMDA, the RSC presented an adventurous season of plays at the Aldwych that included Pinter's *The Birthday Party*, Rudkin's *Afore Night Come*, Beckett's *Endgame* and Roger Vitrac's *Victor*: the last-named was a surrealist piece by a colleague of Artaud's that depended heavily on its protagonist's breaking wind (in performance this was expressed by a loud blast on a tuba specially composed by Guy Woolfenden – not for nothing was this known as 'The Woolfenden Reports'). When Peter Brook's production of Peter Weiss's *The Marat-Sade* was added to the repertory in July, this proved too much for Emile Littler (President of the Society of the West End Managers *and* an RSC governor) who gave an interview criticising the RSC's London programme: 'These plays are dirt plays,' he claimed. 'They do not belong or should not to the Royal Shakespeare Company; they are entirely out of keeping with our public image, and with having the Queen as our patron.'

Others came to Littler's support, including Sir Denys Lowson, an ex-Lord Mayor of London and a member of the RSC's Executive Council. On the other hand, the RSC's actors and directors sent letters of support to Peter Hall and the Chairman, Sir Fordham Flower, and asked that a deputation be allowed to put their case to Littler and Lowson. Peggy was a prime mover behind this and led the delegation that included John Normington, the Equity Deputy, and Tony Church as well as the director, David Jones. Before the party went to see Littler and Lowson in the upstairs boardroom at the Aldwych, a plan of campaign was carefully rehearsed and Peggy, according to Tony Church, was encouraged to appear at her most Dame-like and 'sporting everything bar a Queen Mary toque'.

It was hardly a meeting of true minds. Lowson had the temerity to say to Britain's greatest actress that he was not in the habit of discussing his companies' policies with his employees. According to Peggy, he became extremely heated and, to everyone's astonishment, suddenly asked, 'Do you want to see plays where people jump up and down saying Fuck-fuck-fuck?' After Peggy and her party had retired in some dudgeon, Peter Brook apparently lashed into the two smut-hunters, announcing that the deputation's response had been very mild and that Littler and Lowson were in fact totally despised by the whole company. In the end the whole affair died down, with Lowson choosing not to submit himself to re-election and Littler more or less apologising. It was an unfortunate episode, though typical of Peggy that she should be the actors' chosen spokesman for reason and common sense.

Understandably, after eighteen months of grinding non-stop work, Peggy had a light year in 1965. But it was not solely for reasons of recuperation. Her marriage to Jeremy Hutchinson was breaking up, not because of temperamental incompatibility so much as the strains imposed by the pursuance of separate careers. Jeremy was a thriving and busy barrister; Peggy was an actress whose commitment to the RSC entailed long absences from home. Neither party is keen to talk about the circumstances of the break-up but what is significant is that they remain the best of friends. Looking back now, Jeremy says, 'I always see her as innocent and naïve and very sweet. She's a marvellous mixture

212

of someone with a naïve streak personally and a total shrewdness theatrically. She's also one of the few totally good people I've ever met. There is absolutely nothing nasty in her. She's totally honest about her own behaviour and has – even to this day – an extraordinary youthfulness and open-eyed quality.' Few husbands speak about their ex-wives with such admiration.

Peggy stayed on at her Frognal home with the now grown-up Eliza and Nicholas. She also eased herself gradually back into work. She recorded Cleopatra for BBC Radio. In December she also went on tour to Norway with a one-woman show, *Some Words on Women and Some Women's Words*, that she had devised four years previously. It had started out in 1961 as a show for London University and had gone on to Zurich, Basle, Athens and Israel and done a week in Brighton. Binkie Beaumont had wanted to bring it into the West End but Peggy felt it would be too boring to play it for a straight run.

The show tells us quite a lot about Peggy's taste: her knowledge of the past, her commitment to the present. The first half consisted of portraits of women by male writers: Chaucer's Wife of Bath, Shakespeare's Margaret of Anjou, Byron's Donna Julia from *Don Juan*, bits of *Under Milk Wood* and *Cider with Rosie*. In the second half came women's own words: Mary Tudor's famous speech at Guildhall, Anne Boleyn's letter from the Tower to Henry VIII, a poem by Elizabeth I, excerpts from Queen Victoria's diary, Edith Sitwell's poem written on the day when the atomic bomb fell and a narrative about Hannah Senesh, a Hungarian patriot tortured and killed by the Germans during the war. Peggy played the programme in Oslo's Aula Theatre to a packed house which included the King of Norway. On a stage decorated only with a Gyldenlaers stool and a bunch of flowers, Peggy held the crowded auditorium spellbound, though one feels that an Oslo paper's announcement that 'Dame Peggy Ashcroft kept us imprisoned for two hours yesterday' may have lost something in the translation. She also gave an interview to another Oslo journal that enquired if Ibsen was not a little *passé* in England. Peggy retorted strenuously: 'Ibsen will never be *passé* in England. Myself, I would quite like to play Mrs Alving in *Ghosts* or really I would like to play Irene in *When We Dead Awaken*.' Mrs Alving she was soon to do; Irene, alas, has eluded her.

The following year, 1966, saw Peggy taking another radical departure. She, in fact, gave one of her greatest performances, in John Schlesinger's production of Marguerite Duras's *Des journées entières dans les arbres*, translated by Sonia Orwell as *Days in the Trees*.

Duras is a major writer whose work has never been absorbed into the English theatre. She is seen as difficult, obscure, wordy, dull; in fact, she is subtle, penetrable, persuasive, exciting. Possibly the only English critic who understands her fully is Harold Hobson and he has traced the source of her work to a short story, *Le Boa*, written in 1954. In that, a 13-year-old girl goes every Sunday to the zoo and sees a magnificent boa, with skin shining like steel, devour a live chicken. But what she also sees is the way regret has devoured the life of the virginal old maid who is director of the boarding-school where the girl is a pupil and who accompanies her every week to the zoo. In that story, claims Hobson, lies the seed of all Duras's plays.

That certainly sheds new light on *Days in the Trees* in which we see a greedy, pathetic mother, whose arms are weighed down with gold bracelets, arrive in Paris from an unnamed colony to persuade her son to come home and manage the factory that has made her rich. All her life she has indulged this child. Now he is a hard-faced pimp who makes a living by gambling and procuring clients for the girl with whom he lives. He gambles away the money his mother gives him and returns skint to his flat in the early hours, only to see on the mantelpiece rows and rows of his mother's gold bracelets. They are for him to squander and he knows it. His mother is elated and compares him with those who have succeeded in life, men she despises in spite of her own success.

Critics struggled to find a meaning in all this. Some saw the mother as France and the son as Algeria. But the play is both simpler and more complex than that. On one level, it is a study of love and hate and the indefinable area where they merge. On another, it is a political and psychological vindication of the son who is a destroyer, like the boa, and who has rejected the capitalist virtues of thrift, hard labour and money-making. The mother has created an apparent monster. But, in Duras's eyes, by raising a son without use, love or responsibility, she has created a being wholly free. When Madeleine Renaud played the part in Paris and came to the description of her son as 'ce ... prince' she isolated these words as if they were a definitive verdict.

Peggy's performance was magnificent: a rebuke to those who thought she shrank from portraying vulgarity of soul. It was much more than a skilful assumption of old age. It displayed a profound understanding of character in which every detail was perfect, down to the way she plucked at her dress, fussed with her unpinned white hair, crammed her face with food, carelessly offered charm and then peevishly cut it short.

But such a performance is not achieved without great cost and Peggy went through the last-minute *crise* that is a mark both of her internal insecurity and of her creative power. John Schlesinger – whose brother married Peggy's niece and who therefore has a family connection – remembers a tricky week spent with Peggy and the wig-maker, Kenneth Lintott, getting the costume and the hair exactly right. By the final rehearsals, characterisation and appearance had beautifully meshed. Then, at the first preview, Peggy seemed to lose her grasp of the character. Peter Hall told John Schlesinger he must give her lots of notes. Peggy complained bitterly, saying that she couldn't absorb any more, so Schlesinger got up at five one morning, typed out all his notes and asked Peggy to go away and absorb them on her own. When it came to the first night neither director nor actress was quite sure that what they had worked on would get across. John Schlesinger remembers going down to where Peggy was sitting on a bench just before the rise of the curtain and, more to cheer her up than anything, pointing towards the unseen audience and saying, 'O, fuck 'em.' Peggy repeated his remark several times with astonishing vigour, making an unequivocal gesture to where the customers and the critics were sitting. It is not that she hates audiences: it was simply her way of releasing the intolerable tension. As Schlesinger says, she went on to give a well-nigh perfect performance incorporating every single one of his notes.

What the story reveals is the agony that goes into creating a major performance. As a director, John Schlesinger remarks that he invariably goes through a tortured, sleepless night before embarking on a new play or film; for the stage performer it is even worse, in that he or she has to make the experience live every night for a new audience. But Peggy's greatness shone through every moment of her performance as Duras's aged *parvenu*, beautifully described by B. A. Young in the *Financial Times*: 'This is a truly remarkable creation, this old woman with the vestiges of authority clinging to her like the brave flag on a sinking battleship, while the vulgarities of her youth are openly indulged now that she knows there is no-one to challenge them. You hardly have to be told that her family was poor bourgeoisie, that she only began to make money after she was forty. You see it in the way she wears her expensive clothes and jewellery. The way she pokes her finger into her nostril to clear it; the way she scratches her leg; and you hear it in every exactly placed inflection of Dame Peggy's infinitely malleable voice. She is given every opportunity of showing her paces in this long part; she weeps, she storms, she coos, she gets drunk. One couldn't hope to see it done better.'

One of the remarkable things about Peggy is her constant capacity for surprise. She has spent much of her life playing well-born characters, but can suddenly turn in a stunning performance as a rich vulgarian. She looks demure and is extremely passionate. She can also, as John Schlesinger discovered, unleash ferocious pre-performance nerves. Someone else who learned during the run of *Days in the Trees* that Peggy is nothing like a stereotypical Dame was a young director just making his way up the RSC ladder, Trevor Nunn. On his own admission, Nunn had made a fairly disastrous start with the company and had either seen projects come to nothing or had had his work radically revised by other directors. In that summer of 1966, he felt that his one true, secure friend in the organisation was the Aldwych stage doorkeeper, Cliff. They would often chat about cricket and one evening Cliff invited Nunn into his back parlour to watch the Test Match on his black-and-white television set:

'England were playing the West Indies,' Nunn recalls, 'and significantly failing to hold it together. I was aware there was another figure in the room and, every time an English wicket fell, out of the pitchy darkness came a voice that said things like "O, damn" or worse. I just assumed it was a quite junior member of the company. Then it was stumps and at 6.30 this figure got up and it was a lady wearing a brown suit. It still didn't click who it was and only after she had gone did I realise I had spent half an hour in this tiny little cubicle with Dame Peggy Ashcroft. So I knew from that first encounter that she was much more unconventional and formidable than the surface appearance would suggest: there is something far more extravagant and unexpected underneath.'

Peggy also came to realise the following summer that there was far more to Trevor Nunn than his youthful, Beatle-browed appearance might initially suggest. She was cast as Helen Alving, another doting, indulgent mother in an RSC revival of *Ghosts*. Originally it was to be directed by the American Alan Schneider but he was unavailable and so it was entrusted to Alan Bridges, one of the top British television directors but then inexperienced in the staging of plays. At Peggy's urgent behest, Jocelyn Herbert agreed to design the production though she was busy working on a film at the time, and Miss Herbert soon found she had to contradict some of the director's stranger ideas, such as building a platform out into the auditorium, by pointing out that the people upstairs wouldn't be able to see. She remembers it now as a very dark and sombre production.

When it opened at the Aldwych in June 1967, it seemed to lock Ibsen into a prosaic, low-key naturalism from which he has since been rescued: words like 'slow', 'plodding' and 'dull' were bandied around by the critics. If Peggy came out of it well, it was purely because of her Ibsenite capacity to endow any character she plays with a past and to allow you to see what is going on in their minds. When David Waller's Pastor Manders sat praising her dead husband, her quietly beating finger betrayed her impatience and her true knowledge of Captain Alving's insatiable lust. And when she came to Mrs Alving's great speech about battling the dead conventions of the past ('thick as soot in chimneys' in Denis Cannan's lively translation) a note of vibrant passion came into her voice.

Peggy's Mrs Alving was sufficiently remarkable ('In any anthology of the finest performances of our time,' wrote Harold Hobson, 'this Mrs Alving would surely find a place.') to justify re-working the production. As the original director was now on the other side of the world, Peter Hall invited Trevor Nunn – who had by then shown his mettle with brilliant productions of

The Revenger's Tragedy and *The Taming of the Shrew* – to call some extra rehearsals. Nunn demurred, since he knew nothing about the production. But he went to see it a couple of times and on his second visit asked the stage manager to issue a call for the next morning at 10.30. Back came the message, during the interval, that Dame Peggy was rather tired and would prefer just an afternoon rehearsal. With deep respect, Nunn sent back another message insisting on the morning otherwise nothing would get done. He went back that night to his solitary pad in Highbury Grove and, since his watch was broken and he didn't have an alarm clock, telephoned for an alarm call. 'The next thing I knew,' says Nunn, 'a neighbour was hammering on my door to try and wake me. I discovered my telephone was out of order and the stage manager had finally got a message through to my next-door neighbour. It was now 12.30. I've never been in such a blind panic. I dragged on my clothes without washing or cleaning my teeth and got to the Aldwych at a quarter past one to discover the company had broken for lunch. As they came back one by one, I made the same profuse apology. Peggy was the last to arrive back – slightly late, I might add – and said "Hello, nice to make your acquaintance – I thought you might like this." She produced a cardboard box filled with endless wrapping paper. I finally pulled out a tissue-wrapped object and it was a huge copper alarm clock with a Union Jack imprint and a great bell at the top. She was heaving with laughter – I mean literally hooting. So it was a ghastly first contact but she instantly turned it into a joke with just a touch of punishment to it.'

Despite that initial hiccup, Peggy got on famously with her young director. He remembers that she would often respond to a suggestion with a slightly incredulous 'What?' as if to put one on one's mettle and force one to decide if it was an idea worth defending. 'But,' he says, 'once she has comprehended the notion in her own terms, she is terrifically receptive and shows an innocent and almost adolescent delight in the possibility of trying things. There is a great deal of glee and even girlishness about her in rehearsal and when I was rehearsing with her and David Waller he often appeared, despite the facts, to be the older of the two.' Peggy records in a letter to George Rylands her frustration that Trevor had to leave *Ghosts* to work on a production of his own, and she certainly passed on to Peter Hall her warm feelings about this new young director. This can only have confirmed Hall's own decision that Nunn, at 28, was his ideal successor; and indeed in December 1967 Hall resigned and handed over the reins of the RSC to the young man with the copper alarm clock.

Peggy's openness, her willingness to ally herself with whatever was new and exciting, was not a question of climbing aboard the passing bandwagon but of realising that theatre is a constantly evolving process and that she must change with it. So when she was on holiday in the West Indies after the run of *Ghosts* and received a new play by Harold Pinter, *Landscape*, she read it and quickly cabled back her acceptance. The plan was to do it, under Peter Hall's direction, at the Aldwych in the spring of 1968. But the Lord Chamberlain, then in the last year of his anachronistic existence as a censor, demanded the excision of certain four-letter words. Pinter rightly refused and so the play was first done on the BBC Third Programme in April 1968 with Peggy and Eric Porter.

She fitted in a couple of small film roles in 1968 and returned to John Barton's *The Hollow Crown*. But her next major stage appearance, early in 1969, was in the work of a dramatist, Edward Albee, who deals just as much as Pinter in nameless fears and unexplained mysteries. The play was *A Delicate Balance* and the original plan was that Trevor Nunn should direct it, but he had to take his production of *Much Ado About Nothing* on an American tour and so Peggy's old friend, Peter Hall, came in in his stead.

A Delicate Balance is a much more complex and challenging play than Albee's rancorous marital marathon, *Who's Afraid of Virginia Woolf*: it is, in fact, an extraordinary blend of social comedy and quasi-religious allegory. On the surface, what happens is simple. Agnes, her indecisive husband Tobias and her sister Claire, a dedicated lush, live together in a large American house in a state of workable co-existence: a delicate balance has been achieved with Agnes acting as the fulcrum. Then one day Harry and Edna, the oldest and dearest friends of Tobias and Agnes with whom they've drunk cocktails for forty years, turn up at the house explaining that they feel frightened. They proceed to annex a room in the house. But should they be allowed to stay? Agnes says no, since they bring a plague and no-one can cure it who is not sure of his own immunity. Tobias, on the other hand, begs them to stay, otherwise there is no way of making forty years of social pretence true. In the end, the visitors depart. 'Don't become strangers,' pleads Agnes. 'How could we?' answers Edna. 'Our lives are the same.'

For Peggy as Agnes, the play presented both a technical and an intellectual challenge. It was the first time since *The Heiress* twenty years before that she had essayed an American character. But Peggy's performance was also crucial in deciding whether the play was a condemnation of the superficiality of American friendship or an endorsement of the need to safeguard one's family against the carriers of a mysterious plague: with a slight tilt either way, Agnes could be seen as a monster or a saviour.

As so often with Peggy, the first essential was to get the voice right and to capture the tune of Albee's elegant, parenthetical Jamesian prose. According to Peter Hall: 'The New England sound was absolutely critical. These tonal qualities are as important to her as what she is wearing. The sound in these instances is usually extravagantly right, not to say a caricature; and it gradually fines down until it's hardly noticeable at the end of the play. It's simply part of her work process.'

Her interpretation was remarkable not simply in its tonal accuracy but in its lack of moral judgement. Peggy gave a quiet, elegant, controlled performance full of that peculiar New England combination of serenity and steel: what Harold Hobson excellently called a 'sweet implacability'. Without ducking the issue, she left it to us to decide whether Agnes was the saviour of her family or a woman damned by her refusal of sanctuary to Harry and Edna, and in doing so she added to the beguiling sense of unresolved mystery at the heart of Albee's play. Peggy was like a woman in Balmain clothing tiptoeing round the edge of an abyss. The sense of mystery was intensified by Peter Hall's production which had a surface sheen and polish covering a nameless dread, while John Bury's set gave us an imposing bookcase, marble pillars, swing chairs, the sense of a beautiful American mausoleum behind which was a formless darkness inevitably suggesting death. You came out with the play's philosophical questions reverberating in your mind and longing to see it again.

Peggy had played a gross, vulgar, chain-jangling parvenu in

Days in the Trees and an elegantly tooled woman of steel in *A Delicate Balance*. Six months later she was back on the Aldwych stage in Harold Pinter's *Landscape*, once again making nonsense of those jeremiahs who saw her as an actress always encased in her own form of bourgeois gentility. Here she played, with utter conviction, a lower-middle-class woman armoured against the present but transfigured by a moment of remembered ecstasy. She played it many times over the years and I believe it became one of her finest performances in modern drama: precise, poetic, well observed and endowed with a magical ability to exist in two dimensions at once.

Landscape was teamed at the Aldwych in July 1969 with the same author's *Silence:* two plays apparently demonstrating that our lives on this earth collide, briefly mesh but never lastingly unite. But *Landscape* struck me as infinitely the more enjoyable and accessible of the pair. Two characters, Beth and Duff (no one commented on the fact that they seem to have lost the prefix 'Mac'), sit in the kitchen of the house where they were once employed as servants and which they now seem to own. He is at a table, she sits in a chair. In John Bury's set there was a cleft running across the floor and along the wall behind them. This emphasised the fact that, though married, they live in a state of habitual estrangement. Duff is a robust, vulgar, earthy cellarman who talks of his dog, beer, feeding the ducks; Beth sits downstage dreaming softly of lying with the man she loved on a beach, driving with him in his car, asking him for a baby.

As Martin Esslin pointed out, the play's main image is of the contrast between the tenderness and delicacy of the woman's memory of her past love and the man's brutal coarseness, symbolised by his use of harsh words with strong consonants such as banging, gonging, swinging, slamming. But the interesting question is who the man is whom Beth remembers so tenderly. Is it her husband, Duff, or is it Mr Sykes, her employer? I think the question is left delicately open but Peggy is unusually adamant in thinking otherwise: 'It's definitely her husband she is talking about. That is the tragedy of their estrangement. She is sitting there recalling their past. They are now in separate worlds but sometimes it is as though she hears what Duff has to say but chooses not to reply.'

Many people see the play as two interwoven, elegiac monologues on the disappointment of time, but Pinter's stage directions
make it clear that 'each does not appear to hear the other', which
is rather different from not hearing. Pinter's own view is that:
'Duff refers normally to Beth but does not appear to hear her
voice. Beth never looks at Duff but doesn't appear to hear his
voice. This opened up a lot of interesting moments in rehearsal
about the extent to which they heard each other. As far as I'm
concerned – for what it's worth – I think she hears every word
he says: she's not deaf. But I believe that she is thinking aloud
and therefore he can't hear her. Duff constantly makes overtures
to which there is no response: a door has come down between
them.'

Some have argued the play gained little by being staged rather
than heard on radio. Nonsense. In Peter Hall's production, the
image was all-important: the visual division of the stage, the sight
of David Waller as Duff – stolid, coarse and sturdy – and the
spectacle of Peggy sitting in a humble kitchen chair with a
cardigan draped round her shoulders, hands folded across her lap,
feet splayed slightly outwards in practical brown shoes. But,
vocally, there was also a perfect, musical contrast between Waller's rumbling bass and Peggy's soprano tones with their soft,
gentle cadences leading up to the final, exultant cry of 'Oh, my
true love I said.' Harold Hobson suggested in his column not
once but several weeks running that the play's final line was
worth the whole of *Antony and Cleopatra* in its evocation of the
power of love. Becoming slightly irked with this focus on a single
line, Peggy at one point was heard to remark that if he didn't
stop she might omit it altogether. But Hobson was right on one
point: it was Peggy's recollected joy that was memorable.

Harold Pinter concurs: 'The quality of ecstasy was very strong
in her performance. She fulfilled that part of the play wonderfully.
But there was another aspect of her performance which I remember was really quite formidable which was the door that had
closed in her, that had closed the rest of the world from her, that
she herself had closed. Not, I feel, an ordinary door but a great,
big, clanking iron door that she had pulled down between her
and the rest of the world embodied by her husband. I think David
Waller played it beautifully too so that he could never get through

that door. It's a question of going the whole hog which I think she did, which she is so wonderfully able to do. The whole hog on two counts. One was to shut that door and say it will never be opened. The other was to say I am here and while I am I will recollect my ecstasies – or, if you like, create them.'

While allying herself with the cause of new writing at the Aldwych, Peggy also eagerly threw in her lot with the RSC's new directorial generation at Stratford. By now she was firm friends with, and a close Hampstead neighbour of, Trevor Nunn and his wife Janet Suzman, with whom she had appeared in *The Wars of the Roses*. At Nunn's request, she had also become part of the five-strong team (along with John Barton, Peter Brook, Terry Hands and Nunn himself) responsible for the direction of the RSC: a post that was no sinecure but involved regular meetings to discuss matters of general company policy. Today we hear a lot about the need to democratise the big companies and to ensure that the actor's voice is heard: right from the beginning of Nunn's tenure of the RSC, Peggy had a vital seat on the board.

The role that tempted Peggy back to Stratford in 1969 – her first appearance there in five years – was that of Katharine of Aragon in *Henry VIII* by Shakespeare and, in all probability, John Fletcher. The play itself had not been seen at Stratford since Guthrie's pageant-with-jokes version of 1949. Both it and the key woman's role were awaiting reclamation. Ditched by the king so that he can marry Anne Boleyn, Katharine is far more than the standardised, virtuous wronged woman. She is, in Wilson Knight's phrase, one of Shakespeare's most striking feminine creations: an exact realisation of a particular woman only lately dead and an emblem of dignity in grief. She also displays both at her trial and in her subsequent decline a strenuous regality: 'Though unqueened, yet like a queen and daughter to a king, inter me.'

Looking back, Trevor Nunn, who directed this new production, guiltily feels that in the early stages he did not give Peggy the firmness and security she needs. He observes that she combines 'terrifically productive periods with tremors or sways of fearfulness often about something as simple as the learning of the text.' But he admits that he came to the production, at the end of the first full season for which he felt wholly responsible, 'wiped out and exhausted.' Nunn and his designer, John Bury, were also engaged in a constant dialogue about the nature of the play and the visual style of the production.

Henry VIII came at the end of a Stratford season that included *Pericles* and *The Winter's Tale*. Nunn saw it, in that context, as a late play about a young king's process of self-discovery and about reconciliation achieved through the birth of a child (the future Elizabeth I); Bury, still immersed in the metallic realism of the Hall History Cycle, viewed it much more as a chronicle. On the first day of rehearsal, they presented a design to the company that was a rather uneasy compromise. Two days later, after further discussions, they came up with something much more stripped-down and emblematic. Two weeks later Nunn realised this wasn't going to work and he and Bury produced the final light, white version that combined a permanent toytown backdrop of Tudor London with Brechtian captions that flashed up before every scene. As Nunn says, the discovery process was valuable. The trouble was that for two weeks neither Peggy nor anyone else knew exactly what kind of production they were in.

Despite these initial uncertainties, Peggy had a very clear idea of the character she was playing. Indeed, not for the first time, her total immersion in a role made her almost proprietorial in her attitude towards it. 'Peggy herself,' Nunn recalls, 'had become obsessed with Katharine of Aragon to the point where she brought into rehearsals every day a kind of defence of the character. She was on Katharine's side to the extent that she was against Shakespeare's. She would turn up with extra lines from the historical trial or from Katharine's letters and try and put them into the text. I had to argue that Shakespeare is not interested in that, so it doesn't matter if we are being historically inaccurate. Shakespeare is loading the dice and we have to help him. That is why Katharine is, to some extent, a tragic figure; she is much maligned in this version but the play goes on to other things. But, although we had minor disagreements, I don't think I ever argued Peggy out of her conviction that she was not playing Katharine but that she *was* Katharine.'

In a sense, Peggy was following a basic rule of acting: playing the character from her own point of view. Yet it is characteristic of her that any arguments over the character soon dissolved in laughter. Donald Sinden, who played Henry VIII, recalls a rehearsal of the trial scene where he saw a slight argument developing between Peggy and Trevor and tried to intervene. Peggy turned on him and told him to mind his own ****ing business. 'It was,' says Sinden, 'because she was trying to win an argument when I butted in and got the full force of her anger. But it was over in a moment and it was all hugs and kisses.'

Together with Peggy's concern to do justice to Katharine, however, went a passionate concern for the welfare of the company as a whole. Donald Sinden recalls a long, arduous scene with Peggy when a coffee-break was called and all the young actors dashed off to the canteen leaving himself and Peggy, the senior members of the company, at the back of the queue. He was enough of a traditionalist to be a little put out; Peggy didn't mind a bit.

'The word that Peggy Ashcroft uses more than any other during a rehearsal period,' says Trevor Nunn, 'is the word "company" or "the co" as she always describes it. She will speak when it is not fair on "the co", she will rally "the co" and she knows that she is there to be an example to "the co". She is indeed the shining example of what it is all about. Many actors over the last decade have talked about their passion for greater democracy or for dismantling directorial authority. A lot of the time one knows from actual experience that this is a disguised resentment that the individual concerned does not have a lot of power himself and is not calling the shots. Peggy's sense of democracy is not that at all. It is not sentimental either. She knows that certain people have more responsibility than others. But she does not believe that there is one rule for her and a different rule for everybody else. Absolutely not. There is one rule for the company and she is part of it.'

After the difficulties surrounding its inception. Nunn's production of *Henry VIII* opened in October to considerable acclaim. It also retained enough of Nunn's original purpose to end in a sonorous white hippie Mass celebrating Elizabeth's christening and a ringing declaration, extracted from a speech of Archbishop Cranmer's, exalting 'Peace, plenty, love, truth' (what no one noticed was that Nunn omitted Cranmer's final noun, 'terror', from the list of 'servants to this chosen infant').

Peggy's own performance struck me as a superlative example of what one might term late Ashcroft: sharp, precise and revealing the humanity under the surface regality. 'Clear and economical as a Holbein etching' wrote Ronald Bryden in the *Observer*. By playing the character from her own viewpoint, she also uncovered her contradictions. In the trial scene she was all dignity, restraint and self-possession; then suddenly the restraint broke down and she covered her face and cried 'What will become of me now, wretched lady?' through her hands while, of course, remaining perfectly audible. In contrast, there was a fascinating moment when, at the news of Wolsey's death, she set her chin in a line of senile unforgiveness: she knew she should pardon her old enemy like a good convent-bred girl but couldn't quite bring herself to do so. Peggy gave us a three-dimensional portrait of Katharine's humanity: the resilient toughness as well as the vulnerability of isolation.

Above all, there was the beauty of her speech. Donald Sinden recalls sitting in rehearsal listening to her working on Katharine's long speech in the trial scene. The voice would be raised a bit more here and dropped a bit more there than it had been the previous day. The pauses would be slightly longer or shorter till she had found their precise weight. Peggy's vocal technique, says Sinden, is remarkable. 'She has that gift of the upward inflection that hits the last word in a line. I'm reminded of an actor, Douglas Quayle, who used to say "There's many an old actor sleeping on the Embankment for want of an upward inflection." '

There seemed little danger that Peggy, who in a decade with the RSC had gone from the spitfire Kate in *The Shrew* to the rejected Katharine of Aragon, would ever come to that pass. What is more, she still had within her the capacity for surprise.

CHAPTER FIFTEEN

The Flame of Life

PEGGY EMBARKED UPON a new decade in 1970 in fine spirits. Professionally, she was secure and happy in her relationship with the RSC. Privately, much of her time was absorbed by friends and family. But the great joy of her life was that she had become, during the previous summer, a grandmother. Her daughter Eliza, now living in Paris, had given birth to her first child, Cordelia Manon, and Peggy was inordinately delighted. Her son Nicholas, having begun as Trevor Nunn's assistant on his production of *The Revenger's Tragedy*, was also setting out on his career as a director. Peggy took pleasure and pride in both her children.

In work terms, Peggy remained as loyal as ever to 'the co' while occasionally working outside the expansive empire of the RSC. Amongst the roles one wished she had played is Shakespeare's Volumnia. Indeed, she was twice asked to do so: once by Peter Hall and again by Trevor Nunn for his Stratford season of Roman plays in 1972. But the closest she got to it was the character of the Boss's Wife (who is cast as Volumnia) in David Jones's production of Gunter Grass's *The Plebeians Rehearse the Uprising* at the Aldwych in July 1970. This was a prime example of Peggy's willingness to play as cast and undertake new work, but one cannot say the role greatly exploited her talent.

Grass's play, set in a theatre in East Berlin during the abortive uprising of 1953, was basically an attack on the Boss (i.e. Brecht) for putting his art before his humanity and for being more concerned with his production of *Coriolanus* than with lending his weight to the workers' revolt. As the Russian tanks grind into town, we see the Boss grumbling guiltily over the tape-recording he has made of the arguments with the workers and confronted by his own shame as an expedient fence-sitter.

Peggy as the Boss's Wife obviously called on her own memories of meeting Helene Weigel both in Berlin and during the rehearsals for *The Good Woman of Setzuan* at the Royal Court. She exhibited a hard-as-nails humanity and a flinty, headscarved toughness: Robert Cushman in *The Spectator* picked out as electric one moment when she bent forward with hands on knees to announce 'The people have risen'. But although the people rose, the play didn't. Grass seemed to be having it both ways in attacking Brecht as a hypocrite and then claiming that he was dealing with a universalised figure. But Grass also judged Brecht by the yardstick of Western liberal principles. Brecht was an avowed Marxist playwright and director who had been given his own theatre by the Ulbricht regime. Why should he be expected to join an uprising against it? Would it have made a scrap of difference if he had? Emrys James was in fine form as the slouching, leering, cigar-chomping Boss and Peggy gave a conscientious performance without having much chance to hint at Weigel's own greatness.

Peggy's loyalty, however, was as much to writers as to institutions. In July of the following year she went back to the Royal Court to appear for the second time in a play by Marguerite Duras, *The Lovers of Viorne*. It was undoubtedly an adventurous choice: an austere, enigmatic play about a famous French murderess, Claire Lannes, that made few concessions to obvious theatricality. The only question-mark concerning Peggy's performance was whether it went too far in explaining what Marguerite Duras had left deliberately inexplicable.

The play had its origins in a fascinating case that occurred in 1949. Over a period of weeks scattered fragments of a body were found in open railway trucks in various parts of France. The movements of the trucks were computed by the French police and it was found that their routes had intersected at only one point: under a railway bridge at Viorne. Visiting Viorne the police got an almost instant confession from a 51-year-old housewife, Claire Lannes, who had murdered her miserly husband for reasons that were never entirely clear.

Duras was obsessed by the case. In fact, she wrote two separate plays about it. First came *The Viaduct* (*Les viaducs de la Seine-et-Oise*) which Sybil Thorndike and Max Adrian played in Guildford in a version full of thunderous, dilated-pupil Grand Guignol acting. Then came Duras's second play *The Lovers of Viorne* (*L'amante Anglaise*) that reduced the story to two stark, character-revealing interviews. In the first, an interrogator questions the husband of the murderess. In the second, he interviews the murderess herself.

As is clear, Duras drastically altered the circumstances of the case. The real Claire Lannes killed her husband. But in both plays the victim becomes a deaf-mute cousin, a fat, slummocky maid who kept house for the Lannes for several years. Mme Duras explained the change by saying that to her the Lannes 'are both the French *petite-bourgeoisie*, dead-and-alive from the moment they are old enough to think, killed by the formalism handed down through the ages ... What Claire was killing was death itself.' The implication is that in a sterile bourgeois existence murder becomes the only form of protest against the pointlessness of life.

In performance the play offered an unresolved enigma rather than easy solutions. In the first half, Maurice Denham as the characterless husband answered questions in a dry, sad, sullen sort of way. In the second half Peggy sat under the spotlight in a shabby black dress and stockings with only the tiny, twitching movements of her mouth and the restless fidgeting of her red, rawboned hands hinting at the character's mental disarray and her uncertainty at being dragged from her familiar domestic surroundings.

The play reveals no great secret nor does it explain precisely why Claire was driven to murder. It is true that she had had a lover, a policeman in Cahors who had removed her from God but this in itself was not the motive or the cue for her action. The play is really about a hopeless search for something that can never be discovered.

But did Peggy's performance seek to explain too much? Most

critics did not think so. But Harold Hobson in the *Sunday Times* had profound misgivings: 'There is a wonderful moment when Dame Peggy talks of her lost lover. Her face brims with tears that never fall. But she makes Claire mad. Her mouth works, her fingers endlessly twitch. Her way of life is of utter desolation and it is not surprising that she ended it by murder. In other words, Dame Peggy offers an explanation where it is essential that there should be no explanation. It is very fine but it is not Mme Duras's play. *C'est magnifique, mais ce n'est pas la Claire.*'

Peggy herself remembers working closely on the script with Mme Duras. What she tried to do in performance, without seeking either to motivate or to justify Claire, was to present her irreconcilable contradictions: 'On the one hand, you could say she was totally mad. She had been in love with a policeman in Cahors and then married this stiff nonentity of a man in a dreary town. She was clearly suffering from a neurosis of frustrated sexuality and conceived this totally irrational detestation of her husband's deaf-mute cousin. But the other side of the character is a curious innocence and what I tried to get across was the sanity of the insane: the fact that you are never mad to yourself but only to others and that what you do has a logical inevitability to it. Whether I succeeded or not I don't know.' A majority of the jury thought Yes. What Peggy did, once again, was to play Claire Lannes from her own point of view and present the contradictory facets of a character for whom in the end there seemed no viable alternative to murder.

As an actress, Peggy herself sometimes seems as mysterious as a Duras character. How exactly does she do it? There is no easy answer but in the course of this journey certain clues are beginning to emerge:

Through tonal precision and a faultless ear for sound.

Through emotional identification with a character.

Through the ability to impersonate without disguising her own soul.

Through a surface English restraint concealing a strong sexual passion.

Through a patent detestation of vulgarity and anything done for effect.

But running through all this is a persistent, eager digging to find what makes a character tick without much regard for conservation of energy. It is a quality that Peter Hall, who was shortly to direct her again, commented on: 'In the 30 years I've been working with her – and I say this in no spirit of criticism – I've noticed how quickly she gets tired in rehearsal. That's because of the amount she gives. Michel Saint-Denis told me that he used to instruct her just to mark it and give 50 per cent because if she gave all the time she'd kill herself. But that is the French tradition of *répétition*. Peggy rehearses flat-out and you see her face go absolutely white because she is exhausted. Rosalind and Beatrice are just as tiring to rehearse at that level of intensity as Margaret of Anjou cursing on the battlefield. But I believe that in marking a play you have to find out what the character really is and it's a sacrifice that in rehearsal Peggy gives. I think we're coming near to the heart of her when we speak like that: the givingness.'

Six months after playing Mme Duras's drab, weary French murderess Peggy transformed herself into another of Edward Albee's rich New England matrons in his play *All Over*, which Peter Hall directed at the Aldwych. Duras's play explored the living hell of petty-bourgeois life; Albee's was about the living death of America's financial aristocracy. In a stately New England pile, all polished marble and veneered teak, relatives and friends gather round the death-bed of a famous old man. In a strong RSC cast, Peggy played the dying man's steely, verbally lethal wife, Angela Lansbury was his long-standing mistress, Sheila Hancock his feverishly unstable daughter, Patience Collier his caustic, Thelma Ritter-like nurse. Outside, cameramen and reporters waited for news of the great man's progress. Inside the house, the family reminisced, viciously quarrelled and gradually revealed their own self-absorption and lack of love.

In a sense the play was a rehearsal of familiar Albee themes: the hollowness of loveless family rituals, the preoccupation of a dying culture with verbal style, the fear of the outside world in a collapsing civilisation. But the ongoing theatrical energy that the piece itself occasionally lacked was more than made up for by the cast. And once again Peggy gave a performance, like a shell slowly being cracked open, that revealed the soul-wrenching misery under the dignified façade.

With her silvery hair, expensively simple black dress and gentle New England inflexions, she looked and sounded right. But the involuntary shudder whenever her detested daughter spoke suggested secret inner wounds. And when, at the end, she uttered a great Grecian wail of a cry, it was like seeing a figure of regal conviction and authority falling apart and the old American order cracking up. Irving Wardle recorded in *The Times*: 'The line "Because I'm unhappy" is repeated four times and, as she delivers it from the guts, is comparable to Lear's "Nevers".'

The same morning as Irving Wardle's endorsement of her performance appeared in *The Times*, the paper also carried a letter from Peggy on the sentencing of the Soviet dissident, Vladimir Bukovksy. That a great actress should have an active public conscience is not in itself remarkable, but the even-handedness of her concern with any violation of human rights is unusual. Peggy is certainly not one for knee-jerk anti-Soviet statements. But the letter made it plain that those of a liberal persuasion who deplored the tyranny of the Greek Colonels or the political arrests in Rhodesia and South Africa found their case in no way helped when a Socialist state outdid those countries in terms of savagery of sentence, curtailment of legal defence and the hideous use of 'mental treatment'. A month later Peggy also became a member of an international committee of Western European writers and intellectuals set up to draw attention to political arrests in Czechoslovakia. Peggy is not party political: she simply has an irrepressible and impartial concern with justice and freedom.

In view of her concern with major global issues, it is somewhat ironic that her next stage role was as a lady of the manor threatening to kill herself in protest against a Ministry of Transport plan to build a by-pass through her park. The play was William Douglas-Home's *Lloyd George Knew My Father* which opened at the Savoy in July 1972, and it was to be Peggy's sole venture into the commercial theatre after the foundation of the RSC. Why did she do it? The answer can be summed up in two words: Ralph Richardson. When impresario Ray Cooney offered Richardson the role of General Sir William Boothroyd, he asked him who he would like to play opposite him. 'Edith couldn't do it now,' Sir Ralph mused. Then inspiration struck. 'Peggy,' he said suddenly, 'I might give Peggy a ring.' How could she refuse her old friend?

It wasn't by any means a bad play. Indeed Harold Hobson found unexpected emotional depths in Sir William Boothroyd's long-nursed anger at his wife's infidelity (strangely enough, Brian Clark touched on a similar theme in his 1986 play, *The Petition*, about a reactionary old soldier with a radical wife which Peggy was offered but couldn't do). But although Peggy displayed a talent for comedy that surprised only those who thought of her in terms of Duras and Albee, the play built up with impeccable logic towards the heroine's suicide only to back off at the very end: it seemed a bad case of the West End frights. And although she and Richardson played with all the truthfulness the situation could bear, it was like watching Edrich and Compton going in to bat against a Minor Counties attack. Of course, they scored all round the wicket. Of course, they made centuries. But then so could many other people have done in similar circumstances.

Eight performances a week in the West End was, of course, tiring: Peggy freely admitted as much in her letters and displayed a certain relief that a projected production of *Happy Days* with Peter Hall had been postponed. But she was still heavily involved in matters beyond her own career. Indeed Peter Hall's decision in the spring of 1972 to accept the directorship of the National Theatre, in succession to Laurence Olivier, led to the one real crisis in his close friendship with Peggy.

'The first people I told about my decision,' says Hall, 'were Trevor Nunn, John Barton, David Brierley and Peggy. Peggy was fiercely against it and said it was like crossing the floor of the House. I said I didn't see it like that at all. She said "You can't go and compete with the child you've created." But I said "That's life – everybody competes with their child and their child competes with them." It's almost the only quarrel we've ever had. She questioned me and drove me on this issue and worried about my integrity. She had to satisfy herself that I wasn't being a political turncoat because that would be impossible in her book. We went through a long process of talk and eventually Peggy agreed to join us for the opening plays; but I think that was more out of love for me than out of any desire to work at the National as an idea.'

But while Peggy – as a member of the RSC Directorate – was involved in discussions about a possible future amalgamation of the NT and RSC, chivvying Peter Hall's conscience and playing in the William Douglas Home play at the Savoy, she was also busy helping to plan a gala performance at the Haymarket in October to celebrate Sybil Thorndike's ninetieth birthday. This was a great party with an all-star cast including Olivier, Richardson, Guinness, Scofield and Ustinov, but in a letter to George Rylands Peggy showed her concern with getting the details right. Would it be better to have a reading about Mrs Siddons's Volumnia or Bernhardt's Cleopatra? Which bit of the Bard would be best to open the second half? What was Sybil's favourite piece of Schumann or Chopin? On top of that, there was a Memorial Service for Cecil Day Lewis to attend at St Martin-in-the-Fields and a chance to see a Wednesday matinée at Stratford of Trevor Nunn's *Antony and Cleopatra* with Janet Suzman. As ever, Peggy was deeply involved in the life of her times.

After six months at the Savoy, Peggy handed over her role in *Lloyd George Knew My Father* to Celia Johnson. She too eventually departed, causing Richardson to comment, 'I've had two leading ladies shot from under me and I can't take any more.' But in 1973, after a short holiday, Peggy plunged into an RSC tour of Pinter's *Landscape*, in a revival of the Peter Hall production, and *A Slight Ache* newly directed by Peter James, taking in Croydon, Bath, Nottingham and the Continent.

It was once said that Pinter's female characters were all either mothers or whores. That seems to me a profound untruth. The partnership of Peggy and David Waller in these two plays opened my eyes to the fact that Pinter man either reacts to the unknown with fear and panic or expresses himself in hard, coarse, brutal terms, while Pinter woman, to generalise, represents all that is vibrant, passionate, sexually ecstatic.

In *A Slight Ache*, written for radio in 1958, Pinter shows the intrusion of a speechless, dilapidated, tramp-like matchseller into the lives of a well-heeled, middle-class couple. Invited into their house, the matchseller provokes the householder into a revelation of his snobbery, selfishness, pretentiousness and private terror while his wife lapses into sexual fantasies of her youth. By the end of the play, the matchseller has displaced the husband totally in the wife's affections. She hands her husband the matchseller's tray and leaves the room with the old man. Like Beth in *Landscape*, Flora, the wife in *A Slight Ache*, is middle-aged, childless and yoked to an insensitive man with whom she has long lost contact; unlike Beth, she displays as well as talks about her strong sexual impulses.

What was extraordinary about Peggy's performance in this play was its delicate eroticism which was far more powerful and suggestive than the gyrating mountains of flesh in *Oh! Calcutta!* I still have an image of her winding her chiffon scarf around the matchseller's neck, not with obvious, serpentine seductiveness but with the delirious happiness of a woman releasing instincts long buried. Peggy broke with Pinteresque convention by playing Flora not as a palpable voluptuary but as a gentle, quiet, practical woman in whom passion unexpectedly flares. Harold Pinter's own memory of her performance is very similar. 'It was,' he says, 'very delicate – she caught precisely the balance between the housewife and the erotic woman underneath. But it was such fun too. She was so alive in that play. I think it's this flame of life that she possesses that really informs all she does.'

The 'flame of life' is exactly right. I first saw Peggy playing this double-bill in the Ashcroft Theatre, Croydon: the theatre that in 1962 had been named after her, thus making her the first actress in British stage history to be so honoured. It is, in truth, a rather civic, hard-edged, functional space but she managed to illuminate it with her sexual glow. And her performance in the adjoining *Landscape* was, if anything, even richer than before. She was now, more definably, a middle-aged housekeeper with a slightly 'off' accent; and the contrast between the harsh, brutal monosyllables of David Waller's speech and her plangent cadences was now stronger than ever. But, although she never moved from her chair, it was also a superb piece of physical acting. When the productions moved into the Aldwych in October 1973, Irving Wardle noted in *The Times*: 'Every detail counts: the shape of Dame Peggy's mouth as she relapses into silence, sometimes curved into a child-like smile, sometimes set in a straight, bleak line. The two independent monologues converge and diverge like poetic assonances and half-rhymes.'

It is intriguing that Peggy's increasing commitment to new drama in the late 1960s and early 1970s coincided with an ever-greater concern with public events: it was as if the one fed and stimulated the other. Early in 1973 she took part in a massive phone-in aimed at jamming the Department of the Environment's switchboard in London: organised by the Covent Garden Community Association, the idea was to halt plans to close the old market and redevelop the area (a lost cause). Later that year she joined with Peter Hall, Jonathan Miller, Laurence Olivier and Harold Pinter in writing to *The Times* to protest about the Egyptian and Syrian refusal to issue detailed lists of prisoners after the fourth Arab–Israeli war. In 1974 she co-signed another letter to *The Times* that deplored demonstrations during the Bolshoi Ballet's visits to the London Coliseum (in the event tin-tacks were thrown onto the stage). At the same time the letter announced unequivocally that 'there are many who, like ourselves, will feel unable to attend their performances' specifically because of the dismissal of two leading Soviet dancers, the Panovs, from the Kirov Ballet and the refusal to grant them a visa to go to Israel. In the same year she took part in *A Salute to the Chile of Pablo Neruda* at the Royal Court in aid of professional performers in a country where a military junta had replaced the late President Allende.

I list these activities not to parade her conscience – which she would hate – but simply to demonstrate the breadth of her sympathies and concerns. If she scents any injustice, she just doesn't give up. Harold Pinter confirms this: 'I find her in her dealing with facts as straight as a die and totally unafraid. She doesn't give a damn for her reputation or any possible repercussion. I think she is an object lesson. She is fearless, which is unusual. As people get older, they often say "Oh, there's nothing you can do about the damn world anyway – I think I'll put my feet up." Not for a moment would that ever cross her mind.'

Peggy was now a woman in her late sixties. But she was as far from putting her feet up as she had ever been. Indeed, at a time when most people have reached rose-growing retirement, Peggy was about to annex new theatrical territory and demonstrate her loyalty to Peter Hall by helping him in his struggle to create a new National Theatre company that could move into the long-delayed building on the South Bank. It was not an easy transition for her, because of her emotional loyalty to the RSC; but she was to prove that the flame of life burnt as strongly as ever.

CHAPTER SIXTEEN

Happy Days

IN HER BIOGRAPHY OF Samuel Beckett, Deirdre Bair claims that Peggy turned down the role of Winnie in the first London production of *Happy Days* at the Royal Court in 1962. Far from it. Indeed Peggy once asked George Devine why he had never asked her to play it. 'I didn't think you would want to,' was his simple reply.

But it was Peggy's first role when she joined the National Theatre Company at her beloved Old Vic in the autumn of 1974. It proved to be a baptism of fire – or maybe earth. And as soon as *Happy Days* had opened out of town at the Liverpool Playhouse, Peggy was into rehearsals, again with Peter Hall, for a new production of Ibsen's *John Gabriel Borkman* with Ralph Richardson and Wendy Hiller. Two new roles in Beckett and Ibsen in the space of a little over twelve months: a big undertaking and a sign of Peggy's devotion to her director.

Happy Days, written in English in 1961 and transposed by Beckett into French two years later, is a work of consummate irony. Its heroine, Winnie, spends the first part of the play embedded up to her waist in earth: not sand, as Peggy sharply points out, since that could be blown away. In the second part, only her head still protrudes. You can take the play, according to taste, as a comment on the circumscribed nature of the human condition;

or as a tribute to human stoicism and courage in that Winnie remains implacably cheerful in the face of death and nothingness. To the last, she also maintains her belief in the love of her husband, Willie, although he spends much of the play so absorbed in the reading of his newspaper that he hardly notices her.

Rehearsals began at the Old Vic on 14 October 1974. Alan Webb was Willie; Peter Hall was directing; and, crucially, Beckett himself was there. For Peggy, this was somewhat disconcerting. Her approach to a role is one of steady digging towards psychological truth via tonal accuracy: Beckett regards his texts almost as scores in which words and gestures amount to a musical notation. But Peter Hall's reason for wanting Beckett to be present for the first two weeks was to get the mimetic details exactly right. And indeed Beckett took them through all the physical minutiae of when Winnie takes her possessions out of her handbag – which hand she uses and what she does with her hat and glasses. Peter Hall says that when Beckett directed *Waiting for Godot* in West Berlin he spent six months writing out every gesture and footstep of the production before going in to rehearse: Hall wanted to get the same physical precision into *Happy Days*. 'Of course,' he says, 'for a creative actor, and particularly for Peggy Ashcroft, it was a dreadful corseting. It was a terrifying experience but it gave us what was in Beckett's head. It also gave Peggy a month after he was gone to make it her own and adjust it.'

Peggy is far too diplomatic and admiring of Beckett to admit that the first two weeks of rehearsal were pretty hellish as he gave her every gesture in fine, meticulous detail. What is revealing is her observation that, even with a role as exactly orchestrated as a piece of music, the actress still has to find her own personal route into the character: 'Perhaps it's not so dissimilar from Brecht in that although you've got an artificial set-up – I mean nobody lives buried up to their waist in earth and then up to their neck or talks in total monologue all the time or has all those things in her bag – there has to be an absolute reality. Just as Brecht alienates by not seeking for a situation to be realistic or possible, so Beckett gives you a framework of the impossible; but with both you have to be certain in yourself as a performer of who you are as a character. Mind you, I don't think Beckett would support that at all. It's just a personal approach.'

The key question for Peggy, as always, was how Winnie should sound. Peter Hall records in his *Diaries* that, by the fourth day of rehearsal, both he and she had agreed on an Anglo-Irish lilt with a slight echo of her old friend, Cecil Day Lewis. Peggy recalls an even more potent influence at work:

'I said to Sam one day that I knew how Winnie should speak. He said "How?" I said "Like you." "Oh," said Sam, "I don't know about that." '

But Peggy allowed his gentle, incantatory reading of the text to creep into her own. She realised instinctively what scholars have confirmed: that Beckett is a profoundly Irish writer. A reading of Eoin O'Brien's magnificent book, *The Beckett Country*, confirms the profound influence of the Irish landscape, Irish painting, Irish speech and slang on Beckett's work. Winnie's endless burrowing into her fathomless bag is exactly matched by a love scene in Beckett's unpublished *Dream of Fair to Middling Women*, set on a sandy beach in County Wicklow. And when Winnie cries, 'Come on dear, put a bit of jizz into it,' she is using a good Dublin slang word denoting liveliness or a spritely air. Peggy put a bit of jizz into her Winnie; and the result was a performance gaily flecked with the music of Irish speech.

Even when she had found the right sound for the part, and even after Beckett's departure for Paris, rehearsals were not always easy. As the Hall *Diaries* make clear, the final stages were attended by the agony and doubt that are a built-in part of any actor's nervous system and that in Peggy are strongly pronounced. She has the insecurity of the truly great: even in making a television film with her I observed the hesitation that accompanies perfectionism. In *Happy Days*, of course, she was the play. And a week before the opening, Hall wrote: 'Peg was very obstinate, resisting everything, arguing. She was like a horse who wanted to go and I wouldn't let her. It's the usual tension with her in the last stages of rehearsal. She wants no detailed work, only to run. And yet if things are not working, she finds it impossible to run.' On the afternoon of opening night in Liverpool, there were tears in her eyes as Hall gave her notes. But by early evening she was bright as a button and the performance went exactly as everyone hoped. The ovation was warm, the notices the next day excellent and Winnie, after a week in Liverpool, became a performance to

239

put in the locker ready for use at the Old Vic and eventually far beyond.

Immediately after the Saturday night performance of *Happy Days* Peggy was travelling back south to begin rehearsals for *John Gabriel Borkman*. The production itself could not have come at a more critical time for the National Theatre and everyone knew it. Peter Hall had officially assumed the directorship of the Company in October 1973 and the opening year's work had filled one with misgivings. Hall's own opening production of *The Tempest* had been an over-elaborate Jacobean masque that almost obscured the greatness of Gielgud's Prospero. Olivier's valedictory production of Priestley's *Eden End* was strangely muted and unexciting. There had been a succession of feeble new plays including *The Freeway*, *Next of Kin* and *Grand Manoeuvres*. On top of this, planning became a nightmare because of the crucial delays to the new building on the South Bank, letters appeared in the press criticising the National's capacity to absorb the best technical staff because of its high rates of pay, there were highly public mutterings from disaffected directors still loyal to the *ancien régime* and, as studio theatres came to the fore, there was a widespread feeling that large institutional buildings were white elephants.

John Gabriel Borkman was Peggy's fourth Ibsen play but Hall's first as director. And a fiendishly difficult one he had chosen: one that is equivocal, elusive, poetic. For three acts it apparently exists on the plane of sober realism and then, in the final act, takes off into mountain-top mysticism. Hall had the insurance of a first-rate cast. Ralph Richardson as Borkman, the wealthy financier who has been imprisoned for embezzlement and who paces the upstairs room of his house convinced that his country will demand his return; Wendy Hiller as Mrs Borkman and Peggy as her twin sister, Ella Rentheim, who do batttle for possession of Borkman's son, Erhart; Frank Grimes as Erhart and Anna Carteret as Mrs Wilton, the voluptuous widow with whom he makes off; and Alan Webb as Foldal, Borkman's old clerk. A dream cast, in fact, but one plagued by illness. Alan Webb fell ill at the half-way stage and had to be replaced by Harry Lomax, while Wendy Hiller was forced to miss several rehearsals and returned wheezing and voiceless.

Peggy was clearly not always at ease in rehearsals. She and Wendy Hiller shared a long duologue in the first act that needed careful pacing and timing. She also found the character of Ella difficult to get a purchase on and often fretted over details: the beat of a line, her position on stage. One day there was a problem over a sofa on which she and Richardson had to sit side by side. For Peggy it was too high: for Richardson it was just right. Hall placated Peggy by saying that they would experiment with foam rubber. At Hall's flat that night the phone rang. It was Peggy. 'She asked me,' writes Hall, 'if she was being difficult and I told her she was. She said she was fussed and tired. But her marvellous spirit to surmount crises began to appear when she realised Alan was possibly very ill and the full ramifications of the Wendy situation. Peggy is one of the greatest human beings I know.' That is very typical: a banishment of self-concern when she realises the whole production is in difficulty.

After all the traumas and problems of rehearsal, the production proved to be a turning-point in the National's fortunes and a major success for all concerned. It was an exciting night in the theatre precisely because Hall realised that neither realism nor symbolism are ever absolute or finite in Ibsen, that they seamlessly intertwine. The long opening battle between Peggy and Wendy Hiller also had the edgy menace of Pinter with two people struggling for power. Peggy once said that she loved playing Ibsen because 'the action is always on two levels – we say something and it always implies something underneath.' That was exactly true of her performance here: you sensed the will of steel under the composed, gracious façade. For a start, she had the advantage of looking exactly as Ibsen himself described Ella: 'There is more suffering than hardness in her face. There are traces of great beauty combined with a strong character. Her heavy hair has been combed back in natural waves from her forehead and is completely silver-white.' With a fur hat on top of the silvery hair, she had rarely looked more stunning. But in the long opening scene she also revealed the spinster Ella's desperate, human need for love. When Peggy said of Erhart, 'I want his affection ... his mind ... his soul ... his heart', it was with the ravening hunger of a woman who had long ago lost the father and who had now come to sink her molars into the son. It was particularly touching to see her working once again with Richardson, with whom she had first appeared 49 years before. And his performance, as an ageing Peer Gynt for whom other people were simply things in his dream, was touched by his own unique wild poetry. When his son bade him farewell, Richardson acknowledged his departure with an airy wave of his hand that made you wonder if he had ever apprehended his existence. And when he died he made a strange noise which Gielgud said was 'as if a bird had flown out of his heart.'

The notices were wildly enthusiastic. They realised that the National Theatre Company, in enlisting three magnificent new recruits and cracking a difficult play, had turned a dangerous corner. They also saw that Hall's production had released Ibsen's Nordic poetry. John Barber in the *Daily Telegraph* eloquently wrote: 'As the one sympathetic character, Peggy Ashcroft is most moving as the rejected sister, adding to the papery frailty of the invalid a voice and demeanour that suggest an infinite refinement of spirit.' B. A. Young in the *Financial Times* claimed that Richardson and Ashcroft in the last act offered acting such as is not often seen nowadays – 'not often because it is in a style that has gone out of fashion, speech that is larger than life, characters that are first and foremost characters in a drama.' But behind the awesome grandeur of the final scene lay difficulties that the public never sees. The curtain falls with the main characters on a mountain-top. How are they to get down to stage level in time for the curtain-call? Anna Carteret told me: 'Peggy and Ralph gave these *grandes* performances in the French sense. But the quickest way of getting down the mountain at the end of the play in time for the call was to sit down and slide on their bottoms. I have this treasured memory of Sir Ralph and Dame Peggy sliding down the mountain just like tobogganing children.'

It is my belief that Peggy's commitment to the National Theatre at this stage in its fortunes was absolutely crucial. Just as she had given her backing to Devine at the Royal Court in 1956 and to the RSC at its inception in 1960, so her willingness to cross Waterloo Bridge in the mid-Seventies and work with Peter Hall's company at the Old Vic was vital. The opening year's work of Hall's regime had not been good. There was a lot of talk in the press about the rocketing costs of the new building. Some of Olivier's former associates were not slow to buttonhole journalists at every opportunity and vent their grievances. When Peggy – along with Richardson and Gielgud – threw in their lot with Hall's company they helped to give the National Theatre not merely glamour and prestige but genuine artistic weight.

In March 1975 *Happy Days* was brought into the Old Vic repertoire to a chorus of critical approval. Irving Wardle pinned down beautifully the actress's and director's grasp of Beckett's grave architecture and their sense of the distance that Winnie travels in the course of the play. In the first act, he suggested, Peggy's Winnie was like a rich woman out for a day on the beach surrounded by all her favourite things. By the second, she was simply an immobilised head with eyes bursting out of their sockets. 'And when she speaks,' wrote Wardle, 'it is with a continuous undertone of terror that the words may run out. Silence in Beckett is death; and the stage picture is thus defined as a slow-motion drowning.'

Through the spring and summer of 1975, Peggy continued playing her two immured heroines at the Old Vic: Ella, who recognises finally that Borkman's coldness of heart has turned her into a shadow, and Beckett's Winnie, who faces her desolate future singing a song harsh and out of tune. There was also a gala performance at Stratford in June to raise money for the RSC. Outside the theatre, there were eagerly awaited visits from her family: Nicholas was now running a mobile Caravan Theatre Company that was based in Vancouver and toured the Rockies, while Eliza was living in France. In her letters, Peggy makes it clear how much their visits home meant to her. She also ends one letter, after England had managed to save a match at the Oval with a score of 538, 'And three cheers for the Test Match – at last we do not have to hang our heads.'

Peggy's next major theatrical engagement came on Saturday, 28 February 1976; and a memorable one it was too. The occasion was the National Theatre Company's last night at the Old Vic before the historic move into the new home on the South Bank; the show presented was a charity gala conceived by Val May, *Tribute to the Lady*. The 'lady' in question was, of course, Lilian Baylis; and that the evening was so exuberant, jolly and unsentimental had a lot to do with Peggy's hilarious incarnation of the woman who, 46 years before, had given her her first opportunity to play a wide range of classical roles.

The evening took us through the Baylis years at the Vic from 1912 to 1937, and many of the famous Baylis stories were there. We saw her kneeling at her roll-top desk and praying, 'O God send me good actors – cheap.' We heard her complaining about dramatic critics: 'They form too quick an impression of work it has taken my dear producer and his boys and girls a whole week to prepare.' We also glimpsed her ruthless treatment of actors: 'Quite a sweet little Goneril, don't you think?' she witheringly remarked of some unfortunate *ingénue*. Peggy did not simply impersonate Baylis: she became her. 'It was one of the finest performances,' Peter Hall wrote in his *Diaries*, 'I have seen her give. You can always tell when an actor is absolutely creating. Conventional timing, normality is broken. The rhythm of speech, the rhythm of the body becomes something different. This happened to Peggy tonight. She presented that strange, Cockney, busybodying, strait-laced, crooked-mouthed eternal mother bossing everybody about – and created a genuine eccentric.'

There was one moment of the purest magic when Peggy as this dumpy, bustling visionary threw off her wig, pebble-specs and MA cap and gown and transformed herself in a second into a youthful, radiant Beatrice to Gielgud's gravely witty Benedick. And when, once more Baylis, she told the celebrity-stuffed Old Vic audience that 'All art is a bond between rich and poor' and warned us that 'this theatre must be saved or I shall come back and haunt it', it was as if the fiery angel herself were speaking.

Peggy's miraculous transformation into Lilian Baylis helped to close the National's account at the Old Vic. Just over a week later, on Monday, 8 March, Peggy made history again when she launched a week of previews at the Lyttelton Theatre on the South Bank with a matinée performance of *Happy Days*. She thus became the first actor to address a paying audience from the stage of the National Theatre: the culmination of a tragi-comic, 138-year-long campaign to establish such a building in London. Peggy, who had been the motor behind so many important theatrical enterprises this century, was once more in at the beginning.

I remember the occasion well. A cold, blustery, snow-flecked

March afternoon; coffee and sandwiches for the critics in the upstairs bar; the House Manager walking through the foyers with an electric bell to summon us to our seats. There was little pomp or ceremony. But there was a tangible sense of excitement as, like reconnoitring explorers, we roamed the generous spaces of Denys Lasdun's foyers, discovered the bars and bookshop and got our first glimpse of the spare, functional, proscenium-arch stage. 'The National Theatre is Yours' Tom Phillips's posters proclaimed; and, after years spent in other people's commercial playhouses, there was a feeling that we were entering a theatre in which we were something more than briefly-required guests.

Seeing Peggy's Winnie for the first time, I was also struck by its buoyancy, optimism and musicality. In her floral dress, knitted green hat and gash of lipstick, Peggy seized on the lines 'This is a happy day, this will have been another happy day' which chime, in various forms, through the text like a refrain; yet the unbuckled optimism only served to heighten the desperation of Winnie's plight. It seemed entirely right that the National Theatre should begin its life not with some trumpeted gala event but with Britain's leading actress appearing in a play about survival against the odds by a great contemporary writer. With five productions transferred from the Old Vic in four days the emphasis was on the National Theatre as a working playhouse: a place as much concerned with the present as with the past.

Ironically enough, when the National officially opened on 25 October – with a fairly disastrous performance of Goldoni's *Il Campiello* in the presence of the Queen at the Olivier Theatre – Peggy found herself shut out of the building. It took her an hour and a half to get across a Waterloo Bridge packed with traffic and sightseers and so she was a little late for the scheduled 7.00 p.m. arrival. She had to wait outside for an hour and a quarter until the doors were re-opened.

By October Peggy had, in fact, left the National Theatre and commuted back over the river to appear in an RSC Aldwych production of Aleksei Arbuzov's *Old World*: a rather sentimental Soviet two-hander about a not-so-brief encounter between an age-ing sanitorium boss and one of his flightier patients, an impetuous ex-actress who is now a cashier in a circus. The play gave Peggy the chance to sing an old circus song, to dance the Charleston and to display the beatific smile of a woman who believed love to be sacred. But although it was a pleasure to watch the interplay between her and Anthony Quayle as the stuffy old medico, one kept wondering what had attracted such fine actors, or the RSC itself, to such an old-fashioned and romantic piece. One critic suggested that its appearance at the Aldwych made as much sense as if *Murder at the Vicarage* had been presented at the Moscow Art Theatre; and there was something about the sculpted figures dotted around the stage that suggested neither the director, Terry Hands, nor the designer, Ralph Koltai, had total confidence in the piece. Anthony Quayle, however, recalls that it was a joy to do the play with Peggy and draws an interesting comparison to Celia Johnson, with whom he did another two-hander, *Chin-Chin*, in 1960: 'Working with Celia, I always felt she was a comedian and that there was a devastatingly amusing mind hidden behind those great round eyes. Peggy was equally a pleasure but she was a much more serious personality and brought to the play the instincts of a great classical actress. Peggy took life more seriously. She's a crusader, she's *Pilgrim's Progress* to the end.'

This particular pilgrim made a more unusual progress in 1977. She went to the Citadel Theatre in Edmonton, Canada, to play *Happy Days*, and joined her son Nicholas's Caravan Theatre Company in its tour of the remoter reaches of British Columbia. For Peggy, the whole trip was an unforgettable adventure. She flew to Vancouver and then on to Kamloops, where she joined her son and his family for their mobile theatrical tour: a genuine fit-up company of the kind that survived in Ireland until the late 1960s. Peggy speaks with genuine maternal pride of her son's work – work that seems a product of her belief in exposing children as early as possible to Shakespeare and the riches of theatre. 'I remember,' she says, 'Nick was five when he saw *Much Ado*. A few years later he went to see *The Winter's Tale* and asked if it was a tragedy or a comedy. We told him it was both. He suddenly said that William Shakespeare must have been a very jokey man because when he had a tragic scene he always had a funny one after it. He said he wished he had been alive when Shakespeare was because he'd like to have known if he was really so gay. He meant it in the old-fashioned sense.'

Peggy, equipped with dungarees, cowboy hat and red-check

lumberjack shirt, had a great time accompanying her son's touring theatrical troupe. On one occasion, she was even allowed to appear on stage and speak one line as a farmeress in a play called *Hands Up* about the Canadian train-robber and Ned Kelly figure, Bill Miner. Then it was back to Vancouver for a 15-hour train trip through the Rockies to Edmonton where she was to play *Happy Days* with the Citadel's director, John Neville. Neville, after putting the Nottingham Playhouse squarely on the map, had gone out to Canada in 1972 and made a similar success of the handsome Citadel Theatre. In 1973 he invited Peggy out to do performances with him of *Dear Liar* based on the Shaw–Mrs Campbell letters. In 1977 he invited her out again to do *Happy Days*.

'By then,' says Neville, 'it had dropped out of the Lyttelton repertory but Peter said he would bring it back and we re-rehearsed it with me in the role of Willie. The Lyttelton was the best try-out date I've ever done. When we played it in Edmonton, I always remember there was a little thing that happened every night which was that the backstage crew would come and conduct Peggy and myself to our places on stage. I've never seen that elsewhere and it was a sign not just of the crew's respect and admiration but of their love for the artist. I also listened to her performance every night. With Willie, there are occasions when you can turn off a bit and not listen. But with Peggy, I never wanted to have a little rest: it was like listening to opera.' John Neville, now running Canada's Stratford Festival, is clearly as smitten with Peggy as everyone who comes into contact with her. 'I think,' he says, 'if I had played Romeo opposite her, I would have fallen in love with her. She is a great woman. One reason I adore her is that we support so many of the same causes such as nuclear disarmament; but what is fascinating about her is the way the qualities she has as a person are manifested in the talent.'

Neville was cautious when I asked him how Edmonton took to Beckett. Peggy, however, was more forthright. 'The first night was difficult because we played to a well-heeled, black-tie audience: what they call there "brass-arsed". At the reception afterwards a woman came up to John Neville and said "Mr Neville, is that what you would call a play?" John simply said

"Yes" and turned on his heel. But after the first night the audiences were more responsive. I must say that doing the piece with John made all the difference to the play because Willie became a strong and powerful figure in his performance.' This point was confirmed by Peter Hall: Neville, although he said only 42 words, had a force that increased the vulnerability and sense of dependence of Peggy's Winnie.

Even in Canada, Peggy was still writing home about events that concerned her in London: a slight friction between Peter Hall and Trevor Nunn over the fact that they were both planning to revive the same play (Congreve's *The Double Dealer*); the uncertainty about whether Terry Hands would leave the RSC for the National; and the possibility of doing a play called *Thursday's Ladies* which the director, Clifford Williams, finally rejected as being too French.

Back in London late in 1977 Peggy immersed herself in new projects mainly concerned with films and television. She was, in fact, not seen again on the London stage for the best part of three years: by her standards, an exceptionally long gap. But there was one tragic near-miss when she was forced to withdraw from the cast of Simon Gray's *Close of Play* at the Lyttelton because of injury. It was one of Gray's best plays, and Harold Pinter, who directed it, saw Peggy's enforced withdrawal in the spring of 1979 as a sad tale.

'She rehearsed for a week with this terrible cartilage. Simon Gray will never forget it; nor will I. Nor will anyone else in the room. She was very courageous and insisted on going on, though as she did so, she was more and more often in tears simply out of pain. Nevertheless she charged on indomitably and was one of the funniest things anyone had ever seen. She played a chatterbox of the first order obsessed with trivia and grasped the role quite joyously. With all due respect to the understudy who took over, it was a terrible tragedy for the play when she had to surrender and have an operation since she brought to it something extraordinary.'

After the operation on her knee, Peggy returned to the National a year later to appear in Lillian Hellman's *Watch on the Rhine*: to date, her penultimate performance on the British stage. The part she played – a politically blinkered Yankee matriarch –

could hardly have been further from her own experience, but the historical importance of the play, which dated from 1941, was that it attacked national insularity at a time when the American contribution to the European refugee problem was a firmly closed door. For Peggy the reason for doing it in 1980 was that the problems it dealt with were still relevant: those of national isolationism and the extent to which violence is legitimised by political commitment.

I thought the play was humane propaganda: others found it political melodrama. But, whatever its merits or demerits, Peggy showed once again her ability to understand those formidable American matrons. Her character – said by Dashiell Hammett to be a mixture of Hellman herself and her mother – had the cultivated rudeness of the well-heeled: 'Are those your children or are they dressed-up midgets?' she at one point asked her astonished daughter. Peggy, truculent and downright in specs, played her with just the right mixture of salt, ice and good breeding and showed extraordinary understanding of the kind of ostrich-like old party that she herself could never become.

It was in 1982 at Stratford-upon-Avon that Peggy gave what may well be – though one hopes otherwise – her last major performance on stage. It was certainly one of her finest: the Countess of Rousillon in Trevor Nunn's production of *All's Well that Ends Well*. It was also one that Peggy had been preparing for, mentally, for a long time. Trevor Nunn had first come to her with the idea of playing the Countess in 1979 when he had hoped it would be the opening production in the new Swan Theatre. Convinced that Shakespeare wrote the play for the Blackfriars Theatre rather than the Globe, Nunn felt keenly that its fascinating moral dilemma and ambiguous language demanded an intimate space. But when the building of the Swan was indefinitely postponed through lack of funds, Nunn decided to go ahead with the production in the main house partly on the strength of Peggy's firm commitment.

The conventional view of the play is that the heroine, Helena, is something of a go-getter who uses every trick in the book to win the husband she has determinedly chosen and that Bertram, her elusive prey, is a cad and a snob to reject her so brutally. Shaw, however, sent our thoughts to the right place when he compared *All's Well* to Ibsen's *A Doll's House*, another play about an ordinary young man 'whose unimaginative prejudices and selfish conventionality make him cut a very mean figure in the atmosphere created by the nobler nature of his wife.' Nunn, like Tyrone Guthrie at Stratford in 1959, acknowledged the modernity of the piece by setting it in an Edwardian world with a distinctive mood for each of its main areas of action. The Countess ('the most beautiful old woman's part ever written', according to Shaw) occupied a Chekhovian world of wicker chairs, chiming clocks and melodious nocturnes. The fistula-stricken French king inhabited a Novello court packed with peacock-strutting captains who vaulted, fenced, danced and sported like Ruritanian princes. And when the action moved to the Florentine wars, we were in a world of brass bands, smoke-filled estaminets and peachy nurses all vaguely redolent of *Oh, What a Lovely War!* It was a brilliant production: a realistic fairy tale. And when, in the elegiac final scene, the conservatory doors were flung wide open and Harriet Walter's Helena returned, apparently from the dead, to claim her man, we were in the magical realm of twilit romance.

Peggy was absolutely crucial to Nunn's concept, which was to make us care deeply about the fate of the individual characters. 'The part needed Peggy,' he says, 'more than Peggy needed the part. The Countess is not a tragic queen. She is a recently widowed countess, aware of the strains of mortality, brought up against the fact that her adored son behaves unworthily, and capable of cutting across all notions of class and status in her affection for the orphaned Helena. If the sheer fabric of the person you put on stage as the Countess doesn't have that aura of specialness, then you don't care about the love she is extending to Helena. I am wary of the word greatness since it is difficult to confer valuations of great acting until people have reached a certain age, until you feel that life has tested them and they've come through. But I felt that strongly about Gielgud and Richardson in their later years, particularly in a play like *Home*. And I feel it equally strongly about Peggy. You simply lose yourself in the largeness of her spirit.'

If there was a strong rapport between the director and his senior actress – who shared the same house in Stratford at the time – there was an equally binding one between Harriet Walter and Peggy. Harriet Walter had first met Peggy backstage at the Royal Court the previous year when she had been playing one of Peggy's old roles: Nina in *The Seagull*. She confesses at the time she had been slightly in awe of her while desperately pretending not to be. On the first day of rehearsal she and another young member of the company, Philip Franks, decided to come more tidily dressed than usual out of respect for the Dame: only to find, of course, that Peggy herself was clad in practical working clothes.

But, from that very first day, the relationship between them grew exactly as it does between Helena and the Countess. 'Peggy told me,' said Harriet Walter, 'that she thought Helena was one of Shakespeare's most wonderful heroines and that she wished she had played her. On another occasion I remember sitting on the stairs with her just as if we were two young actresses. I asked her if she still got nervous and she said "Of course." But what I remember is that she was so effortless and I was so tortured. I still like to talk around a scene while Peggy is totally uncluttered in her attitude to work. Years of experience have taught her to go straight to the heart of a scene and do it rather than discuss it. Her questions in rehearsal were also very much about practical things like "Where shall I put my handkerchief now?" But one reason I find Peggy so phenomenal is that in other professions the arteries harden, whereas she seems to have remained so open and young. It stems from her interest in the outside world and from the fact that, as an actor, you put your experience into the work, but the parts also mould and shape you. Working so closely with Peggy, I always felt that her guiding light was Shakespeare himself.'

If that is true, it paid handsome dividends, because the tone and mood of this perfect production was set by Peggy's Countess. She played the role not merely with silvery grace – we knew she could do that – but with an amused tolerance and wit. When, for instance, Helena announced that she, as a physician's daughter, was off to cure the king's fistula, Peggy arched an eyebrow to enquire, 'This was your motive for Paris, was it?', letting us understand that she saw through Helena's protestations. She also treated Geoffrey Hutchings's bent-backed Lavache, supposedly a clown but here transformed into an ancient gardener and relic of the estate, with the most wonderful courtesy and consideration: as Irving Wardle wrote, 'it was as if Ranevskaya had decided to stay behind with Firs.' What was truly remarkable about the performance was the quality suggested by Trevor Nunn: the sense of someone tested by life. When the Countess says to Helena, 'Now I see the mystery of your loneliness and find your salt tears' head' you felt behind the words the wisdom born of life's experience.

Reviewing the 1959 Stratford production, Kenneth Tynan had compared Edith Evans's tranquillised benevolence as the Countess to that of royalty opening a bazaar. No one could possibly have said that of Peggy: she addressed everyone with the democratic openness of an equal. I would argue, in fact, that Peggy found more in the role than her illustrious predecessor – a point picked up by Stanley Wells in the *Times Literary Supplement*: 'The precision of Dame Peggy's characterisation shifts the balance of her role away from poetic generality to personal expression. "Even so was it with me when I was young" is not (as Edith Evans made it) a meditation but a statement. This is a practical woman, warm in her sympathies but capable of ironic detachment, most moving in the little scene with her steward (Bert Parnaby) in which she expresses the dilemma of her divided affections and confesses her grief.'

When the production moved to the Barbican in July 1982 both it and Peggy's performance were greeted with yet more superlatives. B. A. Young wrote that Peggy spoke with such clarity that one longed for another generation of actors of her calibre. But when the production went to New York later in the year Peggy, still suffering the effects of her knee injury and with a long filming stint ahead, felt unable to travel with it. Robert Eddison who played Lafeu in this production sagely remarks that 'Margaret Tyzack who took over was tremendously good but she hadn't lived it like Peggy had.' That was the point. Peggy brought her own life experience to the role. If it does indeed turn out to be her theatrical swansong, it could hardly be a more fitting one, for it proved yet again that one of the mysteries of acting is that it is a judgement of character.

CHAPTER SEVENTEEN

Instant Acting

WHILE MAKING ONE OF her early movies in the 1930s, Peggy was told by a cameraman that if she wanted to be a film star, she would have to get her nose straightened and her teeth fixed.

We owe that man a good deal. He confirmed Peggy's own inner belief that the theatre was where she belonged. He also prevented her being sidetracked into a medium where it is inconceivable that she would have had the mind-stretching opportunities afforded by the British stage. In view of her late greatness in both films and television, it may seem churlish to say that she was better off appearing on stages than on screens large and small. But it is my belief that Peggy has only become a first-rate screen actress because of what she learned in the theatre. In his essay on *Film Acting* Pudovkin, the Russian cinematic pioneer, pays tribute to Stanislavsky's system for training actors: Peggy translated to film and television her ability to understand a character. I also believe that she has got better as a screen actress with the years. Some of her early work is very good; some of it has a certain presentational, theatrical quality; but with age, she has learned the art of allowing her own qualities to shine through, as Peter Hall confirms:

'I think it happens to many people that, as they get older, so they relax more in front of a camera: what they are, they are.

They get richer. It happened to Gielgud and Richardson and it happened to Peggy who just is. She doesn't present it. She just is and the camera comes to get it, whereas in the theatre you have to present. Whether that's conscious or not, she's become a consummate screen actress. It's something to do with getting into your seventies. In a sense, what have you got to lose any more? God preserve us from actors and actresses who think they know how to use the camera. You can see them knowing it.'

Peggy herself, needless to say, is very modest about her transition from stage to screen and her recent successes: 'I do think of myself very much as an amateur of the screen because to me it's a wonderful art and I've never learned it.' I think it's fair to say that, with her latter-day triumphs, she has forfeited her amateur status.

But although Peggy has enjoyed an Indian summer on the screen, one finds – as so often with her – that she was, in fact, involved in British films in their pioneering days. She also started out in life as a keen moviegoer. She recalls seeing *Intolerance*, *The Four Horsemen of the Apocalypse*, Rudolph Valentino and Charlie Chaplin in the Croydon cinemas of her youth. It also amuses her to think that since David Lean is almost exactly the same age and haunted the cinemas of his native Croydon as a boy, they must have been seeing the same films at the same time. But where Lean was unconsciously serving his apprenticeship, Peggy simply thought of films as some remote, exotic world totally outside her own experience.

She first stepped before the cameras at Twickenham Studios in 1933 in Maurice Elvey's pageant-like film of *The Wandering Jew*, starring Conrad Veidt and based on E. Temple Thurston's hack stage-melodrama. At that time British talkies were still in their relative infancy – they had begun in 1929 with Hitchcock's *Blackmail* and E. A. Dupont's *Atlantic* – and the tendency was to raid the theatre for suitable raw material; Elvey's film was given points for ambition and for escaping from the world of bedroom comedy and drawing-room farce but some thought it odd that it took the story of the Jew who insulted Christ and was doomed to wander the world and failed to project it forward into Hitler's Germany. According to the *Observer*, the film was 'just a series of orthodox pageants with wigs by Clarkson and a vast crowd of extras running about in fancy dress.' Peggy looked very beautiful as Olla Quintana, the prostitute who betrays the hero to the Inquisition, but she remembers it now as being 'a terrible film' and certainly not one that filled her with any desire for a life in pictures.

Peggy was used to building a character. What she found disturbing was the fragmented, jigsaw-puzzle nature of filming where the performer was asked to come with a ready-made characterisation: 'instant acting' is what she calls it. It is, of course, even harder for someone playing a small role who has to slot neatly into the existing structure. For most of us, Peggy's five-minute performance as the crofter's wife in Hitchcock's *The Thirty-Nine Steps*, released in 1935, is fascinating in that it reveals the quiet simplicity people found at the time in her stage-work. Her performance is a miracle of lightness and tact, hinting at the lonely lovelessness of her life with John Laurie's crabby crofter and the sexual arousal she feels in the presence of Robert Donat's handsome Richard Hannay. She is full of doe-eyed wonderment as she asks Donat about women in the big cities – 'Do all the ladies paint their toenails? Are they all looking beautiful?' – and rapt attention as she gives him her husband's Sunday-best overcoat containing the hymn-book that will later save his life. Peggy's brief performance tells us that this is a good, repressed woman who has discovered love. But to Peggy, immersed at the time in Shakespeare's Juliet, the process of movie-making was something of a shock.

'I love the film,' she says, 'but I can never rid myself of the dismay I felt when I got to the film studio and I was just put in a nightdress and a plait was tied round my hair and I was put into bed and played the end of my little sequence. I felt this was no way to try and play a part, by doing the last scene first. When you're used to making a part piece by piece from A to Z, it takes a bit of getting used to. It didn't make me long to do more films.'

It is just as well, since Peggy was so theatrically preoccupied in the 1930s that there was little time for movies. Her one other picture of that decade was Berthold Viertel's sober, worthy, crashingly dull *Rhodes of Africa*, which seemed unable to make up its mind what attitude to take towards its imperialist hero. It came out in 1936 – a year in which film output in Britain reached the staggering total of 212 pictures – and it was memorably despatched by Graham Greene in the *Spectator* who pulled no punches about the deficiencies of Peggy's performance: 'Miss Peggy Ashcroft as a most unlikely woman novelist – one imagines she is intended for Olive Schreiner – rebukes Rhodes for his treatment of the Matabele in her usual gentle, carefully enunciated Shakespearean tones, flickering her young romantic Juliet lashes at stated intervals with the effect of too much punctuation.' Such a review was hardly likely to make Peggy feel that she was born for the movies, although she was struck by the technical skill of the film compared to her first effort and has wholly pleasant memories of the star, Walter Huston, and her director.

Although Peggy did not fall instantly in love with the camera nor the camera with her, it is typical of her that she was involved in the pioneering days of BBC television drama. In 1939 she played Miranda in *The Tempest* in the BBC's first television transmission of a Shakespeare play at Alexandra Palace and she was Viola in the Saint-Denis production of *Twelfth Night* transmitted live from the Phoenix Theatre. They whetted her curiosity, but the intervention of war put paid to television drama. And for the cinema Peggy made only three brief wartime appearances. In Puffin Asquith's 1940 film of Esther McCracken's country-house comedy, *Quiet Wedding*, she took over Kay Hammond's role and wardrobe as a sophisticated London flirt with a nutmeg-grater voice (her every utterance 'a daisy of speech' according to the *New Statesman*'s William Whitebait). She also made an eight-minute Ministry of Information short, *Channel Incident*, for Asquith, playing a sporting yachtswoman who hears the call for boats during the retreat from Dunkirk and who dresses up as a man to get the necessary supplies. And in 1942 she was an ATS girl in Carol Reed's propaganda quickie, *A New Lot*.

Peggy didn't appear in front of a film or television camera for another sixteen years. She wasn't asked to and anyway she was too busy. But it is worth remembering that Sir John Gielgud also made no films between 1940 and 1955. Before the war, the British cinema raided the West End stage both for scripts and stars. During and after the war, it manufactured its own. Olivier, as always, broke the rules and leapt lightly over the frontier separating theatre and cinema, but there was a feeling, which persists to this day, that classical theatre had little to do with the naturalistic behaviour required for the camera. Judi Dench, for instance, is very similar to Peggy in that the incandescent glow of truth she brings to the stage has only rarely been exploited by the cinema. As for television, there was a common belief amongst the theatrical stars in the 1950s that they had little to gain, and everything to lose, by appearing in a medium that had all the hazards of live theatre with none of the potent magic. Laurence Olivier once said that he didn't particularly want to appear in a medium where squiggly lines appeared across the screen every time a car went past. One also forgets how intellectually unrespectable, as well as technically primitive, television was in those days: one Sunday paper critic used to delight in calling it 'The Idiot's Lantern.' It was not until pre-recording on film and videotape became standard practice from the late 1950s on that the great stage stars began to ally themselves with television drama.

But it is also true that some of Peggy's early work for the camera – always excepting the Hitchcock film – has a slightly presentational quality. In 1958 she was lured back to the cinema by Fred Zinnemann's film, *The Nun's Story*, in which she plays a Reverend Mother in the Belgian Congo who tries to prevail on Audrey Hepburn as a conscience-torn nun to stay within a religious order. She once admitted that she wasn't terribly drawn to her character but that she wanted to work with the charming Zinnemann and the lovely Hepburn. Looking at the film now one finds that Peggy is sweetly authoritative in her wimple as she shows Miss Hepburn the missionary work the nuns do in the Congo. But, as she articulates crisply and brightly, one feels she delivers the performance to the camera rather than allowing the camera, as she does in her later roles, to eavesdrop on what is there.

Oddly enough, the performance that first showed Peggy's capacity for greatness in front of a camera was her Margaret of Anjou in *The Wars of the Roses*. It was odd because the performance was conceived on a large scale for a large theatre. But when the BBC televised the production at the end of the 1963 Stratford season – with Peter Hall and Robin Midgley rethinking it for the small screen – Peggy had several advantages. She had been playing the role for several months. She was working with a familiar company. She had also based her performance on a wealth of tiny truths within the broad transition from youth to age. Thus the camera was able to pick up almost better than the theatre audience (unless they were in the front rows) such details as her silent smirk at the reading of her marriage contract to Henry and the little shrug she gave at the revelation that Margaret has no dowry. Obviously the grandeur of the whole conception came across on television. Adrian Mitchell poetically observed in the pre-Murdoch *Sun* that 'Peggy Ashcroft's transformation from a kitten to a cobra and finally to a bitter old raven smacked of black magic.' But there was more to it than black magic. There was infinite subtlety as well. Mary Crozier in the *Guardian* noted that in the final play 'she had the cleverest way of faintly suggesting wandering wits' without having to shriek from the rooftops or radiate malignity.

Yet even after this it could hardly be said that Peggy was in ferocious demand as a film or television actress. She repeated some of her stage roles, such as Rebecca West and the Mother in *Days in the Trees*, for television and played Chekhov's wife, Olga Knipper, in a classy Rediffusion show, *From Chekhov with Love*. For the cinema she was mainly called upon to give prestigious little cameos, but never to carry the whole project or motor the production as she did in the theatre.

In Joseph Losey's high baroque *Secret Ceremony* released in 1968, the real star was 8 Addison Road, Kensington, which Halsey Richards designed in 1906 for Mr Debenham of Debenham and Freebody. With its peacock colours and highly wrought (indeed slightly overwrought) mosaics, it walked off with the picture from the nominal stars, Mia Farrow and Elizabeth Taylor. But Peggy and Pamela Brown popped in periodically to provide some eccentric human colour as a couple of dotty, light-fingered old aunts. Peggy had rather more to get her teeth into in Peter Hall's underrated second film for the cinema, *Three into Two Won't Go*, which had the advantage of an Edna O'Brien script based on an Andrea Newman novel. It was a good, coolly ironic film about the wanton destruction of a precarious marriage by a sexy teenager who sleeps with a sales executive at a Midlands hotel and then turns up unexpectedly one day on his doorstep. But it was Peggy as the hero's unwanted mother-in-law who provided some of the best acting. She once again disproved the old *canard* that her natural territory was that of classical drama or upper-middle-class Englishness. Whether dabbing genteelly at her mouth with a handkerchief or enquiring, in the midst of a blazing family row, 'Isn't this a little boisterous?', she was the embodiment of petty-bourgeois virtues and vices and of a generation nervous of emotional display. Peggy was again the mother-figure, this time with Glenda Jackson as a daughter discovering the problems of having a bisexual husband, in John Schlesinger's *Sunday Bloody Sunday*. She even emerged with some distinction ('typically firm in wit' said the *New Yorker*) from Tony Richardson's *Joseph Andrews*, which attempted to repeat the style and manner of *Tom Jones* but which simply proved that lightning does not strike twice in the same place.

After fifty years in the business, Peggy had appeared in only a dozen feature films and a handful of television plays. Partly out of choice; partly because of the old assumption that even when you make a movie out of a stage hit you don't use members of the original cast. The great turn-around in Peggy's screen fortunes came in 1978: a year that began her recent love affair with India and that showed she had a natural talent for what she calls 'the tremendous and difficult-to-acquire art of screen acting.'

During her trip to Canada in 1977 to play *Happy Days* for John Neville, she had had the foresight to pack some solid reading material in her baggage: Paul Scott's *The Raj Quartet* which had appeared in one massive, 2,000-page hardback volume the year before. Reading the book in trains, planes and hotel rooms filled her with a longing to go to India. By a happy accident, almost as soon as she got back to London, she had a phonecall from her agent asking her if she would like to work with James Ivory on a television film to be shot in Jodhpur and elsewhere in Rajasthan the following year. As soon as she read the script, she jumped at the offer: here at last was a film role that was something more than a glittering cameo.

Hullabaloo over Georgie and Bonnie's Pictures, as the film was called, was commissioned by Melvyn Bragg as a two-part special for his London Weekend Television arts magazine, *The South Bank Show*. It was shot in four weeks on a modest budget of £100,000 and was the work of the now legendary team of

James Ivory, producer Ismail Merchant and writer Ruth Prawer Jhabvala who went on to make *Heat and Dust*. Like a lot of this trio's work, it was a subtle, exquisitely comic Jamesian comedy of manners about the collision of two cultures and the confrontation between acquisitiveness and art, the material and the spiritual.

Peggy plays Lady G, an old Anglo-Indian hand and eccentric art-collector who travels overland from Europe in pursuit of a Maharajah's collection of rare miniatures with the aim of bringing them into the safe keeping of the British Museum. Also in pursuit of the paintings is Clark Haven's American millionaire, who gets first access to the collection when he touches the Maharajah's interest in another form of collecting: girls. The pictures are supposedly sent to Calcutta for sale by Victor Banerjee's Maharajah. There is a fire in which they are presumed destroyed, but at the glowingly contented conclusion they are once again displayed in their rightful, palatial Indian home.

For Peggy, at the age of 71, the making of the film was hard work with a schedule that often took her through from two in the afternoon to midnight. But the mood on the set was warm and friendly and Peggy's letters home from the Amaid Bhawan Palace in Jodhpur show her palpable response to India itself. 'Rajasthan,' she writes, 'has the most beautiful, bare, rugged countryside – a little like part of Greece. The town is ancient with modern appendages. The streets teem with people, children, animals, dogs, camels, bullocks, endless horse-tonga (and motorbike tonga) and *thousands* of bicycles. Imagine me driving the most dilapidated van through the streets (no proper hand-brake, a very peculiar green box and a start that nearly didn't). Very enjoyable.'

Peggy's enjoyment comes out in her performance, but more impressive is the way she takes one all round the character of Lady G and shows her multi-facetedness. In her first meeting with the Maharajah, she shows a brisk, brogued downrightness: 'I'm Gwyneth MacLaren Pugh,' she informs him, 'call me Lady G, everybody does.' But she also shows diplomatic skill and low cunning in the way she furthers a liaison between her pretty, hippyish assistant and the Maharajah with his appetite for European girls. At the same time, she displays the sentimental possessiveness of the Raj for everything Indian: 'O the moonlit nights and the nightingales,' she sweetly croons. Henry James once said that he delighted in 'a palpable, imaginable, visitable past', and Peggy conjures up before us the visitable past of the British Raj as she appropriates the Maharajah's personal bathroom, drops bricks and chuckles over the absurdity whereby the Maharajah and his sister still answer to the names of Georgie and Bonnie given them by a Scottish nanny.

A lot of credit, of course, belongs to James Ivory: a quiet, unobtrusive director who always seems more concerned with realising the material and bringing out the best in his actors than with imposing himself. He also allows a story to unfold in the Jamesian manner through a series of reverberations that say everything while seemingly saying nothing. He and Peggy also brought out the best in each other. 'I learned something from Peggy Ashcroft,' he says, 'and that is to go with first instincts. She brought so much to the role and thought it out so thoroughly that if I asked her to do something another way it was never quite as good.' But the educative process was mutual. She says of him: 'I'd never played a leading role in a film before and he taught me how to use the soft pedal, how to bring the performance down for the camera. That was very useful to me.'

From this time on all Peggy's screen performances were illuminated by the valuable lessons she learnt in *Hullabaloo*. Having for many years not even owned a set, she also found herself acquiring a taste for television acting when later in 1978 she came to play Queen Mary in Thames Television's de luxe soap opera about the Abdication Crisis, *Edward and Mrs Simpson*. This was the series that confirmed Edward Fox's star status as the wilful and immature Edward VIII, but it also gave Peggy the chance to show that Queen Mary was more than an ambulatory toque and to play her as a real woman arguing that, for a constitutional monarch, duty came before personal happiness. Playing a character from recent history is always tricky. The audience superimposes their memory of the real person on to the screen portrayal. It can also lead, in less skilled hands, to a Madame Tussaud impersonation. What Peggy gave us was the spirit of Queen Mary with her Corneille-like belief in the imperative of duty. But Clive James in the *Observer* picked out the real point, which was Peggy's ability to translate her talent from one medium to another: 'As Queen Mary, Dame Peggy is quietly giving everyone else on television a lesson in how to act for the camera. Since she so rarely acts for the camera, the secret of her astonishing command must lie not in a specialised training but in a general ability to accept, employ and transcend any set of technical limitations imposed on her. Dame Peggy is a bit of all right.'

Off-screen there were occasionally jarring moments. Marius Goring was also in the series. He had been Peggy's Romeo in 1933 and had once talked eagerly with her and Komisarjevsky about setting up a new company. Now he found there was an unbridgeable political gulf between himself and an actress he still passionately admired: he supported the right of Equity members to perform in South Africa while she vehemently opposed it. On and off the set, the relationship between them never rose above professional courtesy.

But at an age when sustaining a stage performance several times a week required a positive effort of will, Peggy now turned eagerly to television. In 1980 this yielded two marvellous performances – shown within the space of a week – in Stephen Poliakoff's *Caught on a Train* for the BBC and in Dennis Potter's *Cream in My Coffee* for London Weekend Television. In the former, she played Frau Messner, an imperious old Viennese party travelling on a trans-European express with a prickly young publishing PRO. In the latter she and Lionel Jeffries played an elderly married couple returning to the Eastbourne seaside hotel where 45 years earlier they had spent a dirty weekend. Good as she was in the Potter play, her Frau Messner is for me one of her great screen performances.

The shooting of *Caught on a Train* was, once again, extremely tiring. It involved many hours shut up in an imported *wagon-lit* on a disused line outside Peterborough as well as location scenes tramping around Frankfurt station and opera house. Stephen Poliakoff, a stage and screen veteran of 28, was also adjusting and re-writing the script as they went along. But still it was a brilliant performance. Why?

Partly because Peggy, working from the text, brought to the screen an absolutely firm concept of character. 'She was,' she says, 'very clear to me in my mind. She was upper-middle-class Viennese, had a husband who was a Nazi in the war but didn't care for the Nazis herself because they said "Heil Hitler" rather than "Gruss Gott" and caused a terrible servant shortage. One assumes she is a widow, now lives alone and has never had any children. That is why she is half attracted by the young man and half repelled. I was intrigued because she is such an extraordinary mixture: rude, selfish, arrogant yet at the same time perceptive and touching in her appraisal of herself.'

As always with Peggy, the sound of the character went hand in hand with the psychological understanding. She got the BBC Archives Department to send her recordings of the great Austrian singer, Lotte Lehmann, which she used as a model: 'I listened to them over and over, made notes while I listened and tried to get the vowel sounds, which are always the key, exactly right. The problem I always find with filming is that you have to imagine everything in sufficient detail before you begin in order to have a go at once. With the theatre or a studio play, there is time to rehearse and try things out. With filming, it is hit or miss.'

On this occasion, it was definitely hit. Peggy peels layers off the character as if stripping an onion. At first you take Frau Messner for an imperious dame in a fur hat and wrap. You even share the irritation of Michael Kitchen's Yuppie publisher as she demands that he run and fetch her magazines. But Peggy shoots out a wonderful look of pure sexual jealousy as she watches him sizing up the American girl in the seat opposite: this character, you realise, is still very much a woman.

With each scene Peggy gets closer to the core. In the restaurant car she becomes a monster of selfishness. She fumes at the piled-up table ('Really zey should have cleaned zees things'), peers at the menu through lorgnettes as if it were an opera programme, scrapes the plastic table with a fork and starts dropping plates on the floor to get some service. But when she and Kitchen repair to the Frankfurt Opera House during a stopover, she lets you see that this woman is the product of a pre-war world where every caprice was catered for. And there is a marvellous final encounter amidst the detritus of the restaurant car the morning after a harrowing night in which Kitchen was picked up by the police. Was Frau Messner spoilt? 'Always,' she replies with the lightest emphasis. But her own intransigent selfhood enables her to recognise the same quality in the young man. 'You don't really care about anything except success in your work,' she says with brutal truth. As he makes his way off the platform at Linz in the final shot, he passes her still sitting in the restaurant car: proud, stony, erect and lonely.

If one function of acting is to enlarge one's sympathy and understanding, then this is what Peggy achieves in this remarkable performance. Sylvia Clayton in the *Daily Telegraph* shrewdly observed that there is a strong element of folk-tale in Poliakoff's play: it is Peter, the woodcutter's son, fulfilling tasks imposed by an old witch. Yet Peggy takes the character of the old witch and gives her an imaginable past as well as a powerful present and a bleak future. She also combines an elderly dignity with a girlish flightiness that is very Peggy: in everything she does there is an enduring sexuality which is a potent part of her mystery. It was also present in Dennis Potter's *Cream in My Coffee* where she played, very touchingly, a lower-middle-class mouse of a wife confronting the emptiness of her 45-year marriage. It didn't stretch her histrionic muscles in quite the same way as the Poliakoff but it was still instinct with compassion; and together the two roles won Peggy the first of a string of British Academy of Film and Television Arts Awards. Russell Davies in the *Sunday Times* noted that Peggy had stayed away from the 'box' feeling that it was too well-named, too small. 'I can only say,' he added, 'that it is bound to get bigger if she stays in it.'

She did stay in it. And it did get bigger, proving that the domestic screen is capable of containing a monumental piece of acting.

264

CHAPTER EIGHTEEN

Indian Summer

THE STORY IS FAMILIAR, but it bears repeating.

In the autumn of 1980 Peggy was playing at the National in *Watch on the Rhine*. At the time Christopher Morahan was also working at the National as Peter Hall's deputy. One day Peggy walked through the stage door and heard Mr Morahan on the line to Granada Television. There was a momentary pause at the Manchester end of the phone. While Christopher Morahan hung on, Peggy seized her opportunity.

'Christopher,' she said, 'is it really true that you're going to do *The Raj Quartet*?'

'Yes, it is.'

'I'll never forgive you if you don't have me in it.'

'Right, what would you like to play?'

'Barbie.'

So there it was, says Peggy, just a gift from God; though one might add that God was given a sizeable nudge.

Christopher Morahan, who was to be producer and co-director on Granada's *The Jewel in the Crown*, confirms Peggy's version of how she came to be cast. 'She'd been in my mind for *Jewel* before that but, in a funny way, I thought she might be more interested in playing Mabel. But when she suggested herself as

Barbie all other notions fell by the wayside. The fact that she knew the books so well and so desperately wanted to play the part meant that no other casting entered my head.' Significantly, Christopher Morahan was also a part of that extended theatrical family which had woven its way through Peggy's whole career. As a young man, he had studied at the Old Vic School under Michel Saint-Denis and attended classes run by Margaret Harris. The Gielgud-Ashcroft companies also embodied the kind of theatre he wanted to be a part of. And he had got to know Peggy socially when his wife, Anna Carteret, acted with her at the National. For him, casting Peggy as Barbie simply completed the circle.

Because Peggy had imbibed Paul Scott's graphic description of the character, she was extremely well prepared to play Barbie, the ex-missionary teacher who is as much an anachronism in India as the British themselves. As always, getting the sound right was important, though here the basic decision was taken with astonishing swiftness. She was unable to attend the initial mammoth reading of the complete script that Morahan organised in London in the autumn of 1981 before Indian location filming started the following January. So one morning in mid-December Christopher Morahan, his co-director Jim O'Brien, Tim Pigott-Smith (Captain Merrick) and Geraldine James (Sarah Layton) went to Peggy's house in Hampstead for a reading of some of her crucial scenes.

Tim Pigott-Smith had met Peggy when she came to his Stratford school in 1964 and he received from her the Edward Flower Reading Prize. Their paths had crossed briefly again a few years later when he was at the Bristol Old Vic theatre school and she had come to see a first-year production of *Ghosts*. Her first words to him on her Hampstead doorstep were 'Don't I know you?' As he says: 'It was very sweet, very touching. I think it's one of the things that for me marks off all those great performers. They have a kind of common touch. You expect them to be "great" and you go in awe and they're not "great" at all. Their greatness is their extreme ordinariness. They have a great talent but they understand totally how to relate to people.'

The reading itself was remarkable for Peggy's almost instant tonal accuracy. 'She gave us,' says Pigott-Smith, 'a tour of accents.

She felt Barbie should be slightly "off" to get the class relationship with Aunt Mabel. She gave us a complete tour of London "off" accents and then she hit on the Croydon one with which she seemed to be most at home and it just seemed to be the most correct: that slightly affected, fey accent. But she really offered a choice, saying it could be this, that or the other and then turned to Christopher and said "Which one do you think it is?". He said "That one seems to me to be best." But there are also traces of class within that "off" accent, which seemed entirely right for Barbie who had spent her earlier years with posh people. You feel somehow that would have knotted into the character.' Christopher Morahan defines her accent in the role as what George Orwell called 'shabby-genteel'.

The Jewel in the Crown cast and crew set off for India in January 1982 for five months of often arduous location filming in Udaipur, Mysore, Simla and Kashmir. Peggy at the time was still playing the Countess in All's Well at Stratford and flew to India as soon as the season had finished in late January. Peggy and her old friend Rachel Kempson both stayed at Rose Cottage, seven and a half thousand feet up in the Simla hills, as guests of General Gurbash Singh and his wife, Cuckoo. With its view across a valley to the Himalayas and its cherry-trees in full blossom, it was a perfect setting. It could also be fearsomely cold at nights and one evening Peggy went along to Rachel Kempson's room where there was a small electric fire and huddled under the covers with her for warmth. When the houseboy, Nandhi, brought tea to their room, they couldn't help wondering what he made of the spectacle of two mature ladies sitting together under the same blanket.

Peggy came to India with a definite fix on the character of Barbie, but in the process of rehearsing and filming the character grew richer daily. She found herself, for instance, giving Barbie a very idiosyncratic walk. 'We discussed the walk,' says Morahan. 'But it was also the product of the fact that Peggy had recently had an operation on her knee so she harnessed that and used it herself. It wasn't a physical inhibition but she had to be careful and she just felt that a kind of wide-legged, virginal walk really would work. It was both sturdy and innocent. But it was also conditioned by the fact that she was unusually high up at Rose

Cottage and had to be able to walk in quite difficult conditions. But, more generally, what I noticed was that she drew on some hidden well of experience and imagination, so that practically everything she would do in front of the camera had a kind of freshness about it.'

There were occasional mild confrontations such as how to stage the scene of Barbie's fall. She moves her trunk out of the garden shed at Rose Cottage and sets off on a tonga or rickshaw which overturns, spilling her onto the road. Paul Scott apparently made a mistake in depicting the tonga as horse-drawn when in this particular area of the hill-stations it would have been man-drawn. Peggy wanted to play it by the book; Morahan insisted that the tonga be man-drawn. 'No,' he said firmly, 'Scott got it wrong and it is not possible for us to use horses. I absolutely assure you I will make that scene extremely dramatic and very telling.' Which, of course, it was, confounding Peggy's fear that Barbie's fall would seem insufficiently exciting.

Inevitably there were frustrating delays. Tim Pigott-Smith remembers having a blockbuster twelve-minute scene with Peggy which they had to delay shooting for a week as the weather began to fail. But, through his growing friendship with her, Tim Pigott-Smith also gained an insight into Peggy's lifelong mixture of certainty and doubt.

'She was worried,' he says, 'about the sheer amount of text she had to learn. If you've got big chunks on film you've simply got to know it better than you would at the first rehearsal of a play. I used to sit around with her a great deal and just listen to her lines. What intrigued me was her complete awareness of where the character was going and, in contrast, her insecurity as an actress. It taught me a fascinating lesson about acting, in that if you lose that crucial sense of vulnerability, you've had it altogether. She'd say to me "Do you think – is that right?" I kept thinking who was I to tell Dame Peg if it was or wasn't.'

Creating a character in a series of this length is a continual process: the filming forms the character and the playing of it illuminates what the search is for. But when Russell Davies wrote that the medium of television was bound to get bigger the longer Peggy stayed in it, he was nearer the literal truth than he knew. One thing became abundantly clear in India: that the character of Barbie, in Peggy's performance, was steadily growing in importance, so the length of *The Jewel in the Crown* was extended during shooting to accommodate that fact. Christopher Morahan recalls:

'I think the writer Ken Taylor, Jim O'Brien and myself came to the same conclusion as Paul Scott. I have a hunch – and there is no way I can prove this – that Barbie began to write herself. I have a feeling that the third book in the quartet, *The Towers of Silence*, as a piece of creative work didn't quite turn out as conceived by Scott. I think the character began to emerge with great strength and vigour and demand a book of her own. That's my romantic view of it. What happened to us was that we increased our product and made one more episode than originally planned, largely to give space to Barbie's scenes. This happened after we'd been shooting about six or seven months, in the light of what Peggy was doing on film. Because we'd managed our production quite sensibly I was able to demonstrate to Granada that, without any further outlay, I could give them an extra episode. It gave more air to the scenes with Barbie and allowed them to have their full richness. One whole sequence wasn't in the original concept at all – a marvellous scene, directed by Jim, between Barbie and a little Indian boy called Ashok, which Peggy and the rest of us felt would be marvellous to include.'

That particular scene, which I know Peggy is fond of, says a great deal about the deftness of Ken Taylor's script, about the unsentimental realism of Peggy's performance and about the meaning of the whole series. In Scott's novel it is no more than a fragment of dialogue about the flowers that the Indian boy, Ashok, buys daily for Barbie to place on the grave of her former companion, Mabel. In the television version it becomes a moving episode that reveals Barbie's sense of displacement and the declining role of the British in India.

Ashok meets Barbie in the village churchyard and offers to carry her luggage. He says that he has no friends, no gang, and is soon to go away: Barbie recognises in him a fellow outcast. When Barbie sings him a snatch of an old hymn, it reminds her of the importance of Christianity in her life and of the fact that belief is waning. With infinite tenderness, Peggy looks into the boy's eyes and says: 'I am a servant of our Lord Jesus. He is our

Mother and our Father. *Man-bap* ... You don't understand. It's too far away and long ago. The world is grown corrupt.'

Peggy, as Barbie, offers the boy her love; he looks at her with puzzlement, expecting only *baksheesh*. The gulf between her and the boy, between two different cultures, is present in that moment. And when Peggy says, looking at the boy with unanswered love, 'My heart hardly beats at all, it's very tired and old and far from home', she seems to be speaking not only for Barbie but for all the British in India. She plays this scene, which is as touching as anything in the whole 15 hours of the series, with poise, tenderness, affection and a wonderful elegiac melancholy.

It is a sign of Ken Taylor's subtlety that he follows this on screen with a scene that occurs a hundred pages earlier in the novel, between Barbie and Sarah Layton (Geraldine James) on the terrace at Rose Cottage, just before Barbie's departure. Sarah echoes the notion of *man-bap*: Mother-Father, the relationship of the British Raj to India, of Barbie herself to the children she had taught. It was also embodied in the famous and resonant picture of Queen Victoria and India, the jewel in her crown. As *man-bap* is mentioned by Sarah, you suddenly see the light going out in Peggy's eyes at the realisation that her own maternal role is over: that she is now as much a misfit in India as the civilisation to which she belongs. But, as always in her performance, symbolic overtones are quickly brought back to reality. When Peggy says to Sarah that she won't yet be able to invite her to the Peploe's where she is staying because of insinuations of lesbianism she remarks, 'I don't want to push my luck, as the saying is' in a flat-vowelled voice that is pure Croydon.

Location shooting finished in India in May 1982, and by July Peggy was back on stage at the Barbican playing the Countess in the London transfer of *All's Well*. But, though it was the end of her second eastern adventure, it was by no means the end of work on *The Jewel in the Crown*. Shooting continued for another year in a group of Manchester warehouses converted by Granada into a massive four-wall studio known as Botany. By November Peggy was in Manchester shooting daily from eight in the morning till six at night and staying 'over the shop' in Sidney Bernstein's comfortable penthouse flat on top of the Granada building. She found it extraordinary and nostalgic to discover the ground floor of Rose Cottage reconstructed in minute detail with a cyclorama of the Himalayas beyond. Even stranger was being whisked out of Manchester on a 90-minute drive to a Derbyshire village where an old church stood in for St John's in Pankot.

By Christmas Peggy's scenes were mostly completed, but it was to be January 1984 – by which time Peggy had embarked on her third Indian excursion – before the complete 14-part series was shown to the British public. Just what was it that made the series so popular?

Obviously it was a response to the expertness of the acting and direction and the easy collusion, in both Scott's narrative and Taylor's adaptation, between the private and public worlds: personal lives unfolded against a background of historic events. But Peggy gets it right when she says, 'I think it tapped some very sensitive nerve in the British people: a conscience about the role we played in India as well as a certain pride in some quarters. I suspect it was received with a strange mixture of nostalgia and guilt.' She was, in fact, somewhat surprised by the attacks on the series from sources as diverse as Enoch Powell, James Cameron and Salman Rushdie and rebutted them in the course of an interview with Andrew Robinson in *Sight and Sound*: 'Paul Scott's pretty anti-British, although he presents you with some decent people. The most decent and the most rounded is Sarah Layton. Her final comment is: "After three hundred years in India, how can we have produced such a damned, bloody senseless mess?" I wouldn't say that was particularly waving the flag, would you?'

But what was it that made Peggy's Barbie so remarkable? Obviously it has something to do with the way she takes the physical lineaments of the character as described by Paul Scott and fills them out in her own particular way. Scott gives one a very clear image of Barbie: 'The iron-grey hair, cropped almost as short as a man's but softened by attractive natural waves, gave an idea of sacrificial fortitude rather than of sexual ambivalence. Her costume, severely tailored, and made of hard-wearing cloth, did not disguise the rounded shape of her unclaimed breast.' 'Unclaimed breast' is good, since it suggests simultaneously something bra-less and untouched by human hand. But Peggy built on Scott's portrait to give us Barbie's optimism and despair, waddling eccentricity and touching ordinariness, recollected joy and growing awareness that she and her kind are now relics on the dustheap of empire.

My own feeling, however, is that it was Barbie's outsiderishness that Peggy captured so beautifully: the sense that she was always set apart from the clan or the group. And many of the moments from her performance that stay in the mind are to do with aloneness. The image of Barbie sitting on the verandah of Rose Cottage in a Simla sunset quietly weeping for the death of Mabel. The shrieked conviction that 'She is in torment' as Barbie sees Mabel's corpse in the hospital. The characteristic set of the mouth when Clarissa Peploe, with whom she is staying, hints that there has been talk of unnatural inclinations, to which Peggy replies 'It's a difficult thing for an elderly spinster to refute.' The sickened revulsion when Barbie discovers Mildred Layton and Captain Coley noisily making love. Peggy was particularly amused by the way that last sequence so excited the indignation of Mrs Whitehouse. 'When you think,' she says, 'what excesses of copulation you see on the telly, why did that brief sordid glimpse upset her so? Do you think it's because Barbie witnessed it? Do you think it was Mrs Whitehouse herself having a peep through the door?'

Peggy's performance was widely and rightly praised. Richard Ingrams in the *Spectator* described it as 'a *tour de force* which deserves to win every available award for outstanding acting' (it did, including the BAFTA, Royal Television Society and Broadcasting Press Guild Awards). John O'Connor in the *New York Times* wrote that Peggy as the elderly, eccentric missionary turned a rather wispy presence into 'an oracle of judgement'. The Medical Briefing in *The Times* signally praised 'the authentic medical detail' of Peggy's portrayal of Barbie's senility. But the truest note was sounded by the *Times Literary Supplement*, which detected the quality of tragedy Peggy caught behind the loveableness, describing how 'dislodged from one bolt-hole after another, Barbie nighmarishly tumbles from voluble, robust decency into a fierce, dumb despair – something Peggy Ashcroft's unsparing, compassionate performance, with its harsh thickening modulations though chokings of shame and cloggings of bronchitis, rendingly displays.'

That is exactly right. Peggy brought to the role a strong

compassion for a character – a virginal oddity losing her faith and her sanity in a foreign land – far removed from her own experience. At the same time, she obviously dug deep into her own affective memories of solitude and isolation. Christopher Morahan, who was as close to Peggy as anyone, says, 'We would look at this performance with wonder because it had come out of some deep well of experience which was continually stimulating.'

By the time *The Jewel in the Crown* was being shown on British television, Peggy was back in India playing Mrs Moore in David Lean's movie of *A Passage to India*. It was a performance that was to win her sheaves of tributes and shelvesful of awards (including a Hollywood Oscar) but, although Peggy is very reticent about what happened, it is clear that the film was a much less harmonious experience than the television epic. The cast of *The Jewel in the Crown* became a strong family unit and still go on seeing each other. Tim Pigott-Smith, for instance, takes his son Tom round to see Peggy occasionally and she tells him how she once batted with Len Hutton. And when Geraldine James married Joe Blatchley, it was Peggy who read a Shakespeare sonnet at the service while leaning casually up against the church wall. Peggy made many good friends as a result of the Lean film – and, as George Rylands remarks, she has a positive genius for friendship – such as Victor Banerjee, Richard Wilson and Maggie Unsworth. But where the cast of *Jewel*, perhaps because they are more theatrically based, seem to form a loose-knit club, the actors in *A Passage to India* have mostly gone their separate ways in show business.

Unlike Barbie Batchelor, Mrs Moore in *A Passage to India* was not a role that Peggy sought: it seems, in some strange way, to have sought her. In 1960 Santha Rama Rau had done a stage version of the book which moved from the Oxford Playhouse into the West End with Zia Mohyeddin as Aziz and Enid Lorimer as Mrs Moore – a role which Sybil Thorndike later played in a television version. Peggy went to see the stage show at the Comedy Theatre and had her one encounter with E. M. Forster, who irritated her slightly by saying that he hoped that one day she would play Mrs Moore: 'I thought "What me play an old girl like that?" because, although I wasn't that young at the time, the idea had never crossed my mind.' In 1967 the Indian filmmaker Satyajit Ray explored the possibility of filming the book, with Peggy as Mrs Moore, but the idea came to nothing. After Forster's death in 1970, James Ivory and Ismail Merchant also resurrected the idea but once again the project fell through. Finally, the race went to the Lean.

When Peggy was approached in the summer of 1983 about the possibility of playing Mrs Moore, she was at first extremely hesitant. David Lean is famous for his meticulousness and the length of his shooting schedules. As Peggy says: 'Even the experience of India seemed to me almost more than I could perhaps take at my age and for a third time. When I was asked to do it, I said "Mr Lean, I am 76" and he said "So am I", so that shamed me.'

Peggy met Lean for a crucial lunch in June of that year when she was bowled over by his charm and fascinated to discover that they had been young contemporaries in Croydon. But she admitted in a letter that she had problems in 'seeing' Mrs Moore clearly and that she didn't really understand what Forster meant to convey in Chapters 22 and 23. These are the chapters after the incident in the Marabar Caves where Mrs Moore stubbornly refuses to have anything to do with the trial of Dr Aziz and replaces her former Christian tenderness with hardness of heart and what Forster calls 'a just irritation against the human race'. In fact, she sails home on the first available P & O liner to escape the trial, the marriage of Ronny and Miss Quested, and the hot weather. She suffers what Forster sees as the twilit double vision of the elderly: 'She had come to that state where the horror of the universe and its smallness are both visible at the same time.' Peggy says in the letter that she is on her third reading of the book but finds it more and more ambivalent. Equally significant, she remarks that Lean himself loves the character of Mrs Moore but also doesn't understand the change she undergoes and has indeed ignored it totally in the script. One problem in acting Mrs Moore was that Peggy had to make real and manifest a character who in Forster's novel is strange and elemental and in David Lean's movie script blurred and elliptical.

Superficially it may seem as if Peggy, once she agreed to play Mrs Moore, was taking on a character not dissimilar to Barbie: both, after all, are Christian women who in the course of their experiences in India lose their faith. But there the resemblance ends. Barbie is described by Paul Scott with graphic clarity; Mrs Moore is hardly pictured by Forster at all except, in the scene with Aziz in the mosque, as a red-faced old lady with white hair. The mood of the two books could also hardly be more different. Forster's novel is mystical, poetic, suggestive (its title is a reference to Walt Whitman's *Leaves of Grass*) with something of the flowing manner of Eastern philosophy, where Scott's Quartet is specific, historical and precise. No one, to my knowledge, has pinned down the difference between the two writers more perceptively than Peggy herself in her interview in *Sight and Sound*:

'Scott is very objective, whereas Forster is subjective; one is male, one is female almost; one is factual, one is mysterious. Sometimes I think of Forster as being rather Chekhovian and Scott as being, perhaps, like Ibsen. There is much more of *War and Peace* in Scott than there is in *Passage*. The characters are, in a sense, to be argued about: he crystallises them and you can almost see them physically. Forster's characters have a lot of blurred outlines. Nearly all Forster's women are like this.'

In playing the character, however, Peggy had to fill in those blurred outlines for herself. She imagined Mrs Moore as a lady with beads who comes from the outskirts of some provincial city, slightly acid in her relationship with her son, Ronny (rather in the manner of Forster's own mother), and capable of responding to India in a way that the Anglo-Indian military wife rarely did.

During the shooting, which began in India in January 1984, there was plenty of time for Peggy to puzzle out ways of giving details to her shadowy character. There were other vicissitudes to contend with. On one occasion, there was a hotel so auto-cratically run and riddled with damp that it was quickly christened Dampton Manor. More seriously, while shooting the vital scene in the mosque with Dr Aziz, Peggy badly damaged her foot and had to rest for a fortnight.

Furthermore, it is clear that Peggy had ambiguous feelings about her director, whom she once dubbed Magical Mister Mis-topheles. She pays sincere tribute to his enthusiasm, passion and skill and his detailed work on the script, which 'he had practically shot in his head before he got to India.' But that last phrase gives some clue as to why she and David Lean were never tuned to precisely the same wavelength. Lean is a master technician who came to direction via the cutting-room: he has never worked in the theatre which demands an acute understanding of actors' psychology. Early on in the shooting of *A Passage to India* Peggy asked when they were going to rehearse or have a read-through. Apparently the term 'read-through' was not one in Lean's vocabulary; but, to his credit, he was delighted to organise one and found it very instructive. But at this point Lean announced 'There are two characters in this film who are three feet off the ground – Mrs Moore and Professor Godbole.'

This threw Peggy completely. 'It seemed,' she says, 'as if he wanted her to be a mystical and mysterious person whereas I saw her as someone with her feet planted firmly on the ground.' For an actress used to digging into and exploring a character, it seemed to short-circuit the whole process of motivation and discovery. It was as if Lean wanted the ready-made result without the research and the actress–director relationship took a while to recover. One of Lean's methods – to which another actor in the film, Art Malik, pays tribute – is to invite the actor to look through the camera-lens to see the visual effect he is after. For Peggy this meant an awkward clamber up the camera trolley and a sense that she was having to conform to a pre-ordained image. Lean and Peggy shared a Croydon background. But their professional experiences could hardly have been more different and Lean's undoubted genius for relating figures to landscape was palpably at odds with Peggy's Stanislavskyan delving into character.

Peggy spent most of the three-month shooting period in Bangalore but also stayed for a time at the Ootacamund Club in the Nilgiris about ten hours' drive away. She played snooker on the very table where the game was allegedly invented, read voraciously (she was fascinated by V. S. Naipaul's *Area of Darkness* with its funny, moving and depressing account of India) and visited the remarkable and highly progressive Neel Bagh school for village children run by an Englishman, David Horsburgh. It was another actress in the film, Ann Firbank, who had discovered this enlightened school which had no competitiveness and no sport. Peggy was equally fascinated by it and spent a day there reading *The Pied Piper of Hamelin* to the children and, on her return to London, took part in fund-raising evenings for the school. But although her passion for India remains intact, time sometimes weighed a little heavily on her hands and she was not altogether sorry when at the end of March she was able to return home.

But, despite the *longueurs* and temperamental differences on location, the end result, in Peggy's case, is remarkable. Her Mrs Moore on screen is confirmation of Trevor Nunn's point that, when actors and actresses reach a certain age, it is their life experience that really counts. In the classic encounter in the moonlit mosque with Victor Banerjee's marvellous Dr Aziz, Peggy doesn't make a great show of sympathetic curiosity: she just represents it by her very presence. And after the mysterious experience in the Marabar Caves – a literary device that makes little sense when you translate it into the visual literalism of cinema – there is an extraordinary moment when Peggy's Mrs Moore is quitting India and looks out of a train window and sees the Hindu scholar, Professor Godbole. Alec Guinness as Godbole makes a mysterious bowing gesture, half prayer, half supplication: Peggy looks at him out of the train window and watches him with despair and uncertainty flickering across her face. It is a meeting of two enigmas, and the most purely Forsterian moment in the whole film.

When the film was released in 1985, it received mixed notices: slightly guilty ones from many American critics whose fervent hostility to *Ryan's Daughter* fourteen years before had helped to drive Lean out of the cinema altogether, fairly enthusiastic ones in England except from those critics steeped in Forster's novel. But everyone was united in praise of Peggy's performance, and no one understood better than Pauline Kael in *The New Yorker* how much she brought to the role:

'As Mrs Moore, Peggy Ashcroft comes through with a piece of transcendent acting. She has to because Mrs Moore is meant to be a saint, a sage, a woman in tune with the secrets of eternity. Forster never devised anything for her to do; in the novel, she simply *is* a sacred being ... Except for Mrs Moore's brief rapport with Aziz, who tells her she has the kindest face he has ever seen on an English lady, she's simply a weary, practical-minded woman who's very sure of things. She's not much of a mother –

she's quite out of sympathy with her son Ronny – and she has no particular feeling for Miss Quested. She's a cantankerous old lady, yet Peggy Ashcroft breathes so much good sense into the role that Mrs Moore acquires a radiance, a spiritual glow. It makes us like her.'

Although Peggy had carefully kept her counsel and retained her privacy all through her career, the combination of her success in *The Jewel in the Crown* and *A Passage to India* inevitably quickened curiosity about her. She gave a number of interviews and was the subject of a handful of profiles, and when she won a Hollywood Oscar as Best Supporting Actress for her performance in Lean's film, there was a rash of speculative articles about her. But she was unable to answer people's enquiries because she was stricken with 'flu so badly that she was unable to go to Los Angeles for the awards ceremony.

However, her triumph at the Oscars had a rather sad twist to it. She had asked Victor Banerjee to accept the Award on her behalf if she, by any chance, won. But on the evening of the Los Angeles ceremony, Banerjee was emphatically told by the organisers that *nobody* would be permitted to accept the statue on her behalf. He accepted the situation. Then, to the astonishment of himself and David Lean, Angela Lansbury (an old friend and colleague of Peggy's) arrived on stage as soon as the announcement of Peggy's win was made. Later in the week, Peggy received an abject apology from Gregory Peck, on behalf of the Academy, saying that it had all been a terrible mix-up. What was frustrating for Peggy was that, through Victor Banerjee, she had wanted to thank India, above all, for inspiring E. M. Forster and David Lean and for making both the film and the book – as well as her performance – possible. It is a pity that such a generous, Ashcroftian gesture went unnoticed amidst the clatter of the showbiz razzmatazz.

Since her great performance in David Lean's film, Peggy has worked on a number of other projects for film and television. Late in 1985 she found herself battling against crippling laryngitis while on location for a film for TV South called *Murder by the Book*. Not surprisingly, she was full of depressed thoughts about retirement. Being Peggy, she was also full of guilt at the cancellation of professional engagements, including various Sunday recitals. But although she had a severe bout of post-illness blues and although eleven days' filming had to be crowded into six, the resulting film was a pleasurable conceit in which Agatha Christie is visited by an indignant Hercule Poirot at the very point when she is about to kill him off. Nick Evans's script made the shrewd point that the more successful a detective becomes, the more he haunts his creator, until death is the only solution. But the chief pleasure of the film lay in the interaction between Ian Holm and Peggy, reunited for the first time since *The Wars of the Roses*. Holm's Poirot is all sleek, dandified irritation; Peggy's remarkable Mrs Christie, sharp and sly, 'illuminates the play with her candlepower', in the words of Nancy Banks-Smith. No one could have served cocoa laced with potassium cynanide with more sweetly-smiling grace than Peggy.

In 1987 Peggy was heard but not seen, along with John Mills, in the animated film version of Raymond Briggs's *When the Wind Blows*. For Peggy, a one-time Aldermaston marcher and passionate CND supporter, the work was close to her heart. She and John Mills do the voices for a South London suburban couple who, as nuclear war threatens, naïvely follow instructions in government civil defence leaflets: the result is that, after the bomb drops, they find themselves alone in a blasted landscape mumbling the Twenty-Third Psalm. For Peggy the film represented two days' work and half a lifetime's actual beliefs. But one has to admit that John Mills, who privately believes we cannot give up the bomb since it has kept the peace in Europe for 40 years, performs with equal vocal assurance.

Happily Peggy shows no signs of giving up. In her 80th year she appeared, in granny specs and beret, as the seaside landlady, Miss Dubber, in John Le Carré's *A Perfect Spy* on BBC Television. And she appeared in a film, *Madame Sousatzka*, directed by John Schlesinger and based by Ruth Prawer Jhabvala on a novel by Bernice Rubens.

In this she plays an eccentric, twilit old aristocrat who lives in the dank basement of the house she owns and who takes a proprietorial interest in the lives of all her tenants. One cold, foggy November day I found Peggy patiently resting between takes in a house being used for location shooting just off Ladbroke Grove. We talked of this and that: my progress with the book, her impending move from her Hampstead house into a flat, the Olivia Manning series, *Fortunes of War*, then running on BBC Television which she thought highly of. Nothing momentous may have been said; but, simply by her quickness and alertness, she took the chill off a depressing day. As Harold Pinter once said to me, she's a great girl because she's not resigned to anything.

During a break in shooting, John Schlesinger made a number of fascinating points about her qualities as a screen actress. He first worked with her in 1961 on a brilliant TV film for *Monitor*, the BBC arts magazine, which dealt with a drama class at the Central School of Speech and Drama. Peggy had spoken the final voice-over and, he said, had hit the first word in a sentence with explosive emphasis: now he felt there was no trace of mannerism in her acting.

'A lot of directors,' he said, 'take on a great actor and then are frightened of directing them. But in my experience great actors both give you a lot and crave direction. It was true of Olivier in *Marathon Man* and it is certainly true of Peggy. Before we started shooting, she offered me lots of ideas about this eccentric old character who talked with her head tilted to one side. Now we are working, she can be quite beady and tough – she said the other day that I had cut her only laugh in the picture – but her instincts are always right. When you look at her early work for the camera, you realise that she has *become* a great screen actress in her later years. It is difficult to say why except that she has this ability to communicate emotion with absolute honesty.'

Schlesinger is right. His words reminded me of a character in Clifford Odets's *Awake and Sing* who says that she likes seeing Wallace Beery on the screen. When asked why she says: 'He acts like life: very good.'

But meeting Peggy on location on this gloomy, fog-shrouded, Dickensian London day, I was struck by the strange compulsiveness of the born actress. Here she was close on 80 years of age sitting in a bleak room in a dingy London house conserving her energies for the next take and wanting, as ever, to get it right in a medium where, as John Schlesinger says, 'You're trying to get two minutes of first night on film every day.'

One other major project occupied Peggy's 80th year: the

compilation and recording of a television programme called *Two Loves* in which Julian Bream played John Dowland's lute music and Peggy spoke Shakespeare's verse. Julian Bream is a very old friend of Peggy's: he was first introduced to her in the mid-1950s by the poet, Laurie Lee, and has since done countless Apollo Society recitals with her. His account of their collaboration on *Two Loves*, put out by BBC 2 on her birthday, provides evidence of two of Peggy's paramount qualities: insecurity and enthusiasm.

It was Julian Bream who first mooted the notion of their working together on a Dowland–Shakespeare programme. She responded warmly because she believed their music and poetry were complementary. He, not having played the lute for ten years, wanted to re-familiarise himself with the instrument. So he sold the idea to BBC 2 suggesting that it might make a suitable 80th birthday tribute. But, knowing that Peggy didn't want a great fuss made of the event, he kept the timing of the transmission up his sleeve.

'Then one late afternoon,' he recalls, 'Peggy and I were throwing ideas at each other and she suddenly got very despondent and said, "We can't do this – it'll be the biggest switch-off of the year. Why can't we try something else?" I thought there was no point in pressing the matter so I took her out to dinner where we talked of other things and then went back to my place in the country. About four days later the phone rang and it was Peggy full of enthusiasm saying that she had some fresh ideas for the programme. I rushed up to London straightaway and we resumed work as if nothing had happened.

'The next question was where to record the programme. I thought of Elsinore because Dowland had been lutanist to the King of Denmark but Peggy felt it was too gloomy so we settled on Penshurst Place, an Elizabethan mansion with great Shakespearean associations. I recorded the music one day: Peggy did the poetry the next. She was magnificently professional about the whole thing and did the programme virtually on one take. That would be an achievement for anybody but for someone of her age it was extraordinary.

'After we had recorded it, we were talking one day and Peggy suddenly said, out of the blue, "You know, Julian, it would be marvellous if it were shown on my 80th birthday." I have known and loved Peggy for many years and have seen her many times under the joy and stress of creating. I think it's a sign of her intelligence that she takes time to weigh up an idea. Too many of us are impulsive and rush into things saying that's a good idea, let's do it. But it's not always the wisest course of action. You've got to know whether you have the inner capacity to bring it off as well as an integrity of your own in wanting it to be brought off. Peggy, as you know, has great integrity.'

Julian Bream's story confirms what many others have told me: that with any new undertaking Peggy often goes through a period of creative doubt but is always passionate and whole-hearted when it comes to the execution. And, by a happy circumstance, *Two Loves* looks like having a long life: it is being re-created for Radio 3 and then issued as an RCA disc. That is good because it both celebrates Peggy's love of Shakespeare and exemplifies her instinctive melodic gift. As Julian Bream says: 'There is a poetry, a melody, a music in her voice which reveals much of her inner quality. As you get older as an artist what happens is that any bit of dross you've collected on the way becomes meaningless and you can dispense with it. You're left with just yourself. But if you've kept your integrity, you reveal even more magic than you have done before.'

Acting, I said at the outset, is a mysterious business. But perhaps a fragment of its mystery – and the lesson of Peggy's amazing career – is that mimetic virtuosity matters less than inner strength and that only by becoming a whole army of others do you in the end reveal your true self.

Postscript

On Sunday, 20 December, 1987 – two days before her 80th birthday – the theatrical profession gathered at the Old Vic to pay tribute to Peggy. It is fair to say that Peggy, although accompanied by her children, grandchildren and friends, was faintly apprehensive about being lauded in public. In the event the show, *Her Infinite Variety* devised by Tony Church for the RSC, hit exactly the right note. It had none of the dreadful pomp of a black-tie gala. It was more like an informal party made up of extracts from plays Peggy had done and of selections from her favourite poetry and music.

The links were entrusted to Anthony Quayle who had first appeared with Peggy at the Old Vic 55 years previously; to Peter Hall whose first action on being invited to create a company at Stratford had been to approach Peggy; and to Hall's successor, Trevor Nunn, who made her a part of the RSC's directorate and who became a close friend. Peter Hall put it best when he said the evening showed 'the intricate web of relationships, traditions and influences our theatre represents.'

On stage several different generations easily merged. There was Gwen Ffrangcon-Davies, now 91, delivering the Quality of Mercy speech with bell-like clarity and perfect stress and Dadie Rylands, a mere 85, giving us Max Beerbohm's hilarious cricketing account of Benson's production of Henry V ('The fielding was excellent and so was the batting'). There was Judi Dench reminding us of her own great Cleopatra and Helen Mirren, in pearl-grey dress, lending Juliet an impassioned urgency. And, from a younger generation, we had Juliet Stevenson's frisky, betrousered Rosalind, Fiona Shaw's broody Shrew and Harriet Walter's tenderly erotic Viola.

The whole evening was about continuity, permanence, the creation of companies: all things for which Peggy has fought strenuously. And this in the end is the measure of her achievement. I set out on this journey through her career by saying that I would attempt to delve into the heart of her mystery. I no longer think that this is possible. Every actor and actress has an inner creative self which they jealously guard – Peggy more than most – and which they may not always understand themselves. All one can do is to erect a few signposts and hope that they point in the right direction.

But I would argue that Peggy's career is more than the sum total of its parts. She has dignified her profession through her campaigning fervour and has proved that the actor or actress is a part of society rather than apart from it. But more than that, by the force of her example, she has shown her belief in the ideal of permanent companies preferably supported by government subsidy. When she started out on her career, this was not a fashionable view. And even today, when there is a myopic assumption that private sponsorship can take the burden off public subsidy of the arts, the battle has still not been won. The Royal Shakespeare Company, the National Theatre, the regional companies and the Fringe are all vulnerable to an ethos that regards commercial success as the only real criterion of artistic worth. The ideal of permanent companies is one that Peggy has fought for all her life since she knows that, without experiment and occasional failure, nothing of durable value can be created. The best thing that those who admire her can do is to ensure that the philosophy of the casino society does not prevail and that the company ideal is preserved intact.

That, to me, was the significance of *Her Infinite Variety*: it was a tribute to both a rare talent and a radical belief. At the end Peggy herself appeared on stage to deliver Rosalind's Epilogue from *As You Like It*. The voice was as true and clear as ever, the sentiment as heartfelt. I called to mind G. H. Lewes who said of Helen Faucit in parts like Rosalind that she was able to represent the joyous playfulness of young animal spirits without ceasing to be poetical. 'The manner,' he wrote, 'may be light but it sprang from a deep nature.' His words applied perfectly to Peggy. As the house rose to her and her fellow actors applauded, she looked bashful, happy and a trifle dazed. Prompted by Peter Hall, she took a tumultuous solo call and then, with evident relief, escaped into the wings.

Chronology

PEGGY ASHCROFT'S APPEARANCES in theatre, film and television:

1907 Born 22 December, Croydon, Surrey.

1926 First professional stage appearance: Margaret in J. M. Barrie's *Dear Brutus* with Ralph Richardson, directed by W. G. Fay at the Birmingham Repertory Theatre.

1927 Bessie Carvil in Joseph Conrad's *One Day More*, directed by Ralph Neale at Playroom Six.

Mary Dunn in Charles Bennett's *The Return*, directed by Alexander Field at the Everyman, Hampstead.

Eve in George Paston's *When Adam Delved*, directed by Nigel Playfair at the Q.

Joan Greenleaf in John Drinkwater's *Bird in Hand* with Laurence Olivier, directed by the author at the Birmingham Repertory Theatre.

Betty in William Congreve's *The Way of the World* with Edith Evans, directed by Nigel Playfair at Wyndham's.

1928 Anastasia Vullimay in Bernard Shaw's *The Fascinating Foundling* and Mary Bruin in W. B. Yeats's *The Land of Heart's Desire*, both directed by Henry Oscar at the Arts Theatre.

Hester in Sidney Howard's *The Silver Cord* with Lilian Braithwaite and Fabia Drake, directed by Henry Oscar on tour.

Edith Strange in Leslie Goddard and Cecil Weir's *Earthbound*, directed by Henry Oscar at the Q.

Kristina in August Strindberg's *Easter* with Gwen Ffrangcon-Davies, directed by Allan Wade at the Arts.

Eulalia in the Quinteros' *A Hundred Years Old* with Horace Hodges, directed by A. E. Filmer at the Lyric Hammersmith.

1929 Lucy Deren in Molly Kerr's *Requital*, directed by the author at the Everyman, Hampstead.

Sally Humphries in H. F. Maltby's *Bees and Honey*, directed by the author at the Strand.

Constance Neville in Oliver Goldsmith's *She Stoops to Conquer*, directed by Nigel Playfair on tour.

Naemi in Ashley Dukes's *Jew Süss* (adapted from the novel by Lion Feuchtwanger) with Matheson Lang, co-directed by Lang and Reginald Denham at the Duke of York's.

1930 Desdemona in William Shakespeare's *Othello* with Paul Robeson, directed by Ellen van Volkenburg at the Savoy.

Judy Battle in Somerset Maugham's *The Breadwinner* with Ronald Squire and Jack Hawkins, directed by Athole Stewart at the Vaudeville.

1931 Pervaneh in James Elroy Flecker's *Hassan*, directed by Gibson Cowan at the New, Oxford, for OUDS.

Angela in Curt Götz's *Charles the 3rd* (adapted by Edgar Wallace), directed by Mrs Edgar Wallace at Wyndham's.

Anne in Jan Fabricus's *A Knight Passed By* (adapted by W. A. Darlington), directed by Jan Fabricus at the Ambassadors.

Fanny in Marcel Pagnol's *Sea Fever* (adapted by Auriol Lee and John van Druten), directed by Auriol Lee at the New.

Marcela in the Sierras' *Take Two from One* (adapted by Helen and Harley Granville-Barker) with Gertrude Lawrence, directed by Theodore Komisarjevsky at the Haymarket.

1932 Juliet in William Shakespeare's *Romeo and Juliet* with Christopher Hassall, directed by John Gielgud at the New, Oxford, for OUDS.

Stella in Fernand Crommelynck's *Le Coçu Magnifique* (translated by Ivor Montagu), directed by Theodore Komisarjevsky at the Globe.

Salome Westway in Eden Phillpots's *The Secret Woman* with Nancy Price, directed by Miss Price at the Duchess.

Season with the Old Vic Company:
    Cleopatra in George Bernard Shaw's *Caesar and Cleopatra*.
    Imogen in William Shakespeare's *Cymbeline*.
    Rosalind in William Shakespeare's *As You Like It*.
    Portia in William Shakespeare's *The Merchant of Venice*.
    All directed by Harcourt Williams (except for *The Merchant*, directed by John Gielgud) with a company including Malcolm Keen, Valerie Tudor, William Fox, Marius Goring, Roger Livesey, Anthony Quayle and George Devine.
The title role in Arthur Schnitzler's *Fräulein Elsa*, adapted and directed by Theodore Komisarjevsky at the Kingsway.

1933 Season with the Old Vic Company (continued):
    Perdita in William Shakespeare's *The Winter's Tale*.
    Kate Hardcastle in Oliver Goldsmith's *She Stoops to Conquer*.
    The title role in John Drinkwater's *Mary Stuart*.
    Juliet in William Shakespeare's *Romeo and Juliet*.
    Lady Teazle in Richard Brinsley Sheridan's *The School for Scandal*.
    Miranda in William Shakespeare's *The Tempest*.
    All directed by Harcourt Williams.
Inken Peters in Gerhard Hauptmann's *Before Sunset*, adapted and directed by Miles Malleson at the Shaftesbury.
Film: Olalla Quintana in *The Wandering Jew* with Conrad Veidt, directed by Maurice Elvey.

1934 Vasantasena in Carl Zuckmayer's *The Golden Toy* with Ion Swinley and Nellie Wallace, directed by Ludwig Berger at the Coliseum.
Lucia Maubel in Pirandello's *The Life that I Gave Him* (adapted by Clifford Bax) with Nancy Price, directed by Frank Birch at the Little.

1935 Therese Paradis in Beverley Nichols's *Mesmer* with Oscar Homolka, directed by Theodore Komisarjevsky on tour.
Juliet in William Shakespeare's *Romeo and Juliet* with John Gielgud, Laurence Olivier and Edith Evans, directed by John Gielgud at the New.
Film: Mrs Crofter in *The Thirty-Nine Steps* with Robert Donat, directed by Alfred Hitchcock.

1936 Nina in Anton Chekhov's *The Seagull* with Stephen Haggard, Edith Evans and John Gielgud, translated and directed by Theodore Komisarjevsky at the New.

Film: Anna Carpenter in *Rhodes of Africa* with Walter Houston, directed by Berthold Viertel.

1937 Lise in Maxwell Anderson's *High Tor*, directed by Guthrie McClintic at the Martin Beck, New York.

The Queen in William Shakespeare's *Richard II* with John Gielgud and Michael Redgrave, directed by John Gielgud at the Queen's.

Lady Teazle in Richard Brinsley Sheridan's *The School for Scandal* with Leon Quartermaine, directed by Tyrone Guthrie at the Queen's.

1938 Irina in Anton Chekhov's *Three Sisters* (translated by Constance Garnett) with Gwen Ffrangcon-Davies and Carol Goodner, directed by Michel Saint-Denis at the Queen's.

Portia in William Shakespeare's *The Merchant of Venice* with John Gielgud, directed by Gielgud and Glen Byam Shaw at the Queen's.

Yeliena in Michael Bulgakov's *The White Guard* (adapted by Rodney Ackland) with Michael Redgrave, directed by Michel Saint-Denis at the Phoenix.

Viola in William Shakespeare's *Twelfth Night*, directed by Michel Saint-Denis at the Phoenix.

1939 Isolde in Stephen Haggard's *Weep for the Spring*, directed by Michel Saint-Denis on tour.

Cecily Cardew in Oscar Wilde's *The Importance of Being Earnest* with John Gielgud and Gwen Ffrangcon-Davies, directed by Gielgud at the Globe.

Television: Miranda in William Shakespeare's *The Tempest*, directed by Dallas Bower (BBC).

Viola in William Shakespeare's *Twelfth Night*, directed by Michel Saint-Denis (BBC).

1940 Dinah Sylvester in Clemence Dane's *Cousin Muriel* with Alec Guinness, directed by Norman Marshall at the Globe.

Miranda in William Shakespeare's *The Tempest* with John Gielgud, directed by George Devine and Marius Goring at the Old Vic.

Film: The Woman in *Channel Incident*, directed by Anthony Asquith.

1941 Mrs de Winter in Daphne du Maurier's *Rebecca*, directed by George Devine on tour.
Film: Fleur Lisle in *Quiet Wedding*, directed by Anthony Asquith.

1942 Cecily Cardew in Oscar Wilde's *The Importance of Being Earnest*, directed by John Gielgud at the Phoenix.
Film: ATS Girl in *New Lot*, directed by Carol Reed.

1943 Catherine Lisle in Rodney Ackland's *The Dark River*, directed by the author at the Whitehall.

1944 Ophelia in William Shakespeare's *Hamlet* with John Gielgud, directed by George Rylands at the Haymarket.

1945 Titania in *A Midsummer Night's Dream*, directed by Nevill Coghill at the Haymarket.
The Duchess in John Webster's *The Duchess of Malfi*, directed by George Rylands at the Haymarket.

1947 Evelyn Holt in Robert Morley and Noel Langley's *Edward, My Son* with Robert Morley, directed by Peter Ashmore at His Majesty's.

1948 Evelyn Holt in *Edward, My Son* at the Martin Beck, New York.

1949 Catherine Sloper in Ruth and Augustus Goetz's *The Heiress* (adapted from Henry James's *Washington Square*) with Ralph Richardson, directed by John Gielgud at the Haymarket.

1950 Beatrice in William Shakespeare's *Much Ado About Nothing* with John Gielgud, directed by Gielgud at the Shakespeare Memorial Theatre.
Cordelia in William Shakespeare's *King Lear* with John Gielgud, directed by Gielgud at the Shakespeare Memorial Theatre.
Viola in William Shakespeare's *Twelfth Night* with Alec Clunes, directed by Hugh Hunt at the Old Vic.

1951 The title role in Sophocles' *Electra* (translated by J. T. Sheppard), directed by Michel Saint-Denis at the Old Vic.

Mistress Page in William Shakespeare's *The Merry Wives of Windsor*, directed by Hugh Hunt at the Old Vic.

1952 Hester Collyer in Terence Rattigan's *The Deep Blue Sea* with Kenneth More and Roland Culver, directed by Frith Banbury at the Duchess.

1953 Portia in William Shakespeare's *The Merchant of Venice* with Michael Redgrave, directed by Denis Carey at the Shakespeare Memorial Theatre.
Cleopatra in William Shakespeare's *Antony and Cleopatra* with Michael Redgrave, directed by Glen Byam Shaw at the Shakespeare Memorial Theatre.

1954 The title role in Henrik Ibsen's *Hedda Gabler* (adapted by Max Faber) with George Devine, directed by Peter Ashmore at the Lyric Hammersmith, the Westminster and on a European tour.

1955 Cordelia in William Shakespeare's *King Lear*, directed by George Devine, and Beatrice in William Shakespeare's *Much Ado About Nothing*, directed by John Gielgud, on a European tour and at the Palace Theatre, London.

1956 Miss Madrigal in Enid Bagnold's *The Chalk Garden* with Edith Evans, directed by John Gielgud at the Haymarket.
Shen Te/Shui Ta in Bertolt Brecht's *The Good Woman of Setzuan*, directed by George Devine at the Royal Court.

1957 Rosalind in William Shakespeare's *As You Like It* with Richard Johnson, directed by Glen Byam Shaw at the Shakespeare Memorial Theatre.
Imogen in William Shakespeare's *Cymbeline*, directed by Peter Hall at the Shakespeare Memorial Theatre.

1958 Julia Rajk in Robert Ardrey's *Shadow of Heroes* with Moegens Wieth, directed by Peter Hall at the Piccadilly.
Film: Mother Mathilde in *The Nun's Story* with Audrey Hepburn, directed by Fred Zinnemann.
Television: Julia Rajk in *Shadow of Heroes*, directed by Peter Hall (BBC).

1959 Eve Delaware in J. M. Sadler's *The Coast of Coromandel* with Eric
Porter, directed by John Fernald on tour.

Rebecca West in Henrik Ibsen's *Rosmersholm* (translated by Ann
Jellicoe) with Eric Porter, directed by George Devine at the
Royal Court and the Comedy.

1960 Katherina in William Shakespeare's *The Taming of the Shrew* with
Peter O'Toole, directed by John Baton at the Shakespeare
Memorial Theatre.

Paulina in William Shakespeare's *The Winter's Tale* with Eric
Porter, directed by Peter Wood at the Shakespeare Memorial
Theatre.

The Duchess in John Webster's *The Duchess of Malfi* with Eric
Porter and Max Adrian, directed by Donald McWhinnie at
the Aldwych.

1961 Appeared in *The Hollow Crown* devised by John Barton at the
Aldwych and *Some Words on Women and Some Women's Words*,
devised by herself, at the Senate House, University of London.

Emilia in William Shakespeare's *Othello* with John Gielgud,
directed by Franco Zeffirelli at the Royal Shakespeare Theatre.

Madame Ranevsky in Anton Chekhov's *The Cherry Orchard* with
John Gielgud, directed by Michel Saint-Denis at the Royal
Shakespeare Theatre and the Aldwych.

1962 Appeared in *The Hollow Crown* on tour throughout Europe
(where she won the Paris Festival Théâtre des Nations Award).

Television: Madame Ranevsky in *The Cherry Orchard*, directed
by Michel Saint-Denis (BBC).

1963 Margaret in William Shakespeare's *The Wars of the Roses*, directed
by Peter Hall and John Barton at the Royal Shakespeare
Theatre.

1964 Margaret in *The Wars of the Roses* at the Aldwych, the Royal
Shakespeare Theatre and on the BBC where it was co-directed
by Peter Hall and Robin Midgley.

Madame Arkadina in Anton Chekhov's *The Seagull* (translated
by Ann Jellicoe) with Peter Finch, directed by George Devine
at the Queen's.

1965 *Television*: Rebecca West in Henrik Ibsen's *Rosmersholm* (translated by Michael Meyer), directed by Michael Barry (BBC).

1966 Mother in Marguerite Duras's *Days in the Trees* (translated by Sonia Orwell) with George Baker, directed by John Schlesinger at the Aldwych.

Television: Mother in *Days in the Trees*, directed by Waris Hussein (BBC).

Mrs Patrick Campbell in Jerome Kilty's *Dear Liar* (adapted from the correspondence of George Bernard Shaw and Mrs Patrick Campbell), directed by Christopher McMaster (Granada).

1967 Mrs Alving in Henrik Ibsen's *Ghosts* (adapted by Denis Cannan) with John Castle, directed by Alan Bridges at the Aldwych.

1968 *Film*: Aunt Hanna in *Secret Ceremony* with Elizabeth Taylor and Mia Farrow, directed by Joseph Losey.

Television: Olga Knipper in *From Chekhov with Love* (translated by Moura Budberg and Gordon Latta), directed by Bill Turner (Rediffusion).

1969 Agnes in Edward Albee's *A Delicate Landscape* with Michael Hordern, directed by Peter Hall at the Aldwych.

Beth in Harold Pinter's *Landscape* with David Waller, directed by Peter Hall at the Aldwych.

Queen Katherine in William Shakespeare's *Henry VIII* with Donald Sinden, directed by Trevor Nunn at the Royal Shakespeare Theatre and the Aldwych.

Film: Belle in *Three into Two Won't Go* with Rod Steiger and Claire Bloom, directed by Peter Hall.

1970 Volumnia in Gunter Grass's *The Plebeians Rehearse the Uprising* (translated by Ralph Mannheim) with Emrys James, directed by David Jones at the Aldwych.

1971 Claire Lannes in Marguerite Duras's *The Lovers of Viorne* (translated by Barbara Bray) with Gordon Jackson, directed by Jonathan Hales at the Royal Court.

Film: Mrs Greville in *Sunday, Bloody Sunday* with Glenda Jackson, directed by John Schlesinger.

Television: Sonia Tolstoy in James Forsyth's *The Last Journey*, directed by Peter Potter (Granada).

1972 The Wife in Edward Albee's *All Over* with Angela Lansbury, directed by Peter Hall at the Aldwych.

Lady Boothroyd in William Douglas Home's *Lloyd George Knew*

My Father with Ralph Richardson, directed by Robin Midgley at the Savoy.

1973 Beth in *Landscape*, directed by Peter Hall, and Flora in *A Slight Ache*, directed by Peter James, both by Harold Pinter, on a European tour and at the Aldwych.

1974 *The Hollow Crown* in Ottawa.
Lilian Baylis in *Tribute to the Lady*, devised by Val May, at the Old Vic.

1975 Ella Rentheim in Henrik Ibsen's *John Gabriel Borkman* (translated by Inga-Stina Ewbank and Peter Hall) with Ralph Richardson and Wendy Hiller, directed by Peter Hall at the Old Vic.
Winnie in Samuel Beckett's *Happy Days*, directed by Peter Hall at the Old Vic.
Mrs Patrick Campbell in *Dear Liar* with John Neville, directed by Edwin Stephenson at the Citadel, Edmonton, Canada.
Film: Lady Gray in *Der Fussgänger* (*The Pedestrian*), directed by Maximilian Schell.

1976 *Tribute to the Lady* at the Old Vic.
Lidya Vasilyevna in Aleksei Arbuzov's *Old World* (translated by Ariadne Nikolaeff) with Anthony Quayle, directed by Terry Hands at the Aldwych.

1977 Winnie in Samuel Beckett's *Happy Days*, directed by Peter Hall at the Lyttelton and the Citadel, Edmonton.

1978 *Film*: Lady Gee in Ruth Prawer Jhabvala's *Hullabaloo over Georgie and Bonnie's Pictures*, directed by James Ivory.
Television: Queen Mary in Simon Raven's *Edward and Mrs Simpson*, directed by Waris Hussein (Thames).

1980 Fanny Farelly in Lilian Hellman's *Watch on the Rhine*, directed by Mike Ockrent at the Lyttelton.
Television: Frau Messner in Stephen Poliakoff's *Caught on a Train* with Michael Kitchen, directed by Peter Duffell (BBC).
Jean Wilsher in Dennis Potter's *Cream in My Coffee* with Lionel Jeffries, directed by Gavin Millar (LWT).

1981 Countess of Rousillon in William Shakespeare's *All's Well that*

Ends Well with Harriet Walter, directed by Trevor Nunn at the Royal Shakespeare Theatre and the Barbican.

1982 *Television*: The Rat-Wife in Henrik Ibsen's *Little Eyolf* (translated by Michael Meyer) with Anthony Hopkins, directed by Michael Darlow (BBC).

1984 *Film*: Mrs Moore in *A Passage to India* with Judy Davis and Victor Banerjee, directed by David Lean.
Television: Barbie Batchelor in *The Jewel in the Crown* (adapted by Ken Taylor from Paul Scott's *The Raj Quartet*), directed by Christopher Morahan and Jim O'Brien (Granada).
Appeared in *Six Centuries of Verse* with John Gielgud and Ralph Richardson, directed by Richard Mervyn (Thames).

1986 Lilian Baylis in *Save the Wells*, devised by Val May, at the Royal Opera House.
Appeared in *The Hollow Crown* at the Swan.
Television: Agatha Christie in Nick Evans's *Murder by the Book* with Ian Holm, directed by Lawrence Gordon Clark.

1987 *Film*: Hilda (voice only) in an animated version of Raymond Briggs's *When the Wind Blows*, directed by Jimmy T. Murakmi.
Television: Miss Dubber in John Le Carré's *A Perfect Spy* (adapted by Arthur Hopcraft), directed by Peter Smith (BBC).
Appeared in *Two Loves*, a celebration of William Shakespeare and John Dowland devised and performed by herself and Julian Bream (BBC).

1988 *Film: Madame Sousatzka*, based by Ruth Prawer Jhabvala on a novel by Bernice Rubens, directed by John Schlesinger.

Index